The Institutional Standards Factory

Intellectual Technologies Set

coordinated by
Jean-Max Noyer and Maryse Carmès

Volume 11

The Institutional Standards Factory

Precursors, Foundation, Methods, Future and Technical Promise

Henri Hudrisier

iSTE

WILEY

First published 2026 in Great Britain and the United States by ISTE Ltd and John Wiley & Sons, Inc.

ISTE Ltd
27-37 St George's Road
London SW19 4EU
UK

www.iste.co.uk

John Wiley & Sons, Inc.
111 River Street
Hoboken, NJ 07030
USA

www.wiley.com

Library of Congress Control Number: 2026939330

British Library Cataloguing-in-Publication Data
A CIP record for this book is available from the British Library
ISBN 978-1-78630-967-9

The manufacturer's authorized representative according to the EU General Product Safety Regulation is Wiley-VCH GmbH, Boschstr. 12, 69469 Weinheim, Germany, e-mail: Product_Safety@wiley.com.

Contents

Foreword

I first met Henri Hudrisier a quarter of a century ago, when we both had the opportunity to share our interest in the Text Encoding Initiative (TEI), which today forms the basis for any work carried out in the field of digital humanities. However, it was in Beirut, at the Sommet de la Francophonie in 2002, that I truly understood how passionate he was about anything to do with standards. I was struck by his ability to create a common vision at the very point where disciplines, cultures and courses seemed to diverge. Both of us, in our own way, carried a convergent message on the need to structure texts so that they could be shared better – a project that naturally found a reflection in the principles of the TEI and in our continued efforts for standardization in the documentation domain. In the enthusiastic intellectual engagement that marked Francophone meetings, Henri already embodied this conviction that standardization was not only about standards but was also about the men and women who were dedicated to constructing a shared language in service of human knowledge.

Beyond this vision, we have often had debates on the fundamental pillars of standardization: creating consensus, the regular updating of standards and the accessibility of standards. A consensus guarantees that standards are created from a collective agreement between stakeholders, thus giving them legitimacy and ensuring they are adopted. Regularly updating standards is essential if standards are to remain in phase with evolving practices, technologies and user needs. Finally, the accessibility of standards – both legally and technically – allows them to be consulted, understood and easily applied by the general public. These three principles ensure not only the stability of standards but also that they are adaptable and have a long-term impact.

Henri Hudrisier has also helped me see firsthand what a key role standardization plays in generating prosperity, both economic as well as social. By establishing common frameworks of interoperability, standardization facilitates exchanges, reduces development costs and promotes innovation by allowing actors to focus on the added value rather than on technical compatibility. It creates ground for agreements between institutions, companies and researchers, thereby stimulating collaborations and the emergence of sustainable ecosystems. Further, by ensuring that resources are accessible and reusable, especially in the digital and information field, standardization strengthens the spread of knowledge and equal opportunities. Far from being a simple technical constraint, it acts as a strategic driver of development and competition on a global scale.

Finally, Henri and I share the essential idea that standardization is, above all, a human adventure, founded on interactions, listening and cooperation between individuals from diverse milieux, disciplines and cultures. It is not a technical exercise, but a collective process where every vote counts, where disagreements feed debates and where compromises are an art. It is a form of intellectual diplomacy, where the common goal is to construct shared, sustainable and inclusive reference frameworks. Across committees, open discussions and interdisciplinary contributions, standardization reflects a deeply human dynamic: the desire to come together to build a common language, not to homogenize but to enable diverse uses. This collaborative, patient and committed dimension is what makes standardization a deeply social and ethical field.

The fabulous work that Henri Hudrisier has carried out in compiling the information in this book makes it possible to understand these fundamental themes and many others by learning about them with historical context, which shows how deeply standard production is associated with scientific and industrial development in human societies. Indeed, every page is an account of an adventure, of another step forward in the standardization journey and the promise of a new ambition to follow.

This is a book that you can dip into at random to latch onto a technological theme or the processes that govern standardization, a little like you might browse through a dictionary. However you use it, you will leave with a sense of having learnt, or rather understood, many things and with the desire to learn much more about them.

Laurent ROMARY
Director of Scientific Information and Culture at Inria
(Institut national de recherche en sciences et technologies du numérique
– National Institute of Scientific Research and Digital Technologies)
President of the ISO 639 Maintenance Agency
Ex-President of Committee ISO TC 37 (2016–2024)

Preface

The question of consistency across domestic and international use of jargon in the field of standards is a recurring problem, posing a significant barrier to mutual comprehension. It hinders the social acceptance and democratization of norms as well as the entry of new experts into the field. This is a problem with natural language as well as the use of abbreviations, acronyms and other references (norms, committees, processes, etc.). We think that this question is an essential one and we also discuss it with a view to the future in the conclusion.

Standardization requires specialized knowledge and precise, technical vocabulary and, notably, it makes extensive use of abbreviations and acronyms:

– to denote organizations; for example: ISO, ITU, JTC 1, BSI, AFNOR;

– to refer to norms; for example: ISO 9000;

– to identify the committees or subcommittees that carry out work on norms.

For example, we have ISO/TC 22 (road vehicles, technical committee no. 22), which is divided into multiple subcommittees (SCs) and working groups (WGs). Thus, ISO/TC 22/SC 37 corresponds to subcommittee 37, which is dedicated to electrically propelled vehicles. ISO/TC 22/SC 37/WG 5 is more specifically dedicated to the energy transfer requirements for these vehicles. With over 843 technical committees and subcommittees in the ISO (as of 2025), in addition to the committees and subcommittees from the ITU[1]

1 International Telecommunication Union or Union internationale des télécommunications.

and IEC[2], standardization covers a wide range of domains: industrial, societal and environmental. As in other technical or scientific disciplines (physics, chemistry), experts must communicate with each other through rigorous and recognized international formalism[3]. This includes (1) precise symbolism for the terms being used and (2) standardized syntax to bring together various elements. Conveniently enough, this formalism is Anglophone. A common koine is essential, and any attempt at translation, especially of the acronyms, threatens the stability of the whole structure. To prevent any confusion, this formalism must be internationally recognized. Translating certain acronyms or abbreviations risks causing confusion. For example, looking at just two languages that use the same script: French uses CT (Comité Technique) for technical committee, abbreviated as TC in English. There would be complete bafflement in a group of 10 experts who, between them, speak six different mother tongues and use four different writing systems. This could be especially confusing if this modifies the reference of the same standard.

The exclusive use of English for the abbreviation of committees, standards or processes allows us to minimize linguistic challenges and to ensure that experts from any linguistic background can discuss the same subjects without any ambiguity. For instance, an English speaker and French speaker would face considerable difficulty in speaking to each other if one spoke about NATO and the other about OTAN, or one used OMS and the other WHO[4]. Although English abbreviations are preferred in most instances, in some instances the abbreviation reflects the fact that an organization was originally founded in another country using their language as the official language, for example, the ITU is the International Telecommunication Union, but the French abbreviation (UIT) reflects the organization's original French name.

Whenever the scope of a committee or working group is introduced (summaries that define the scope of the work carried out or the applications

2 The International Electrotechnical Commission.

3 This is a problem at an international level as well as within each national or linguistic group.

4 "WHO verifies Niger as the first country in the African Region to eliminate onchocerciasis". This citation may sound confusing when read out loud. See: https://www.who.int/ news/item/30-01-2025-who-verifies-niger-as-the-first-country-in-the-african-region-to-eliminate-onchocerciasis#.

implemented), by convention the description will be presented between brackets: <…>[5].

May 2026

5 Refer to the conclusion, section C.3. These symbols' UNICODE names are: U+3008: left angle bracket (<); U+3009: right angle bracket (>).

Acknowledgments

Standardization is a friendly and collaborative activity. I was welcomed into this world by experts and professionals from national and international bodies as one of their own, and they have all patiently helped me explore this world, which may seem wreathed in mystery to the newcomer.

Jean-Michel Borde was my first mentor. An engineer with AFNOR, he was given the task of supporting many technical committees (especially those related to ICT, multimedia and documentation). He soon encouraged me to redeploy my university research goals. In a seeming coincidence, my first article co-authored with Jean-Michel Borde was for the journal *Solaris* under the direction of Max Noyer. I can never thank him enough for his attention to my work on standardization and the inclusion of this work within this collection is a testament to that. At the AUF (Agence Universitaire de la Francophonie, the University Agency of Francophonie), Didier Oillo, Digital Director, was my constant support. The rectors Michel Guillou and then Michèle Gendreau-Massaloux successively amplified a policy of standards development that they had already begun with Michel Le Coz, Pierre-Jean Loiret and Frantz Fongang. For over 20 years, Mokhtar Ben Henda, from the Bordeaux Montaigne University, has been my partner in the AUF delegation as the liaison with the ISO. From Montreal to Hanoi, from Abidjan to Beirut, from Toronto to Melbourne, we met hundreds of friends and colleagues, all of whom were eager to share their pedagogic resources.

The interoperability of all languages in the world remains an exciting area of standardization. Nadine Lucas (CNRS) was the first to introduce me to the fascinating complexity of ideographic writing, and Jacques André (INRIA) introduced me to the subtlety of the basic theory of glyphs and the diversity in the digital coding of writing systems.

My Arab, Berber and Malagasy colleagues, and the various speakers of partner languages to French, stood side by side with us to take on the challenge of interoperability among global languages. Other friends, notably Claire Scopsi, initiated me into the essential formalism of standards for multimedia, documentation and library and museum cataloguing. Laurent Romary, who did me the honor of penning the preface to this work, introduced me to the terminology of standardization and taught me the fundamental difference between onomasiology and semasiology. Lou Burnard (Oxford) introduced me to the TEI. Renan Mouren led me to discover smart cities or sustainable cities and communities and Juliette Pupin introduced me to ancient Hanseatic measurements. The MPEG group particularly fascinated me, as its work reminded me of my own early research into audiovisual media and multimedia. A special thank you to Françoise Préteux, chairperson of AFNOR-MPEG, for his warm welcome into this research group. Alain Vaucelle, whose thesis I supervised, became my personal instructor in audiovisual media and multimedia. In 1999, Renaud Fabre, the then president of University Paris 8, put me in charge of a standardization mission. It is thanks to him that I spent over two decades within ISO/IEC JTC 1/SC 36. Ghislaine Azémard, chairperson of ITEN UNESCO Chair, placed her trust in me and accepted a research topic that was quite atypical at the time, as did François Mellet, a close friend who is no longer with us. I express my warmest gratitude to Imad Saleh and Khaldoun Zreik, of Laboratoire Paragraphe, as well as my colleagues, friends and former students at University Paris 8, in AUF, in the Maison des sciences de l'homme, in the ITEN UNESCO Chair, and in countless other standardization bodies, research centers and universities around the world. Being a part of JTC 1/SC 36 has been extraordinarily rewarding. Within this community, I found many friends, publishers, university professors and professionals, all of whom were brought together by education and online training. Jacques Perriault, who is no longer with us, was the AFNOR chair for many years. We were friends for almost 50 years. He was succeeded by Renaud Fabre, Philippe Portelli and, today, Yolaine Bourda. At the international SC 36 level, successive presidents, Franck Farance (United States), Bruce Peoples (United States), Mike Collett (Great Britain), Øverby Erlend (Norway) and today my close friend Jon Mason (Australia), who also helped look over this book, have each led SC 36 in their own inimitable way and ensured the SC continued to progress. It is impossible to name the hundreds of experts (Russians, Ukrainians, Chinese, Japanese, Koreans, Kenyans, Indians, New Zealanders, Americans, Europeans) with whom I maintain ties of friendship and who expanded my own horizons. I hope each of them feels included in this expression of gratitude, as this work is the fruit of a long collaborative effort.

I thank both the French and English teams at ISTE Ltd for all their hard work. I would like to especially acknowledge Akhila Phadnis for her involvement in the translation of this book. Many thanks also to Jon Mason and Liddy Neville for agreeing to proofread this book as friends as well as established anglophone ISO experts.

I wish to extend my immense gratitude to Max Noyer, who supported, guided and reassured me. And my special thanks to Jean-Michel Borde, Geneviève Vidal, Mokhtar Ben Henda and Christiane Spièro for their patient and friendly proofreading.

Abbreviations and Acronyms

ADL	Advanced Distributed (or Defense) Learning
AFNOR	Association française de Normalisation (French standardization association)
AG	advisory group
AHG	ad hoc group
AICC	Aviation Industry CBT (computer-based training) Committee
ANSI	American National Standards Institute
AUF	Agence universitaire de la Francophonie (Francophonie University Agency)
BA, later BSA	British Association for Science Advancement
BIPM	International Bureau of Weights and Measures (Bureau international des poids et mesures)
BMP	Basic Multilingual Plane
BSI	British Standards Institution
CASCO	Committee on Conformity Assessment (ISO)

CBT	computer-based training
CCIF	Consultative Committee for International Telegraphy and Telephony
CCITT	Consultative Committee for International Telegraphy and Telephony (this has become the ITU-T)
CD	committee draft
CEN	European Committee for Standardization
CENELEC	European Committee for Electrotechnical Standardization
CGS	centimeter, gram, second
CGPM	General Conference on Weights and Measures (Conférence générale des poids et mesures)
CIB	Committee Internal Balloting system
CIGRE	International Council on Large Electric Systems (Conférence internationale des grands réseaux électriques)
CIPM	International Committee for Weights and Measures (Comité international des poids et mesures)
CISPR	International Special Committee on Radio Interference (Comité international spécial des perturbations radioélectriques)
CJK	Chinese, Japanese and Korean (UNICODE)
COPOLCO	Committee on Consumer Policy (ISO)
CSC/FIN	Council Standing Committee on Finance
CSC/NOM	Council Standing Committee for Review of Nominations
CSC/OVE	Council Standing Committee on Oversight

CSC/SP	Strategy and Policy Committee
DARPA	Defense Advanced Research Projects Agency (formerly ARPA: Advanced Research Projects Agency)
DCMI	Dublin Core Metadata Initiative
DEVCO	Committee on Developing Country Matters (ISO)
DIS	draft international standard
DIN	Deutsches Institut für Normung (German Standardization Institute)
DoC	Department of Commerce
DoD	Department of Defense
DSA	Digital Services Act
ERTMS	European Railway Traffic Management System
FDIS	final draft international standard
FOAF	Friend of a Friend
GAFAM+	Google, Apple, Facebook (later Meta), Amazon, Microsoft + (others)
GIS	geographic information systems
GOST-R	Federal Agency on Technical Regulating and Metrology
GPS	Global Positioning System
ICANN	Internet Corporation for Assigned Names and Numbers
ICT	information and communication technologies (often simply IT, information technologies)
IEC	International Electrotechnical Commission

IEEE	Institute of Electrical and Electronics Engineers
IEEE/LTSC	IEEE/Learning Technology Standard Committee
IETF	Internet Engineering Task Force
IGF	Internet Governance Forum
ILOM	International Organization of Legal Metrology
IMTFE	International Military Tribunal for the Far East
INCITS	International Committee for Information Technology Standard
INRIA	Institut national de recherche en sciences et technologies du numérique (France) (National Institute for Research in the Sciences and Digital Technologies)
INSEE	Institut national de la statistique et des études économiques (France) (National Institute for Statistics and Economics)
IS	international standard
ISA	International Standards Association
ISDN	Integrated Services Digital Network
ISO	International Organization for Standardization, acronym used across all languages
ISO/CS	ISO Central Secretariat
ISO 9000	family of standards for quality management
ISO/IEC 27000	family of standards for digital information security management
ISO 45000	family of standards related to health and safety in the workplace

ISO 14000	family of standards for environment management
ISO 22000	family of standards for food safety management
ISO 26000	family of standards for social responsibility
ISO/IEC 27001:2022	standard for cybersecurity and privacy protection
ISO 31000	family of standards for risk management (companies and organizations)
ISO 37001	family of anti-corruption standards
ISO 50001	family of standards for energy management
ISO-PAS	Publicly Available Specification
ISOC	Internet Society
ITU	International Telecommunication Union (UIT – Union internationale des télécommunications)
IWA	International Workshop Agreement
JIS	Japanese Industrial Standards
JISC	Japanese Industrial Standards Committee
JPEG	Joint Picture Expert Group
JTC	joint technical committee
JWG	joint working group
KATS	Korean Agency for Technology and Standards
MKS	meter, kilogram, second
MPEG	Moving Picture Experts Group
MSS	Management Systems Standard

NB	national body
NBLO	National Bodies and Liaison Organizations
NP	new proposal
OECD	Organization for Economic Cooperation and Development
OSI	Open Systems Interconnection
PC	project committee
RFC	Requests for Comments
RSRE	Royal Signals and Radar Establishment
SA	Standards Australia
SAC	Standardization Administration of China
SC	subcommittee
SCC	Standards Council of Canada
SCG	Strategic Coordination Group
SDG	Sustainable Development Goal
SI	International System of Units (Système international d'unités)
SR	systematic review
TC	technical committee
TCP-IP	Transmission Control Protocol – Internet Protocol
TMB	Technical Management Board (ISO)
TPM	Technical Programme Manager
TR	technical report

TS	technical specification
UNIPEDE	Union internationale des producteurs et distributeurs d'énergie électrique (International Union of Producers and Distributors of Electrical Energy)
UNSCC	United Nations Standardization Coordination Committee (1946–1947)
VA	Vienna Agreement (between ISO and CEN)
W3C	World Wide Web Consortium
WD	working draft
WG	working group
WSC	World Standards Cooperation (ISO, IEC, ITU)
WTO	World Trade Organization
WTO-TBT	World Trade Organization Technical Barriers to Trade Agreement

National Standards Organizations

ABNT	Associação Brasileira de Normas Técnicas
AFNOR	Association française de Normalisation
ANSI	American National Standards Institute
ASI	Austrian Standards International
ASN	Institut Sénégalais de Normalisation
BIS	Bureau of Indian Standards
BSI	British Standards Institution
BSJ	Bureau of Standards Jamaica

DIN	Deutsches Institut für Normung
DS	Danish Standards Foundation
DSM	Department of Standards Malaysia
GOST-R	Federal Agency on Technical Regulating and Metrology
ICONTEC	Instituto Colombiano de Normas Técnicas y Certificación
INSO	Iran National Standards Organization
IPQ	Instituto Português da Qualidade
IRAM	Instituto Argentino de Normalización y Certificación
JISC	Japanese Industrial Standards Committee
KATS	Korean Agency for Technology and Standards
KEBS	Kenya Bureau of Standards
NBN	Bureau voor Normalisatie
NEN	Royal Netherlands Standardization Institute
PKN	Polish Committee for Standardization
SA	Standards Australia
SABS	South African Bureau of Standards
SAC	Standardization Administration of China
SASO	Saudi Standards, Metrology and Quality Organization
SCC	Standards Council of Canada
SE UkrNDNC	Ukrainian Scientific Research and Training Center for Standardization, Certification and Quality Problems

SFS	Finnish Standards
SII	Standards Institution of Israel
SIS	Swedish Institute for Standards
SN	Standards Norway
SNV	Swiss Association for Standardization
TSE	Türk Standardlari Enstitüsü
UNBS	Uganda National Bureau of Standards
UNE	Spanish Association for Standardization
UNI	Ente Italiano di Normazione

Introduction

Standards, like laws, are often seen as obstructions to free will until the day the absence of standards, or the flouting of a standard, results in catastrophe, accidents[1] or simply annoyances: being unable to charge your phone, incompatibilities between software, or problems using non-metric units of measurement. Like the law (and standards and legislation have a synergistic and sometimes ambiguous relationship with the law), technical standards are often misunderstood. Very little is known about standardization outside the specialized milieu within which standards are developed and their professional implementation in organizations.

The conceptual universe, which includes guidelines and technical standardization, is difficult for non-specialists to understand, as it has two related and synergistic aspects. Both these aspects were essential for the worldwide progress of the industrial age, and today's neo-Industrial age. Without national and international standards, without initiatives for standardization within organizations and cartels, this Machine Age would never have come to be. Communication networks, railways, canals, distribution networks for water, gas, electricity and telecommunications, and, a fortiori, modern-day media and the digital world – none of these would have progressed beyond being objects in a global cabinet of curiosities. Note that 19th-century civil engineering work, especially the railroads, required the standard production of girders, rails, screws and rivets, which could be used in a modular manner and were certified in both quality and dimensions, created by cartels or professional groups like the

1 Buildings without anti-earthquake standards, tools without safety, unregulated food ingredients or poorly controlled chemical pollutants.

Master Ironworkers. All the institutional standards are developed by a vast, interprofessional and international community of experts. This community develops a growing corpus of national or best international standards which, until recently, almost exclusively pertained to products or market services. However, today these institutional standards also concern environment and social issues[2].

The production of institutional standards soon became a virtual collegial space, which is spatially widely distributed but well-coordinated, overseeing the conception, discussion, voting and publication of standards. However, this shared and collaborative enterprise is exclusively powered by the community that has come together to run it: industrial, economic or policy decision-makers, scientists, inventors, engineers, military actors and certain permanent employees of standardization organizations. With very few exceptions, their defining quality is a passion and desire for the growth of specific technological branches. They are also constantly careful to move forward taking into account other branches, which may already have defined standards that can be shared, in order to avoid reinventing the wheel. We use the term *production of standards* deliberately. While a standard is the outcome of thousands of debates among parallel committees in the well-regulated, democratic space of international standardization bodies (ISO, ITU, IEC), it is not just an abstract ideal but a definite product that constitutes a universal, common good. Of course, this project has evolved considerably since it was first proposed. Today, the corpus of standards is planned in a dynamic and future-oriented manner, with upstream quality checks.

The concept of an "industrial standard" is eminently distinct from the concept of an institutional (national or international) "standard". An industrial standard is internal to an organization and governs the manufacture of a product, assuring the user of the quality of the product and its interoperability, but only with respect to a range of products from the same company, or a group of companies. On the other hand, an institutional standard is more general and lays down characteristics with which specific products or services must comply across all national or international organizations. They also differ in nature: an international or national standard is a published guideline, while an industrial standard (often kept confidential by a company) regulates the manufactured standard product. In

2 Notably, the SDGs, the UN's Sustainable Development Goals.

this sense, industrial, but also institutional standardization was the bedrock of the Industrial Era. Both institutional and industrial standardization revolutionized modes of production, use and exchange between companies (interoperability and quality), which led to exponential growth in the scale of production[3]. National or international standardization is essential when there are too many competing industrial standards, which is counterproductive for producers and users. However, since the standard is not the product but a textual document, a virtuous cycle must be set up. Since every company has a copy of this domestic or international standards, they can use it to develop their "industrial standard" and manufacture products that comply with the guideline characteristics, supplementing them with innovative features to gain a competitive edge over their rivals. A new standardization cycle (or revision of existing de jure standards) then begins to produce standards for these new innovations.

Chapter 1 studies the forerunners of standardization. Although we begin in ancient times, it was only around the 19th century that we saw the combined advent of machines, the immediacy of the telegraph, electricity, locomotives (1874) and the Bureau International des Poids et Mesures (BIPM, 1875)[4]. Such organizations institutionalized a universal metric system among nations, brought in by the French Revolution. However, it was the electricians who first saw the need to invent standards and then establish the Spirit of Electricity[5], and industrialists needed to be able to measure electricity, manufacture consistent products and use it without any risks in factories and households.

Over 25 years, in successive congresses on electricity, an international elite group of scholars and industrialists working on electricity would go on to create and rationally organize the objective and the actual establishment of an international organization to standardize electricity and electromagnetism. This was the IEC, which was officially created and established in London in 1906. This was the culmination of a century of creation of standardization

3 The construction of railway station concourses, thanks to the standards for rails and beams created by master ironworkers.

4 This began with the independence of the United States and the French Revolution and ended before the First World War.

5 For the Great Exhibition of 1937, Raoul Dufy created *La Fée électricité* (*The Spirit of Electricity*) a historic, allegorical painting measuring 600 m^2, which today hangs in the Museum of Modern Art in Paris.

organizations, the history of which is studied in Chapter 2. Chapter 3 is entirely dedicated to the IEC, which was the true inventor of modern-day standards production. Chapter 4 demonstrates how the production of standards became generalized. The First World War galvanized and thus standardized industrial production in the countries involved in the war. Between 1917 and the late-1920s, all developed countries founded their own national generalist standardization organization. Unlike the ITU and IEC, these national organizations were generalists, that is, they designed standards for all industrial branches. From 1927 onwards, they were federated within the ISA[6] following the model and methods of the IEC. The Second World War was another event that led to a new round of standards production led by the ISO. While the ITU and IEC retained their autonomous status, all three international organizations set up their headquarters in Geneva in the second half of the 1940s and worked closely with each other.

The convergence of information and communication technologies encouraged the ISO and IEC to found a highly strategic joint committee, which allowed the common discussion and definition of standards to regulate ICT[7]. This committee, ISO/IEC JTC 1[8], is the sole focus of Chapter 5. From the 1980s, ICT radically transformed society itself, but more specifically also the information technology sector. Up to now, standardization had been the preserve of a small, international group of seasoned experts. However, the global community of computer scientists had another objective: they wanted to rapidly put in place a globalized digital system, for which they needed common regulations[9]. The ISO, IEC, ITU and, more specifically, JTC 1, proposed standards. However, their publishing and collegial qualitative control processes were too slow for computer scientists[10]. No one had yet thought of making competing standards, *stricto sensu*.

From the 1980s onwards, the standards produced by digital consortia grew in number, especially those related to the Internet and Unicode,

6 International Standard Association.

7 Sometimes IT, sometimes ICT, for information (communication) technologies.

8 ISO, IEC, joint technical committee no. 1. We will see that there are two other JTCs.

9 Modern computing cannot exist without globally shared codes and standards.

10 They were sponsored by militaries and large companies: they wanted things within a few keystrokes.

dedicated to the interoperability of writing systems from around the world. Niche consortia were founded, especially for the digital humanities[11] and Open Archives. However, the latter were only for academic purposes and never became commercial.

From the 2000s onwards, ISOC and W3C[12] sponsors began large-scale appropriation and misuse of the Global Digital Commons, which had been built by the pioneering Internet consortia. Big Tech[13] began to offer users tools that were "convivial" but also addictive. The price for using these applications was to give up your data and sometimes your conscience. Standardization organizations, *stricto sensu*, have already started working on this and the solutions they are working on have already produced results. This subject is studied in Chapter 6. The steps taken to resist Big Tech's misuse of data are examined in the conclusion.

11 The TEI and Music Encoding Initiative (MEI).

12 The Internet Society and World Wide Web Consortium.

13 Or GAFAM+, for Google, Apple, Facebook (today, Meta, Amazon and Microsoft), and other companies play the same role.

1

The Forerunners of Standardization

The use of standards to aid in the progress of humans, and even other species, dates back to the dawn of time. The storage, duplication and transmission of genetic material leads to the reproduction of similar beings, standard individuals adapted so that a species might survive the competitive processes of evolution. Beyond this primordial genetic stage, among evolved species, epigenetics allowed a species to pass on standard know-how and knowledge (feeding yourself, protecting yourself and so on) to their descendants and other similar beings to increase their chances of survival and promote the well-being of those communities. This holds true for the species *Homo*; however, it is not the only species passing on information – consider nests, termite mounds, beehives, corals and beaver dams. However, the long line of hominids is certainly the line of species that has produced the highest number of tools or made the most modifications to the environment. The use of language by *Homo sapiens* allowed technology to spread far and wide. The basis of each language is the *lexicon*, which allows users to understand categories of beings, objects or events that are considered to be *standard*. All societies require norms, in the broadest sense of the term. Complex societies, with highly specialized tasks, must quickly distinguish between norms practiced by the community as a whole and *standards* that apply to specific sections of that society: these are technical standards[1].

1 Within politically organized societies, there emerges the requirement to share certain norms not only within the nation (or a league of nations), but on a more global scale, as peaceful trade is set up.

It must be emphasized that language, followed by writing, is not the only means of transmitting knowledge and techniques, but it becomes the primary support for performative recording of these standards. Numbers and calculations are simply a subset of writing and significantly prefigure writing. At the same time, numbers govern the normative formalization of weights and measurements[2] especially and are an essential feature of a sovereign power. The discovery and subsequent cultural codification of the technical drawing were also a fundamental dimension of the power of standardization. The architectural forms of a city, the designs and purposes that formalized mechanical techniques used by artisans or in war machines – these are all modes of transmission of technical standards. This chapter presents a few forerunners of modern standardization, pre-dating the contemporary period. For this, 1776 is a convenient marker for Americans[3], a well-known date and effectively approaching the end of the pre-industrial age, which had a wealth of early standardization methods.

1.1. Standardization in Antiquity: writing, knowledge and metrology

The Greek alphabet was one of the earliest normative bases of Western civilization (and, of course, of the Greek world initially). It was the reason it transformed into a society that invented another way of thinking and of transmitting science as distinct from technology. There have been many commentaries on the influence of writing, through technical progress in producing writing, the supports used, and in printing. Despite being the subject of much criticism, Havelock's theory regarding the fundamental contribution of the Greek alphabet to the creation of the *Greek miracle*, resulting in the globalizing transformation of Western civilization, is a perfect description of this key point in standardization in Western cultures (Havelock 1981). It does not matter whether it was really the Greeks who invented the very first alphabet. What is certain is that they were able to standardize a short writing code, which was capable of recording (capturing) speech completely and which was easy to learn and, therefore, easy to share widely. This produced a new cultural ecosystem, both communicational and political, which had never existed before.

2 Closely linked to proto-coins and then coins.

3 The French Revolution – 1789 – is a similarly striking date for European historians.

Writing, money, networks: inventions of Antiquity, inventions of modernity

Based on concrete evidence from digs, Clarisse Herrenschmidt, an archaeologist and a fine linguist, demonstrated the continuum between proto-writing and the practice of exchanges (whether monetary, linguistic or informatic) within networks:

> Like the *bulla or cylinder seals*, on to which a seal was printed, whether an Eastern seal representing the sender's signature, or a Lydian or Ionian seal indicating the authority issuing the stamp, the packet carried its own identification: the IP address of the machine that issued it (I am ignoring data encryption for the time being). What remains are the geographic and cultural aspects. The stamp seal circulated between Uruk and Syria, between Suse and the Iranian plateau, while the cylinder seal circulated between the Lydian empire of Sardis and Ionian cities. These signs were created to circulate over more or less vast expanses, politically heterogenous in any case. From the start, these packets traveled around the world: this was the true birth of the Web: exchanges between CERN physicists and their colleagues across the Atlantic. The people who exchanged stamps seals and cylinder seals, those who exchanged the packets, may not have spoken the same language, but they certainly shared a code: dice in the old Eastern world, weighted precious metal and a complete alphabet in the Asia Minor of the 7th century BCE, international English and the interconnection protocols and standards used for computers in the late 20th century CE. These writings built upon one another. An arithmetic writing was deployed through the means of money that was minted based on the complete alphabet; writing computer code uses linguistic and arithmetic writing, and contributions from the industrial development of writing, including information technology and the telephone: writing code starts with the premise that languages, beings, the world itself can all be written using numbers. (Herrenschmidt 1999, p. 63)

Box 1.1. *Money, the forerunner of writing and digital networks*

Within this new ecosystem, it became possible to discuss and argue each new proposition of a dialogue and, above all, it was easy to record these debates in writing. A new skill thus emerged, which was no longer simply the *summation of technical discussion* but a perennial process of recording speech, which would form the basis of agreement between experts (artisans, philosophers, savants, traders or buyers). And so began discourse on *technology*[4], which was distinct from *science*. Using these new social competencies and by theorizing on the universe itself, everything seemed possible to the Greeks: questioning their own mythology by distinguishing the physical from the metaphysical, or questioning politics by distinguishing between tyranny and democracy, which, of course, was also their creation. Language itself became a science with the study of grammar, measuring the world through geometry, the essence of knowledge with logic, and, through rigorous association of arguments, it became a means to test the veracity of a proposition.

Disparities in writing culture between Ancient Chinese and Greco-Roman civilizations

Two writing cultures, two cultures that transmitted knowledge and know-how, and two kinds of social and institutional organization for technoscientific governance existed contemporaneously, without any real contact, at the Western and Eastern ends of Eurasia. It is clear that norms around writing, produced by tens of generations of speakers, readers and writers, do not lead to the same social institutions (democracy vs. bureaucracy and empire) nor the same modalities of differentiating (or not differentiating) between technology and abstract science. This leads to specificities in the diffusion of technical knowledge and, therefore, in the modes of standardizing this knowledge. Within both these writing regions, technology did not evolve in the same way over the next thousand years: it was the ideographic world that had the initial advantage. They produced woodblock printing, resulting in text and images that could be widely shared. It was partly thanks to these early books that China could so widely propagate the sophisticated technologies that they had already used for centuries: metallurgy, hydraulics and multi-tube seed drills, for example. As a result of this, these two different writing cultures had different cultural, social and technological futures[5].

Box 1.2. *Other writing families, other technological and social cultures*

4 From later Greek *tekhnologia*: literally *discourse on techniques* (see Hudrisier 1999, pp. 54–56).

5 For a long time, in Egypt, Mesopotamia, the Indian subcontinent and China, writing was almost entirely an exclusive profession practiced by scribes.

Other populations around the world had asked similar questions, but thanks to the alliance formed between the Greeks[6] and their Roman conquerors, a brilliant civilization emerged that first the Renaissance and then the Enlightenment, rediscovered, amplified and reactivated, and which even today serves as the foundation of European civilization, resulting in the globalized industrial civilization that continues today.

It was thanks to the significant spread of writing among the ordinary people that Athens, and then Rome, could establish standards for weights, measurements and coinage. They also standardized certain sensitive activities that were of importance to the State and its citizens: architecture, urbanism, maritime activities (especially military ones), as well as innovations that had to be preserved through the granting of privileges: creating monopolies[7].

Constructing a town is a fundamental competence among evolved, sedentary civilizations. Aristotle defined this as the fundamental philosophical requirement: "Poiesis is the disposition to produce accompanied by rules" (Aristotle 1997). Three centuries later, in Rome, Vitruvius penned a series of texts not only on architecture but a variety of technical subjects. Vitruvius was a mechanical engineer as well as a military and then civil engineer who served under Caesar during the Gallic wars, and through his *Ten Books on Architecture,* he brought together the processes of engineering sciences in a single book. Like Archimedes and Pythagoras before him, he established a close link between theory and practice: "Architecture is a science that embraces a wide variety of study and knowledge; it knows and judges everything produced by the other arts. It is the fruit of practice and of theory" (Vitruvius 1914). In doing this, Vitruvius was a *standardizer* in the modern sense of this term. He defined a good

6 It must also be highlighted that, to pay homage to the primacy of Greek as well as for international equity, the abbreviation ISO is no longer officially a reference to the International Standard Organization but to the ancient Greek ἴσος, *isos*. This allows the organization to sidestep the thorny question of promoting English over French or Russian (these being its three official languages). Thus, officially, the abbreviation is no longer the abbreviation of the English name (International Organization for Standardization), the French name (Organisation internationale de normalisation) or the Russian name (Международная организация по стандартизации).

7 Etymologically *monos* = single and *polein* = to sell.

architect not only as one who could choose from a catalogue of *styles*[8] that which was best suited for use with the structure, but also a person who could propose rules (*norma*) and was able to reason between theory and practice.

In the Greco-Roman world, we encounter norms in multiple domains: rhetoric, poetic meter, metrology, military and maritime organization and so on. The fact that the *Pax Romana* lasted five centuries was not purely chance. The Romans, of the Republic and then the Empire, were able to establish solid institutions. They had the wisdom to bring about *religious syncretism*[9] and, above all, they put in place a normative framework for exchange: land and sea routes that were well-maintained and under military protection, Greek and Latin (or rather koine[10]) as the bridge language, as well as unified weights, measurements and coinage, which simplified business and allowed trade to prosper:

> Ancient Greece considered the question of monopolies to protect innovations very early on. The oldest known mention is derogatory. It concerns the Greek colony in Sybaris, in Southern Italy, in the 6th century BCE. Athenaeus of Naucratis wrote to Rome in 228 CE in his magnum opus *Deipnosophistae* (Scholars at the Dinner Table): "If a cook among them were to invent a new, very delicate dish, no cook other than the inventor would be permitted to prepare this for one year, so that each of them may try to surpass the other by making similar discoveries." [Later, Aristotle] "complained multiple times about the practice in certain nation-States of conferring monopolies. (Lapointe 2000)

In fact, legal historians consider that the attribution of *privileges* or *monopolies*, awarded on a case-by-case basis, was in existence well before the emergence of any laws on patents[11]. We can, however, highlight this mode of having an innovation acknowledged by governments. While distinct from the question of technical standardization, monopolies and then patents, like norms, are a means for States to govern technologies. This is thus a

8 *Stýlos*, στῦλος = column. A distinctive feature of Doric, Ionic and Corinthian styles.

9 They were able to establish, through consensus, an interoperability of pantheons, not only between Greek and Roman religion, but also Egyptian and Mesopotamian religions.

10 A standardized linguistic form of the various spoken Greeks, based on an Attic dialect, to facilitate exchanges.

11 Which was legally formalized in Europe, notably in Venice in 1474 and Great Britain in 1624.

subject that is very closely related and complementary to questions of standardization, which we only briefly mention.

The Roman system of weights and measures is particularly interesting, having endured over the centuries, across the expanse of the Empire. *Measurement standards* were submitted to the Capitol as well as other cities in the Empire. Additionally, the principal routes were marked by *milestones*, which were an omnipresent metrological reference, and any number of archaeological traces of these remain.

This system formalized a subtle division of units into multiples and sub-multiples, sometimes in a decimal base, sometimes founded on other numerical systems[12] depending on the professional use. This desire to adapt measurement norms to a variety of practices (social, professional or scholarly) can be seen in all civilizations that developed a system of measurements, a calendar and symbols for trade exchanges. Thus, Babylonian astronomers developed systems for calculating and measuring angles that were much more sophisticated than systems to count livestock or measure grains, which were developed in the same civilization at the same time.

However, in Rome, metrological norms were institutionalized and imposed uniformly across the Empire, whether it was to measure length, area, or volume[13]. The units, as well as their multiples and sub-multiples, were organized according to scales that were adapted to metrological requirements as well as the understanding and capabilities of the users.

All units of measurement were based on two or three numerical bases, sometimes more. Let us look at the example of units of length. These were initially structured based on corporal comparisons, which was practical for daily commerce: threads, fabric, wood. The base unit, the standard for which was submitted to the Capitol, close to the Forum, was the *pes* (foot, or 0.29 m). Its sub-multiples included the *palmus* (palm, 0.074 m) and *digitus* (finger, 0.018 m). Its multiples were sometimes organized across several numerical bases in order to allow the addition of different units to arrive at an exact measurement for some common objects:

– *palmipes* = 1 foot + 1 palm = 20 thumbs = 0.37 m;

12 Decimal, duodecimal, hexadecimal or sexagesimal for angular and hourly measures.

13 Or measuring the capacities for liquids or granular materials.

– *cubitus* or *ulna* (elbow or ell[14]) = 1 foot + 2 palms = 24 thumbs = 0.44 m;

– *gradus* (degree) = 2 feet + 2 palms = 0.74 m.

Depending on the profession, the scales of magnitude and the units would vary. For land surveyors, calculations were essential and the decimal base prevailed [15]:

– *gradus* (single step) = 2.5 feet = 0.741 m;

– *passus* (double step[16]) = 5 feet = 1.482 m;

– *pertica* (perch) = 10 feet = 2.964 m.

On a larger scale:

– *actus* (track) = 120 feet = 35.56 m;

– *stadium* (stade[17]) = 625 feet = 185.25 m;

– *milliarium* (Roman mile) = 5,000 feet = 1,482 m;

– *leuga* (Roman league[18]) = 7,500 feet = 2,223 m.

The assessment of areas, called quadrature, required more complex computations. The base unit was the *quadratus pes* (square foot = 875 cm^2). The most common multiples included:

– *decempeda quadrata* or *scripulum* = 100 square feet = 8.75 m^2;

– the rectangular metrological unit, the *jugerum*, met the needs of laborers and wine-growers, focusing on units of measurement that were adapted to rectangular plots and were easier to use. Thus, the *jugerum* or the

14 It must be noted that the *elbow*, divided into 24 *thumbs*, was the ideal measurement to assess objects using your own body. It corresponded to the distance between the tips of the fingers and the tip of the elbow. A textile merchant could combine the action of unwinding a bobbin or roll of cloth with the act of measurement using nothing but their arm.

15 In Latin, as in many other languages, the lexicon of numbers is primarily a decimal one. However, while ill-suited to commercial exchanges, this decimal base is essential for calculations using an abacus.

16 The *double step* and *perch* were useful in measuring the dimensions of a room.

17 The *arpent* and *stade* were used for agricultural measurements.

18 The *mile* and *league* made it possible to calculate distances between cities. A *Roman league* was the distance that could be covered on foot in around 30 min.

track was an area of 240 feet multiplied by 120 feet, or 28,800 square feet, approximately 2,520 m^2.

On a more complex metrological scale, land records or assessing the area over which an Empire extends, geometricians and astronomers turned to geodesic techniques involving angular measurements to assess areas across vast territories. This operation, known as centuriation (*centuratio*), was distinct from localized land surveying. Based on limits or high points, they would triangulate and map large regions[19].

Monetary units are a particular case in point: there were large variations in the value and metallic and alloy composition of the *as*, *sesterce, denier* and the *aurei* between the third century BCE and the end of the Western Roman Empire. While devaluation allowed the authorities to write off State debts, the names of the coins as well as their relative hierarchy remained unchanged in order to preserve fiduciary value[20].

After the fall of the Roman Empire, Charlemagne tried to retain the universality of Roman weights and measurements. While the names for the units survived in Europe until the advent of the metric system, universal metrology was lost. A monumental statue of Roland of Roncevaux still stands in Bremen (a former Hanseatic town): the distance between the pointed knee guards of his armor served as the standard measure for the *Bremen ell*.

This precious heritage of Roman metrology was preserved in England alone, thanks to William the Conqueror and, as we will see, this benefitted the British Empire and the United States.

1.2. The stages of the standardization of text before printing

From *poetic meter* to digital publishing, over millennia all civilizations have innovated in order to standardize, record and pass on the *word*. The terms themselves testify to this: the *Iliad* and the *Odyssey* were composed in *dactylic hexameter*[21]. As in many cultures, it was thanks to the *meter* (or,

19 See Decramer (2002, pp. 137–150). Spatial technologies have replaced these skills.

20 A value in which we trust (*fides* = faith). Master weights as well as a minting workshop were found in the temple of Juno, overlooking the Forum in Rome.

21 In Greek: ἕξ (*héx*) = six and μέτρον (*métron*) = measurement.

more broadly, *poetic meter* and *musical rhythm*) that oral literatures were passed on and preserved. The appearance of the book was a fundamental stage, especially the emergence of the *codex*, which progressively replaced the *volumen* (a book in scroll form), from the first century CE onwards. Printing marked a major transformation and, even today, we are far from comprehending the full impact of the digitization of books and writing.

In the Greco-Roman world, authors, who were generally from the patrician class, dictated their works[22] to scribes (often slaves or freedmen) whose responsibility it was to transcribe this work. From the first century CE, Rome saw the emergence of a true Republic of Letters. Authors organized public lectures and exchanged corrections. A number of successful books had circulation figures that are comparable to figures from our own times (between 1,000 and 2,000 copies), traveling to the ends of the Empire. The first ancient form of a book was the papyrus scroll, which imposed a sequential reading of the text. However, the *intelligent reader* (one who was adept at *inter-legere* or "reading between the lines") was not satisfied with closely perusing two or three[23]. To deepen their understanding, they would spread out armfuls of volumen across their table, thereby creating folds, enabling them to *ex-plicare* (*unfold*), that is, understand something hidden within the folds of the text[24].

The emergence of the codex in the first century CE marked a significant cognitive revolution (Goody 1979). This form freed the reader from the necessity of reading sequentially and allowed them to gain a more global understanding of the text. When reading a scroll, in order to follow the thread of a discourse, the text had to be tagged systematically[25] (in the Gospel, for example[26]: John, book 4, verse 48). The codex simplified reading, thanks to a table of contents and systematic numbering of pages,

22 With a few exceptions, this practice continued until the Renaissance.

23 In Latin, *pagina* is both the *page in a book* and *plots in vineyards*. The analogy becomes clear when you imagine several columns of text juxtaposed in a section of a scroll, like well-aligned rectangular plots in a vineyard.

24 *Lire à Rome* (Reading in Rome) (Salles 1992) as well as *Rome : l'esprit des lettres* (Rome: The Spirit of Writing) (Porte 1993) are two fundamental books, from which we have taken most of the information given here.

25 This prefigured XML tagging of texts, which became essential because of their undifferentiated digital form.

26 This was the same across all books in scroll form, especially the books of the Quran and Torah.

which rendered these tags useless. Thus, the reader benefitted from a panoptic view of the text, allowing easier understanding and a more flexible manner of reading. A notable fact is that the codex was first adopted for technical, scientific and historical texts and its use for literary, religious and poetic texts was much slower.

From the High Medieval period, Charlemagne, with the help of his Palatine Academy, especially Alcuin, embarked upon the project of a normative overhauling of how reading and writing were taught. He standardized new codes, especially punctuation:

> With the new *Carolingian minuscule*[27], the beginning of sentences could easily be identified thanks to the initial majuscule of the first word. There also emerged punctuation marks similar to musical notations [...] However, the concept of the word still remained unclear [...] In the 12th century, the words were clearly individualized and, when the copyist had to split a word at the end of a line, he would insert a hyphen. Punctuation, both within sentences as well as at the end of the text, was indicated by a point. (BnF n.d.a)

At the end of the Medieval period, the progressive standardization of books marked a turning point. Formatting was codified in order to meet the needs of exchanges of manuscripts between clerks in the Christian world: a central reference text, flanked by drop case letters, rubrics, explanatory areas of text framing the main text, as well as marginal notes and illumination. These typographic standards catered to specific uses of these texts: reading to monastic assemblies, *readers-commentators-authors* working in libraries, or again, monks meditating in their cells upon the writings of leading Doctors of the Church. There was a spectacular growth in the market for handwritten books: between the 10th and 12th century, demand doubled and then tripled. It was in this period, the late Medieval period, that the technological and economic balance around books was overturned. As books went beyond the conventual context, which had been strictly regulated thus far, the secular production of manuscripts also required *standards approved by institutions*.

27 From the Latin name for Charlemagne: *Carolus Magnus*.

1.3. The *pecia:* de jure standardization of a manuscript

The *pecia* is a term that is relatively unknown outside of specialists who study manuscripts. However, thanks to this system, the handwritten book saw considerable growth three centuries before the invention of printing. This was the time that the earliest universities were founded, such as the university of Bologna (1088–1158) and the Sorbonne (1200–1215). These new intellectual centers generated an increasing demand for books, which began to be published in the proper sense of the term. This production was carried out under the strict and normative control of the university. Contrary to what one may think, paper (which was widely used in Europe a century before printing) was not the material used for the handwritten copies of the books. In fact, the quality of these early papers was poorly suited to writing and made it practically impossible to strike through a word. Furthermore, the material was fragile. Thus, parchment remained the best suited material to produce these handwritten manuscripts.

In Latin, *pecia* means "a piece" (in this context, *a piece of* skin, generally mutton). By extension, therefore, it referred to a fragment of parchment (folded *in folio* to form four pages, or *in quarto* for eight pages) on which the copyist would write. To guarantee that the copies remained faithful to the reference manuscript, usually held by the university, the *stationer*[28] had to first have invested in *exemplaria*[29], the copy of which had to have been certified as a true copy of the original. Each *exemplar* was made up of tens of *pecia*, each of which contained four to eight folios that could be simultaneously copied by several copyists. The stationer would rent their *peciae*, generally for a week, which was the time taken by a copyist to make a copy. If there was high demand and the *pecia* had been rented many times, this meant that the book was selling well, thus allowing the stationer to recover their initial investment. Stationers thus became *accomplices of the university*: both entrepreneurs and guarantors of handwritten publishing, they ensured that academic production was standardized and certified. Each university's *commission for petitions*[30] exerted strict control over the entire process: they ensured texts conformed to the reference, the prices being

28 Publisher-bookseller, giving us the term "stationery" today.

29 One *exemplar*, many *exemplaria*.

30 *Petitioners*, in the older sense of "representatives of authority".

charged for the texts were fair and that the production standards were rigorous. All these requirements were precisely defined in detailed rules[31].

1.4. Printing and engraving: tools of standardization

Before 1500, printers of *incanubles* (the very first printed books) had to mimic medieval manuscripts. They were printed on vellum, the only material made of skin that was suited for printing, and the first fonts sought to reproduce Gothic handwriting, which was then in vogue. However, this soon brought up many problems that were almost insurmountable.

For the typographic composition of his 42-line Bible (1452–1455), Gutenberg had to have more than 290 different characters: initial letters, median letters, final letters, and isolated letters, not to forget ligatures and other characters that connected letters to each other (Wild 1995). This process made it possible to mimic handwritten manuscripts; however, it quite significantly complicated the printing process and increased costs. Despite this, 180 copies of the first book were made.

Starting from the second edition, called the 36-line Gutenberg Bible (1461), close to a hundred characters disappeared from the first typeset case. Typographic standardization had begun. From 1500 onwards, and within a few decades, the typeset case stabilized to carry around 100 types, divided into four sections[32].

There were precursors to typography standardization. Printers such as Nicolas Jenson (1420–1480), established in Venice, participated in this by engraving the Roman-style letters (in contrast to Alde Manuce's italics) to mimic handwriting. This evolution resulted in a fundamental technical and cultural transformation: the radical split between the printed text and handwritten text.

---

31 For more information on the concept of *pecia*, an important source is the article by its modern re-discoverer, Jean Destrez (1923).

32 A typeset case or type case was a wooden box divided into compartments. Each compartment would contain different typographic letters. A specific drawer or case for capital letters was fitted above the case holding the other letters, leading to the terms "uppercase letters" and "lowercase letters", which are used even today.

Font production was quickly industrialized. Permanently engraved steel printing punches could be used to create a large number of copper molds ("matrices") for different characters. This allowed smelters to produced re-usable letters made of lead. From the 16th century onwards, certain European states published the first royal technical standards to ensure that the collections of lead types with different printers would be interoperable, compatible with each other, and long lasting. These decrees defined certain font measurements, the height of the characters and the typography point.

In the early decades of the 16th century, bookstore catalogues expanded considerably: technical volumes, scholarly works and, of course, secular literature.

For a manuscript to be copied, the parchment had to be smooth so that the quill would not snag on the fibers. On the other hand, printing a sheet (which would then be folded to create a "quire" of 4–8 pages) required an absorbent material. Paper that could not be used for handwritten documents was easier to produce and, fortuitously, it replaced parchment. Printers developed oil-based inks which had longer drying times but were easier to print on to paper. The techniques of arranging pages over one large sheet that would then be folded to form quires followed the same principles as those used for a *pecia*.

The format of the codex remained almost unchanged from the 1st century to the 21st century. There have only been marginal changes in technical details: the material (papyrus, parchment, paper) and the binding (quire stitched together, or glued together to be cut by the reader). The formats depended on the number of times the sheet was folded: *in folio, in quarto, in octavo, in 16ths*, and in exceptional cases, *in 32nds*[33].

The printing press was thus the first truly modern industry, involving a number of actors: authors, booksellers-editors, printers, stationers, binders, punch engravers, smelters of characters and the manufacturers of the press itself[34]. This industry operated based on standards that guaranteed the

33 In the 18th century, this format was often reserved for libertine novels.

34 Various types of presses were developed to manufacture paper pulp, then paper, as well as for binding and, of course, printing.

interoperability of tools and the homogeneous production of the semi-finished products. For example:

– standardizing the dimensions of a stationer's tools: presses, trays and a frame with a screen stretched over it;

– de jure typographic standards that were often defined with State support.

Typographers played an essential role in the standardization of printing: Claude Garamont[35], Christophe Plantin[36], Pierre Simon Fournier (who created the *Fournier point*, a typographic measurement that was the predecessor of the *Didot point*[37]), John Baskerville, etc.

Printing became the catalyst for the systematic collection of knowledge. As David Hume wrote to his publisher, "The power which printing gives us of continually improving and correcting our Works in successive editions appears to me the chief advantage of that art"[38]. Even today, *publishing* remains a major tool for the evaluation and universality of science.

1.4.1. *The* Grecs du Roy *and the standardization of the typographic point*

The *Grecs du Roy*, which was a set of Greek typeface punches commissioned for King Francis I of France, represents a fascinating study in typography. This typeface responded to the difficulty with scholarly study of Greek texts at the time and, above all, responded to the need to collect and translate texts so that publishers could disseminate them among a wider, educated public. This enterprise thus became one of the chief humanistic standardization challenges of the Renaissance. The central challenge

35 Known as the creator of the Garamond fonts (with a "d" and not "t"), which were notably used by the Venetian publisher Alde Manuce.

36 The *Plantin* font was one of the sources of inspiration for *Times New Roman*.

37 The Didot dynasty, which created font families as well as de facto standards for correcting proofs.

38 Cited by Élisabeth Eisenstein (1991). In the same work, she explains that printing enabled astronomical observations to be gathered and compared exhaustively, allowing Copernicus's heliocentric theory to emerge. She highlights the role of the standardization of astronomical texts and tables, which allowed the inconsistencies in the geocentric model to be more clearly seen.

was that as with any handwritten text, the *standards for the letter forms* necessarily change and transform over centuries (from the seventh century BCE in Byzantium to the fifteenth century CE) and between regions (from Sicily to the Indus). Francis I, on the advice of Guillaume Budé, desired to make his kingdom the center of humanistic studies. He therefore decided to create printed versions of the Greek manuscripts from royal collections. Following the King's commission, between 1543 and 1555 Claude Garamont engraved the punches that would allow the printing of the characters that are today known as the legendary *Grecs du Roy* (the King's Greek letters). The original punches, preserved in France's *Imprimerie Nationale* (National Printing Press), are today considered historical monuments. Garamont engraved three different sizes: a medium size or *gros romain*, a small size or *cicero*, and a large size or *gros parangon*. These letters were designed by faithfully reproducing the Greek writing and multiple ligatures of Angelo Vergecio, a Greek copyist and calligrapher from Crete who was active in Venice between 1530 and 1538 before being put in charge of King Francis' royal collection of Greek manuscripts in Fontainebleau.

The *Didot typographic point* is another example of standardization and also posed a challenge for metrological standards. To a non-specialist, establishing a metrology of typography may seem easy. The apparent ease with which we select a font size for a typeface in a word-processing software today seems to indicate that there is a universal measurement for typographic writing. However, typographic points have been standardized to respond to the needs of professional typographers working with traditional lead fonts, as was the case in artisanal presses even in the 1960s.

To understand why such a measurement was useful, it helps to move away from quantifying the dimensions of text typed in a word[39]. In reality, the only data that an author would be interested in would be the number of characters, with or without spaces. The remaining considerations are for publishing and typesetting. Printing, which earlier measured characters in the *Didot point*, today uses the *pica*[40].

---

39 This criterion is not very relevant except for knowing whether a text will take up a greater or lesser number of pages.

40 A DTP (desktop publishing point), often called a *pica point*, corresponds to 1/72nd of the international inch, or 0.351 mm or 0.94 of a Didot point.

However, it would be erroneous to think that this measurement is universal. In typography, each character font must consider the area occupied by the *eye* of a letter (the printed part of the character), which falls within the *height of the font*[41], a rectangular shape defined by the height of the mold and measured in the *Didot point*. The typographer-printer must have a unit of measurement that allows them to set texts in horizontal lines. The typographic point, adopted by consensus, guarantees a perfect alignment of lines regardless of the font used.

By the end of the 19th century, American and British printers began to use typographic points based on the *pica*, which is 1/72nd of the international inch. Many disputes broke out over how to precisely define this value, which was a crucial commercial question for dominating the font market. For the amateur typographer in us all, the typographic point (*Didot* or *pica*) allows us to appreciate the relative size of the characters within the same font. In simple terms, size 8 < 9 < 12 < 14, etc. However, neither the *Didot point* nor the *pica point* is meant to allow us to understand the volume of the texts. They define a graphic chart. It must be emphasized that in 1978, the standard AFNOR NF Q 60-010 was published, defining the Didot point as the typographic unit of measurement in the international system. However, in 1975, the ISO had proposed a Didot point measuring 0.375 mm (or 0.2584% smaller), a value that was never adopted. It must be recognized that even among the most specialized standardizers, there has never been any consensus on the universal definition of the typographic point. The problem therefore remains just as complex today.

Today, certain publishing houses still share *galley proofs* before confirming that a text is *ready for the press*, although these are now the exceptions rather than the norm. In this context, it is still useful to have a knowledge of a small set of standardized proofreading signs.

1.4.2. *A revolution in perspective: standardizing a point of view*

With the appearance of perspective in art, it soon became a standard point of view and one that is fundamental even today in photography and cinema. The mastery of illusion in relief features emerged in Italy in the

41 Height of the inside of the mould in the direction of the letter. Not to be confused with the *character height*, which is the distance between the letter in relief and the base of the character in lead.

14th century. In 1425, Brunelleschi definitively imposed a point of view of a one-eyed, immobile spectator through a public demonstration in the Florence Baptistery. He presented the public with a *tavoletta*, a board pierced with a hole on which he had painted the Baptisery's façade. The painting stopped at the roof of the building and the tablet had a metallic mirror fixed to the portion above this, reflecting the sky. The spectators would look through the hole, holding a mirror in the other hand, thus superimposing the painting on the actual view.

Following this, the evidence of the illusion created for a single, fixed eye became the norm: *conical perspective* became the pictorial convention[42]. Leon Battista Alberti (1404–1472) theorized this principle in *De Pictura*, where he recommends that "a painter be instructed in the liberal arts, as far as possible, but [...] above all, that he have a good grasp of geometry" (Alberti 1435). Let us not let the dates mislead us, however. Brunelleschi's demonstration took place in 1425, and the first handwritten Latin edition of *De Pictura* dates to 1435 – however, this book was printed only in 1540, around 100 years after Brunelleschi's demonstration.

The question of whether perspective was discovered or rediscovered from ancient knowledge is not of interest to us here. In a highly illuminating article, Luce (1953, pp. 308–321) cites Vitruvius, who talks about lost Greek texts (especially Democritus's *Actinography*), saying they describe: "how to draw the lines corresponding in the natural way to eyes and propagation of rays from the specified center point". What interests us here is that this discovery led to a radical cultural, scientific and technical transformation in the Renaissance, not only in painting but also in geometric thought. Certain painters and theoreticians explored the limits of this concept through techniques such as anamorphosis, slowed perspective and foreshortening.

This standard conical perspective would be implemented in the *camera obscura*, the *camera lucida*, the physiognotrace and film and digital cameras. This is the conventional representation through which we analyze the world even today. It can be said that thanks to this discovery and the social adoption of all its facets, whether esthetic or theoretical, there was an unprecedented transmission of technical knowledge. Perspective laid the foundations for technical design and had a lasting impact on our perception

42 From the 15th century, Masaccio, Francesco di Giorgio Martini and Piero della Francesca rivaled one another for pictorial and geometric skill.

of beings and objects, including technical objects. In line with this, we can state that it was only through a radical change in his point of view that Leibniz was able to propose the concept of the modern binary number system.

1.4.3. *Engraving and the standardization of technical presentations*

From the Renaissance onwards, there was significant technical progress made in the field of engraving. While the earliest engravings on copper appeared around the 14th century, wood carvings had existed for much longer. Some incunabula (books printed before 1500) were illustrated using woodcuts[43]. From the 15th century, intaglio engraving became widespread, especially to diffuse the work of painters. However, unlike woodcuts, these new techniques that required engraving on copper were incompatible (we would say *non-interoperable* today) with text typography. To print using a woodcut, ink is applied on the design in relief on the block, which is perfectly compatible with the printing of texts. The engraved block, cut to the same character height[44] as the characters in the texts, can thus be directly included in the compositor for the composition of the final page. On the other hand, engraving on copper (through etching or chiseling) required a separate printing process: after inking, the excess ink had to be wiped away, with ink only remaining in the etched depressions. The image was then transferred onto a dampened sheet and pressed using a specific press that was different from the presses used for typography.

Until the 19th century and the invention of wood engraving, traditional woodcuts offered a much lower level of precision than engraving on copper. For scientific and technical books, publishers therefore printed texts and

43 For example, *De Re Militari* (1483), the first printed book to include illustrations (woodcuts) and which discussed military techniques. Another example is the *Nuremberg Chronicle*, printed in 1493 and illustrated with 1,800 woodcuts.

44 The standard height of typographic characters is 0.918 inches in North America and Great Britain. This is the height of the character measured from the foot to the face of the type. In France, this measurement is 23.56 mm or 62 points, a measurement standardized in 1723 through a Royal Decree specifying that there must be 10 lines to every half *pied du roi* (older unit of measurement of length).

illustrated plates separately, which led to a strict separation between image and text[45] in the books. This separation would last until the middle of the 19th century, notably seen in the case of Diderot and d'Alembert's *Encyclopédie* where the plates were published in a separate volume (Diderot and d'Alembert 1751).

Gradually, technical works benefitted from integrated explanations that allied texts and images. Apart from perspective, the illustrations now included complementary plan views, elevated views, and cross-sections, whose geometric construction followed rational rules. From this point onwards, the reader of a technical project was no longer looking only for an illusion of perspective, but a standardized rationality that led to the emergence of technical design. In her essay on technical design, Madeleine Pinault-Sørensen clearly illustrates the progressive inclusion of images within technical design and decision-making processes. She says:

> Colbert gives technical design an importance that it had never before enjoyed. He wanted design to play the double role of memory and progress, and to use image to present all the monuments and machines in the kingdom in order to glorify the reign of King Louis XIV. [He created a] *Bureau des dessinateurs* meant to establish maps and plans in the kingdom and then [he founded] the *École royale des Ponts et chaussées* in 1747 [...] The students received scientific and technical training. They had to know about architecture and the art of sketching, be able to prepare quotes for wooden or stone bridges and other public works and establish maps and trace them carefully in watercolors. [It was again Colbert who] gave a strong impetus to arts and professions by creating craft production centers and research programs for the Royal Academy of Sciences. (Pinault-Sørensen 2003)

Colbert was also behind the publication of the earliest plates for *Arts and Professions*, for which a truly standardized visual syntax was developed, with a series of illustrations for each profession. This model would be repeated in the plates used for the *Encyclopédie*:

---

45 A standard enforced in publishing, which necessarily led to cognitive patterns being formed.

> Each art would begin with a plate that served as the frontispiece, in the top third was a sketch, a 'condensed meaning' [...] summarizing the chief operations, and in the lower two-thirds, the descriptions of the tools. The following plates would only contain a description of the objects. (Pinault-Sørensen 2003)

Diderot and d'Alembert's *Encyclopédie* also had a rationalized dictionary, initially only textual, with close to 3,000 plates (2,885, to be precise), although only 30 plates were initially planned. This *Encyclopédie* had a lasting impact on how the European elites in the 18th and 19th centuries thought about technology. It established a true standard for technical description in text, but with close association with images that were systematically codified and referenced. These images were annotated with indices (numbers, letters, scales) corresponding to the textual commentary on the plates. However, the contemporary standardization of design was carried out by Gaspard Monge by standardizing the corpus on descriptive geometry (which was scattered until this point) and by closely associating theory with a renewed practice of technical design (see section 2.2.2).

1.5. Metrological uniqueness, the engine of metrological prosperity

Although Great Britain and the United States were the last to adopt the metric system, we must not forget that, from the 11th century onwards, England had been the first country in modern times to unify its systems of weights, measurements and currency. Inherited from the Romans, this system was enforced by law and lasted for a millennium. William the Conqueror (1066–1087) had been able to establish stable fiscal institutions like the Exchequer and a general inventory of wealth in the kingdom in his *Domesday Book*, all by putting in place a unified system of weights and measurements, which was made legally binding throughout the kingdom in order to simplify data collection. It must be highlighted that by creating a list of feudal lands without creating a cadastral survey, the *Domesday Book* favored the barons by attributing vast lands to them. In the 16th century, this led to the highly unequal dynamic of *enclosures*[46]. Further, in 1624, English industry had a patents office (*Statute of Monopolies*). This social inequality favored high finance, trade (especially maritime trade) and industry. While the rest of Europe tried to move away from its feudal structures, Great

46 This dynamic indirectly pushed poor farmers toward factories run by aristocrats.

Britain had already entered into industrial modernity, and this was in large part thanks to its metrological unicity[47].

The marine or nautical mile

The nautical mile is equal to 1,852 m, which is 1 min of latitude. In a fluid space like the sea (or sky), when one is far from the coast and without any fixed point of reference, the only possible references in earlier times were astronomical angular references. These were calculated using a sextant and the measurement of longitude using a marine chronometer. In this context, decimality was a counterproductive concept. As we saw earlier, these instruments were instead graduated into degrees of angles, formed by dividing a circle in a geometrically logical manner (6 × 60° = 360°, or six chords whose length is equal to the radius of the compass). In the geodesic system, the equatorial circle measures around 40,075 km, that is, an average length of around 1,855.3 m for 1 min of longitude at the equator. In 1929, the *international marine mile* was fixed by convention to 1,852 m, a universal value that was gradually adopted by all countries.

Box 1.3. *The nautical mile – an angular measure of length*

However, it would be wrong to assume that the Anglo-Americans were completely uninterested in a decimal metric system. British and American astronomers had approached this question, chiefly by trying to establish coherence between units of length, weight and time. Nonetheless, in daily life, the subdivisions of units of measurement and of English money offered greater flexibility than the decimal system, which only allowed a single division (2 × 5). For example, the *mile*, which was equal to 1,760 *yards*, can be then divided by 2 five times. The *yard* is equal to 3 *feet*, itself divisible into 12 *inches*. It is the same for other units, especially for currency, which makes it easy to use in everyday life and for trade. The British thus tended to retain these advantages.

If there is one domain where British sailors – or indeed any sailor or aviator in the world – have not given in, it is nautical measurements.

In Europe, until the 18th century, there was a counterproductive diversity of weights and measurements. Jaucourt's entry for *Measurement* in Diderot

47 Direct effect (weights and measurements) or indirect effects, such as the Domesday Book and enclosures.

and d'Alembert's *Encyclopédie* highlighted the total absence of coherence between the different systems:

> Entry: MEASUREMENT (*Government thereof*). It can be imagined that people would never agree to work in concert with the same weights & the same measurements; however, this is very possible in a country under a single master. Henry I, the King of England, established the same weights and measurements across all his lands; this was the work of a wise legislator, which he fully implemented in his kingdom and which has always been proposed in vain in this one. In 1321, Philippe V wished to execute it but died. Louis XI had the same thought, because, he said, a State must have only one law, one weight and one measurement. Do not protest that this was a specious project, full of problems in execution, and which upon closer study proved to have been in vain and a conflict of words, as the prices of things quickly follow their weight and measurement. Would it not be more natural to avoid this step, to prevent it, to simplify and facilitate the course of internal trade which has always been difficult, when we must constantly have in mind and before us rates of the weights and measurements of the various provinces in a kingdom, to adjust one's operations to this? (Chapelle et al. 1751)

By the end of the 17th century, the different European countries in the continent wished to unify their units of measurement without aligning themselves on any existing system, or adopting the English measurements. Taking the dimensions of the Earth or the length of a second pendulum allowed them to arrive at a universal consensus to define inter-coherent weights and measurements. In 1668, the English scholar John Wilkins proposed a coherent system of three units of measurements related to each other through astronomy and physics. In 1583, Galileo theorized the simple pendulum, apparently after having observed the oscillation of a pendulum in Padua cathedral, synchronized with his pulse. In 1659, the Dutch astronomer and physicist Christian Huygens established an algebraic relationship between the time, length and weight of a pendulum, and then filed the patent for the first pendulum clock. In 1665, Jean-Dominique Cassini (the first of a dynasty of astronomers) constructed a heliometer to update the sundial meridian line that had been installed in the San Petronio church in 1575. This brought him great renown and as a result he was appointed the astronomer at the Royal Observatory in Paris in 1669. He was thus an example of the hunt for scholars that all European states were engaged in.

John Wilkins's proposition in 1668 was a major methodological advance toward a *coherent scientific metrology*[48]. Several propositions emerged in parallel to promote a decimal system, notably by defining multiples and sub-multiples for units, which simplified calculations. In 1670, the French priest and scholar Gabriel Mouton proposed a universal unit of length, based on the measurement of a terrestrial meridian, defined according to a decimal system. In 1675, Tito Livio Burattini suggested that this unit be called the *metro cattolico* (universal measure). In 1703, Leibniz published the *Explication de l'arithmétique binaire* (Explanation of Binary Arithmetic). By theoretically extending to infinity the number of possible numerical bases, Liebnitz consequently reduced the primacy of the decimal system.

The English, who were pragmatic, did not concern themselves overmuch with the unification of weights and measurements. However, as a seafaring nation, their Parliament founded the *Board of Longitude* in 1714. This was a committee of experts in charge of allocating contracts and granting loans or subsidies to develop methods to determine longitudes, especially at sea. The compensation was fixed as a function of the precision of the proposed techniques and instruments: £20,000 for a method that determined the longitude within 30 nautical miles (56 km) or a half-degree; £15,000 for a precision of up to 40 nautical miles; £10,000 for precision within 1° (60 nautical miles). This gave the English a considerable advantage in the invention and improvement of measuring instruments. In France, a *Bureau des Longitudes* was only established in 1795, by the Convention, and its role was limited to scientific coordination and publication.

1.6. Measuring the Earth: metrology's scientific quest

Astronomers have been obsessed with measuring the earth since ancient times:

48 The following measurements were thus coordinated: (1) a *universal length* from which followed the computation of a *universal volume*; (2) a *universal mass*, defined as the quantity of rainwater contained in a cube whose edge was equal to the universal length; (3) a universal length, fixed at 38 Prussian inches, equivalent to the *length of a pendulum, the half-oscillation of which is equal to one second* (which itself is a non-decimal sub-unit of a 24-h day).

> In 205 BCE, Eratosthenes designed and carried out an experiment to measure the meridian of the earth from two points: Syene (located above the first cataract of the Nile, today known as Aswan and famous for the dam) and Alexandria. Eratosthenes, like all Greeks (at least since Anaximander in the 6th century BCE) considered the Earth to be a sphere [...] The city of Syene is almost on the Tropic of Cancer [...] At the same time, in Alexandria, 5,000 stadia to the north (i.e, around 800 kilometers from Syene), on the same meridian, the short and decentered shadow of an obelisk of known height was measured. This measurement made it possible to calculate the angle that the sun's rays made with the vertical, that is, 7.2 degrees. [Bernard Champion concludes by noting that] three centuries earlier, Eratosthenes was right and not Ptolemy. Eratosthenes had thus estimated the Earth's circumference at 250,000 stadia, or, taking one stadium to be 157.50 meters, 39,600 kilometers. This estimate was close to the actual figure of 40,000.07 kilometers. (Champion 2007, pp. 135–160)

An error of only 400 km over 360°! This was a level of precision that the *Board of Longitude* would undoubtedly have found remarkable. However, over the centuries, and even today, Ptolemy has remained better known than Eratosthenes, whose name is almost unknown.

In 1617, the Dutch physicist Willebrord Snell used triangulation to measure the distance between Alkmaar and Berg-op-Zoom, separated by 1°, with a margin of error of 4%. In 1670, Jean Picard and Christiaan Huygens measured one degree of the Paris-Amiens meridian. This triangulation was again used in 1701 by Jean-Dominique Cassini. In 1735, Charles-Marie de La Condamine was order by the Academy of Sciences to measure the length of 1° of the arc of the Earth's meridian close to the equator[49]. After many difficulties, the expedition completed this measurement of three degrees on the Quito meridian.

It was during this long quest that La Condamine adopted:

> the idea of using the length of a second pendulum at the equator, at the altitude of Quito, as the natural measure [...] defined by the gravitational attraction of the Earth rather than an

49 Maupertuis and Celsius carried out other measurements in Lapland. In retrospect, these were considered to be less precise than La Condamine's measurements.

> arbitrary measurement, like the *pied du roi*, which would provide a *standardized instrument for all nations to use.* (La Condamine 1751)

By comparing these meridian measurements, whose degrees appear longer in the South than the North, a controversy arose over the shape of the Earth. It set the Newtonians (who believed the Earth was swollen at the equator and flattened at the poles, like a mandarin) against the Cartesians (who believed the converse, that the Earth was more rounded at the poles and flattened at the Equator, like a lemon).

1.7. Turgot, standardizer of metallurgy and metrology

In 1775, Turgot, who was then a Minister under Louis XVI was preoccupied by the question of weights and measurements and wrote to Charles Messier, astronomer and a member of the Academy of Sciences:

> 3 October [1775]. M. de Condorcet must have told you [M. Charles Messier, 1730–1817], of the project that I established through exact experiments on the precise length of the pendulum, which, it appears to me, must serve as a common reference and comparison term for all measurements that will be easy to reduce to this. However, the rotational movement and the shape of the Earth will vary depending on the different latitudes, the weight, and consequently, the length of the pendulum that is used to create oscillations of equal duration. We must therefore resolve to choose the length of the pendulum at a fixed latitude as the matrix measurement [...] the 45th degree, which passes close to Bordeau, seems appropriate to me [...] I had therefore resolved to request an astronomer to come here in order to carry out all the necessary observations to establish the length of the pendulum. (Turgot 1775)

However, Turgot's fall from power led to the project being abandoned before Messier could set out[50]. Turgot was, however, a remarkable politician,

50 Editor's note on Turgot's letters: "The unification of weights and measures in France had long been demanded; it was discussed at the Estates General of Orléans in 1560. If Turgot's ministry had lasted six more months, the metric system would have been fixed thirty years earlier".

energetic and exceptionally cultured. A friend of Voltaire and the Encyclopédistes (he had authored several articles in the *Encyclopédie* himself), he was a physiocrat, yet not dogmatic. When he was a tax collector at Limoges, he had written a thesis called *Mémoire sur les mines et carrières* (Brief on Mines and Quaries) and another on *Marques des fers* (Protection of Native Iron), in which he protested against the protectionist standards imposed by the *Maîtres de forges (*Master Smiths):

> These standards are harmful to the specific requirements of industrial use [...] To prohibit the importation of foreign iron, therefore, is to favor the iron master not only at the expense of the domestic consumers, as in the ordinary cases of prohibition, [...] Now there are certain kinds of iron which our Kingdom does not supply, and which must be obtained abroad. With regard to steel, it is well known that very little of it is produced in France, that this kind of production is only just in the experimental stage, and that, however successful the trials may have been, it may take half a century perhaps before enough steel can be produced in France to supply a reasonable part of the use made of it by manufactures. (Turgot 1773)

2

The 19th Century: The Establishment of Institutions

Contemporary institutional standards were formally organized and developed over the 19th century (broadly speaking; strictly speaking from 1789 to 1906) both at a domestic as well as international level. The radical change that took place in the 19th century was that norms were no longer local technical standards defined by a few corporations or manufacturers and enforced by royal decree by the ruler. There were now techno-professional, scientific and even political communities that came together across developed nations to implement a concerted standardization process. In this second chapter, we first describe the invention and then gradual creation of the earliest international standardization bodies over the course of the 19th century. However, we also study the political, economic and scientific context that allowed the development of these norms or were forerunners to these standards. It was only toward the end of the 19th century that there arose an urgent need to regulate two domains of cutting-edge technology: electricity and telecommunication. The ITU, in 1906, provided the building blocks for future international standardization organizations. It must be highlighted that because it was so technologically specialized, the IEC was relatively protected from direct State control from the beginning[1], while the ITU, on the other hand, is even today an organization run largely on diplomatic accord between States.

In the 19th century, industry and commerce aspired to conquer the world. Out of all of this desire for universality, the strongest force emerged in the

1 Only scholars or engineers could meaningfully participate in the discussions.

late 18th century and early 19th century with the creation of *standardized units of measurement*[2]. While it was quickly seen that the standards for the telegraph system and electricity needed to be international, the metric system (and metrology in general) was largely determined by each sovereign government, and it was only in 1875 that a universal organization was founded – the Bureau International des Poids et Mesurese (BIPM[3] or the International Bureau for Weights and Measurements). This was established through a convention in 1875 that was first ratified by 17 countries from Europe and North America[4]. As a result, the BIPM is not an international standardization organization like the ITU or IEC. The BIPM units depend on science and, by extension, the technology that is required to manufacture and refine the usual instruments of measurement, especially the reference standards. It was largely between 1790 and 1850 that scholars around the world truly recognized that a difficult balance had to be maintained: not depending on companies (this was the role of the engineer) nor being restricted by country of origin. Above all, they had to be true to universal logic and reason. This is why the BIPM, the metrological standardization organization founded in 1875, is truly unique and is indisputably an international standardization organization.

This century that saw the foundation for the *modern* creation of national and international standards is also compelling because of its incompleteness. Machine working required metallurgical and mechanical standards for large-scale growth. Railways required rules for organizing international traffic. Central Europe, following Berlin's leadership, was able to attempt setting up an international organization to meet these requirements. However, all other attempts to implement international industrial standardization failed in the 19th century. This was a century of competition between industrial standards, alliances cartels and *comptoirs* (common sales agencies) organized by forge owners. Most notably, it was the period that saw Great Britain acquire monopolies because of its significant progress in metallurgy compared to European metallurgy. Moreover, it was the first country to institute national standards and establish the first *generalist*

2 The term itself is not polysemic by accident. It conveys the meaning of a unit, as in unit of measurement, and is also related to *unity*, implying universality.

3 For ease of writing, throughout this book BIPM will be generally used in a broader sense to refer to all the institutions founded in 1875, headquartered at Sèvres.

4 These institutions endow these units with their universal symbolic rationality.

national standards organization in 1901. However, we look at this in Chapter 3 and, in more detail, in Chapter 4.

2.1. The French Revolution: metric system and telegraph

The American War of Independence in 1776 and the French Revolution in 1789 ushered in a new era globally, which would eventually lead to the bourgeoisie and industrial development. For British and American historians, 1689, the year of the *Glorious Revolution* in Great Britain (which saw the overthrow of the British Monarch, James II, and the establishment of his daughter Mary and her husband William of Orange as the rulers of Great Britain) and American Independence in 1776 were events that marked the end of an era, in the same way that the French Revolution of 1789 was the year of transformation in France. These events marked the end of the *early Modern period*, the Classical period and the age of nations and the divine right of kings. Historians mark this as the beginning of the *Modern period.* These technical historical terms do not imply "Modern" and "Contemporary"[5] in the colloquial use of the terms. The important fact here is that in technological history, this was the beginning of the industrial age and, therefore, accompanied by the rise of a new social, economic and political order. The history of these three countries, the United States, France and Great Britain, is intimately linked. France helped the Americans in their War of Independence, which led to its own economy failing, leading the French King Louis XVI to call together the Estates General (the Clergy or the First Estate, the Nobility or the Second Estate and the Commoners or the Third Estate), which precipitated the French Revolution. The British Empire had to recover from the loss of the United States, but was already ahead of France in industry, maritime development and commerce (helped here by unified weights and measurements). This was the industrial and metrological modernity that the French elites of the Third Estate aspired to achieve in 1789 by adopting the metric system[6], as well as the semaphore telegraph

5 The Modern era is variously seen as the period starting from 1500 (the early Modern period) and extending up to the early 20th century. Contemporary history commonly defines the period following WWII up to the present.

6 They thereby aimed to offer the world a universal metric system.

system that Chappe presented before the Revolutionary Government, which was at war[7].

French political history, however, is eventful. In the first phase of the French Revolution (from 1789 to 1792), the objective was to force the King to accept a constitutional monarchy, but before this could happen Louis XVI tried to flee (which was treated as treason), leading to his downfall, the triggering of war with Austria, the establishment of the French Republic and the execution of the king. This marked the onset of the second, extremist, phase of the Revolution in which all the elites were either executed or forced to work with the Republic. This ended in the Reign of Terror, followed by the third phase of the Revolution that began with a return to the objectives of the first phase but ended with the coronation of Napoleon I. This led to a more pernicious form of absolutism and unleashed violence across Europe, even though Napoleon's dictatorial reign was accompanied by technical and scientific modernization (which was occasionally arbitrary).

2.1.1. *The decimal metric system at the heart of the Revolution*

Talleyrand-Périgord, the great French diplomat, was the Bishop of Autun and also one of the major actors in the first phase of the Revolution. He was at the forefront of all reforms and in early March of 1790, he rose to address the Tribune on his "Proposal on Weights and Measurements", which he had printed and distributed to all the deputies:

> Messieurs, the countless variety in our weights and measures, and their bizarre denominations, necessarily cause confusion in ideas and difficulties in trade [he retraces the diversity highlighted in the *Encyclopédie*]. Nothing can justify such abuse. It is the Assemblée Nationale's duty to annihilate this. I will not revisit what we have learned from history concerning political economy [the Romans, Charlemagne, La Condamine]. Finally, the significance of this reform revealed itself to the quick mind of M. Turgot, who was able to appreciate it and he was going to give it his name when he left the Ministry. Today, you will do

7 Chappe's telegraph system was an immediate military advantage and was unanimously adopted.

> what this great man regretted not being able to do [collaborating with other nations]. The National Assembly will write a letter to the Parliament in England to engage it in competing with France in finalizing the natural unit for measurements and weights; consequently, under the auspices of both nations[8], officers from the Academy of Sciences in Paris will meet with an equal number of members chosen from the Royal Society of London [...] Each nation will use this measurement to create its standard references, which it will then carefully preserve such that if, centuries later, any variation is seen in the sidereal year, these standard references can be used to evaluate this and, from here, to associate this important point in a *world system* with a significant authority, that of the National Assembly [...] Each municipality will be sent a certain number of new weights and measures that will be freely distributed by them to those to whom this change will prove costly; such that eventually, just six months after this is sent, the older measurements will be abolished and replaced by the new ones. (Talleyrand-Périgord 1884, pp. 104–105)

Two months after Talleyrand's proposal, the National Assembly adopted the principle of standardizing weights and measurements (May 8, 1790). Charles de Borda, Condorcet, Lavoisier and Tillet were sent as delegates to Spain, England and the United States to finalize the definition off the unit. While initially in favor of the pendulum, the United States and England changed their opinion in late 1790 and opted for a measurement related to the earth's arc, which seemed easier and more universal. The French Academy of Sciences deliberated and appointed a commission, which set up a decimal project based on a quarter of the Earth's meridian. What remained was defining a base unit. On March 26, 1791, Condorcet proposed an ambitious and universal metrological project before the deputies (who had become the Constituent Assembly):

> Considering that, in order to establish the uniformity of weights and measures, it is necessary to fix a natural and invariable unit

8 Talleyrand was not naive in saying this. In the 1780s, he had been a close associate of Calonne (Louis XVI's Comptroller General of Finances) and had thus attended the signing of the Eden-Rayneval Treaty, a free-trade agreement between France and Great Britain, signed in 1786.

> of measurement, and that the only way to extend this uniformity to foreign countries and to engage them in accepting a system of measurement, is to choose a unit that has nothing arbitrary about it and which is not specific to the location of any people on the globe, […] adopt the value of the quarter of the earth's meridian as the base of the new system of measurements, which will be a decimal one: the necessary operations to determine this base, especially measuring the meridian arc from Dunkirk to Barcelona, will be relentlessly carried out. (Condorcet 1791)

However, the triangulation work was interrupted several times during the Reign of Terror. The scholars were arrested and accused of espionage[9]:

> In 1793, the Convention adopted the meter and three months later, the Academy of Sciences was shut down but several members were part of the temporary Commission on Weights and Measurements. Lavoisier was arrested. In 1795, the Executive Commission for Public Education was given charge of the weights and measurements project. (Boyé n.d.)

The Convention did not wait for the work to be completed and decided, instead, to adopt a provisional system based on the work carried out by Condamine, Maupertuis and Cassini. Reference weights and measures were created and the Metric System became one of the Articles in the French Constitution of 1795: "There shall be uniformity of weights and measures throughout the Republic" (Law of 1st Vendemiaire, year IV, September 23, 1795, Article 371)[10]. The new measurements were enforced and teachers had to teach French schoolchildren and the local authorities the new system. In June 1798, under the Directoire, Talleyrand (who had spent the intervening years in England and then the United States before returning to France) invited allied and neutral nations to participate in the determination of the final references for the meter and kilogram:

> On 22 June 1799, the definitive prototype reference standards in platinum, for the meter and kilogram, were presented to the Conseil des Cinq-Cents (the Council of the Five Hundred), and then the Conseil des Anciens (the Council of Elders) by a

9 The reason: they climbed to the top of bell towers with telescopes!

10 See: https://revolution.chnm.org/items/show/409.

> delegation comprising of foreign scholars and members of the Commission of Weights and Measurements of the Institut National. The reference standards were then given to Camus, the Keeper of the Archives of the Republic, who then locked them into a steel double cupboard, locked with 4 keys, hence their name: "Meter and Kilogram of the Archives". The meter is (then) a flat ruler with a rectangular cross-section […] The law of 19 Frimaire of the year VIII (10 December 1799) [proclaimed these] the definitive reference standards for the measurement of length and weight throughout the Republic. The hallmark of the Republic must be applied to these new measurements. (Février n.d.)

The reformation of the new measurements, called MKS (meter, kilogram, second), was associated with the implementation of decimal multiples and sub-multiples. At this time, French society was only partially literate. Further, as in almost all societies, there were broadly three worlds of metrology:

1) The world of the scholars, especially astronomers and physicists, as well as engineers. Meridian calculations are angular calculations, most often expressed in a base of 60 and requiring the use of trigonometric tables as well as whole number calculations where decimality is indispensable.

2) The intermediate social category of the Good Man of the Enlightenment – literate, curious about science, not necessarily familiar with mathematical nuances, but frequently required to confront financial computations. The worlds of industry, banking and wholesale and international trade were all related to this world.

3) The ancient world, largely unfamiliar with writing and even more so with complex calculations. This was the world of the *boutiques*, said to be reactionary and almost illiterate, that the Revolution had wanted to eradicate.

2.1.2. *The Republican Calendar and decimality under the Terror*

It would be completely wrong to think that the *metric system* (associated with a unified and consistent system of weights and measures) was wholly invented and gifted to the world by the deputies of the Revolutionary Constituent Chamber fueled by the ideal of a reason-led government. This was, of course, the heroic historical account that even today is a simplified summary, a reassuring narrative. The fact is that the deputies claimed to be men of the Enlightenment as well as rigorous scholars but found it difficult to avoid being manipulated within the pseudoscientific commissions that Revolutionary extremists had set up and tightly controlled in order to be able to put in place an extremist, hardline vision of the decimal system, weights and measurements and, above all, the *Republican Calendar*.

However, since Leibniz's article "Explanation of Binary Arithmetic" was published in 1703, the international community of scholars in the late 18th century was aware of binary numbers, therefore relativity, and also the fundamental importance of the *decimal system*. Examining articles on these subjects, which the members of the Convention must have read (numbers, binary, fraction, quantity, calculus, measurement, area, quadrature, weight, volume, time, second, calendar, velocity, etc.), we can see today how ideology can prevail over reason. From August 1792, the positive aspects of the reform were pushed to the background. The extremist Montagnards governed through terror and forced scholars to take on two projects: *weights and measurements* and the *Republican Calendar*.

From July 14, 1789, the idea of proclaiming a new era of liberty circulated within the revolutionary press. The day after it was created, the National Convention met and decreed that from this day onwards (fortuitously the first day of the autumn equinox), all public documents would be dated as being the first year of the French Republic. The symbolic intent was clear and praiseworthy; however, its implementation depended on a handful of ideologues led by a surprising guru: Charles-Gilbert Romme. A Calendar Commission was appointed within the Committee of Public Education: Lagrange, Lalande and Monge were the scientific leaders; however, Romme took over very quickly. The parliamentarians quickly turned both these commisions into *political commissions* (the Weights and Measurements and Calendar Commisions) and manipulated or silenced the scholars, who were held hostage by them. The Calendar Commission soon abandoned the idea of reconciling the Gregorian calendar with this new calendar.

However, as certain members tried to (timidly) put forth, the Gregorian calendar was born out of patient efforts to reconcile the lunar logic of using 28-day months with a solar year[11] of approximately 365 and a quarter days, first standardized by Julius Caesar (46 BCE, who replaced the Republican

11 See, for example, Parisot and Suagher (1997).

Roman calendar) and then readjusted by Pope Gregory XIII in 1582. The priority of the Reformers was to eradicate everything that alluded to saints, religious feasts and the God who rested on the seventh day! Romme proposed new names for 12 months, made up of 30 days each and divided into three 10-day cycles, with 5 "intercalary" days at the end of the year, and a sixth day added every leap year. The day would now be 10 h long (instead of 24 h), with each hour being decimalized: each hour was 100 decimal minutes, and each minute was 100 decimal seconds.

Months and days in the Republican Calendar:

– autumn (names ending in-aire): vendémiaire, brumaire and frimaire;

– winter (names ending in -ôse): nivôse, pluviôse and ventôse;

– spring (names ending in -al) germinal, floréal and prairial;

– summer (names ending in -or): messidor, thermidor and fructidor.

The names of the days were composed of an ordinal prefix and the suffix -di (*dies* in Latin = day). Thus, the 10 days in each cycle were as follows: primidi, duodi, tridi, quartidi, quintidi, sextidi, septidi, octidi, nonidi and décadi. Since the Republican Calendar had only 360 regular days, the remaining days before the next year began were called the *sanculotide days* (after the Sans-Culottes, or the name given to the working-class people, many of whom drove the Revolution): 17 September: the Day of Virtue, followed by the Day of Genius, followed by the Day of Work and the Day of Opinion up to 21 September, the Day of Rewards. Every 4 years a day was added: this was the Festival of the Revolution and called the leap year[12].

Box 2.1. *Terminology of the Republican Calendar*

Although the related Commission for Weights and Measures developed a meter, kilogram, second system, all references to the last unit vanished with this calendar! Certain clockmakers made new watches and clocks or a clockface with both systems. The Republican Calendar had a fascinating and outlandish history. In its initial version, the year, months and days in the 10-day cycle (*décade*) were simply designated in an ordinal manner: "The third day of the first décade of the fourth month of the second year of the

12 Romme did not wish to use the term "bissextile", preferring the term "sextile". He was unaware that the Romans used this to indicate that one day was doubled (*bis*) every 4 years.

Republic!" When questioned by the deputies of the National Convention, Romme took on board certain criticisms and a new commission was appointed, in October 1793, to create a new nomenclature for the months and days! It was Fabre d'Églantine[13], a renowned poet, who proposed a list of nature-based names for the months, which would be memorable and facilitate the use of this system.

A few criticisms had emerged in the meantime – those who wanted universalism instead of the fanaticism of liberty, and those who fought for reason. Both these concerns were swept aside. What the Montagnards wanted was a radically new, decimal calendar. However, Romme was not ignorant. From 1779 to 1786, he had tutored the son of the Russian count Stroganov. He frequently engaged with Euler at the Academy of Sciences in St. Petersburg. It is hard to understand why, after Robespierre was executed, he joined the *Crétois*, extremist deputies[14] who wished to continue with the Reign of Terror. This choice led him to the guillotine on June 17, 1795 – though he succeeded in stabbing himself just before climbing onto the platform. His final words were, "I die for the Republic". Historically, this was a terrible period. The guillotine came down endlessly. Many scholars from the Academy were killed and, on August 8, 1793, the Royal Academy was dissolved. A few scholars, notably those who were working on the weights and measurement project, or on the calendar, faced legal troubles. Delambre, Borda and Laplace were arrested. Lavoisier and Jean-Sylvain Bailly were guillotined. Condorcet killed himself to avoid being executed. Despite its inherent contradictions, the *Decimal Hour* decree was only abrogated on April 17, 1795, when a moderate majority came back to power. However, the Republican Calendar was such a significant symbol of the Republic that it would take more than a simple decision to remove it from public consciousness.

We must consider what a complete upheaval the enforced adoption of such a disruptive calendar would have meant for the French. The implementation of a 1-day cycle and the removal of almost all festival days except the *décadi* (every 10th day, the equivalent of Sunday) and the five *s*

13 Fabre d'Églantine wrote the libretto of the comic opera *Laure et Pétrarque* (1780), which had a famous song alluding to Marie Antoinette. Having become a Montagnard (the radical section after the Revolution) during the Reign of Terror, he was guillotined on April 5, 1794.

14 The name, *Crétois*, came from the fact that they sat on the highest benches in the Assembly, the *crête* or "crest".

days would have been an unprecedently violent change. The calendar almost doubled working hours and we can imagine that the moderate bourgeois government who succeeded the Reign of Terror were in no hurry to return to a 7-day week and the varied Christian holidays. Further, once implemented, this *Era of Liberty* became a powerful national symbol. There were successive amendments, changes in certain details and a move to legalize the use of both the Republican and Gregorian calendar, until, finally, in 1806, Napoleon definitely ended the use of the Republican Calendar.

2.1.3. *The metric system before the standardized body in Sèvres*

France benefited from the revolutionary spirit that helped institutionalize a system of weights and measurements founded on the meter, kilogram and second (MKS). It standardized this system over all its territories and enforced its adoption in regions it conquered. However, it was also the first nation to abandon this system. An unsettling order dated 13 Brumaine, year IX (November 4, 1800), decreed: "The decimal system of weights and measurements will be definitely executed across the Republic from 1st Vendémiaire, year X (23 September 1802)". The decree added:

> To facilitate this execution, the denominations given to weights and measurements can be translated in public documents and in everyday speech, using the following French terms [...] the Kilogram can be called the Pound; the Centimeter, the Finger; the Liter, the Pint. (Février n.d.)

Fortunately, there was a reaction from the elites in the country. Schools continued teaching the metric system, but it took 40 years for a law dated July 4, 1837 to state:

> From January 1, 1840, all weights and measurements other than those established by the laws of 18 Germinal, year III, and 19 Frimaire, year VIII, constituting the decimal metric system, will be prohibited under the penalties laid out in Article 479 of the Penal Code. (Février n.d.)

The irony of history was that Switzerland adopted the metric system in 1803, the Netherlands in 1816 and Greece in 1836. Drawing a veil over the last three decades of failed experiments, after 1830 the French government once again took action to promote the universality of the metric system. The practice of exchanging physical objects that serve as standard references with other counties became generalized. Thus, when the Meter Convention was set up in 1875, the BIPM was set up at Sèvres. This international organization exists even today and we examine the details of its foundations more closely in section 2.8.

2.1.4. *Chappe's technological and institutional innovations*

There were many forerunners to the aerial transmission of visual signals: smoke signals, beacons, maritime signals using flags, etc. However, Chappe's telegram system and, to a certain extent, other similar systems developed in Europe in the early 19th century were a significant advance. These systems allowed users to exchange predetermined signals as the Romans had done, but with much higher efficiency. Chappe's secret vocabulary was composed of 8,464 terms. Further, it was possible to transmit messages using an alphabetic code, allowing texts to be precisely transcribed, letter by letter. Aerial telegraph systems quickly proved advantageous, providing sophisticated and rapid communication[15], although they were dependent on weather conditions and it was near impossible to use them at night. It must be highlighted that well after the Morse telegraph system was set up in Europe, certain arial telegraph systems remained functional until the first undersea cables were laid over short distances, like the Calais strait.

The real merit of the system developed by Chappe, his brothers and a cousin, Léon Delauney[16], was how they rationally systematized the aerial telegraphy process. Semaphore was optimized, telescopes were installed between neighboring relay stations, the optimal distance between towers was determined and a sophisticated code was developed, a precursor to future electric telegraph codes[17]. This system was made possible due to the Chappe semaphore system, comprising a regulator with two wings that acted as

15 A message and its response could travel between Paris and Lille in just a few hours, a feat that could never be matched on horseback.

16 Léon Delauney, the cousin, is largely forgotten today but played a major role in developing Chappe's numerical code.

17 For a more detailed explanation, visit: https://www.dcode.fr/alphabet-chappe.

indicators. With these three components, it was possible to compose messages based on the precise position of each component:

– In correspondence mode, the regulator had to be either horizontal or vertical.

– While composing signals, it was placed in a left oblique position (which interrupted transmission).

– The right oblique position was reserved for what were called "regulation signals" (emergency, fog, interruption in service, etc.).

– The two indicators (the "wings" on the regulator) were used to code the message itself. Theoretically, it was possible to create 196 distinct signals: the regulator had two useful positions, and the indicators seven useful positions. But in practice, to avoid errors, only 98 were used, 6 of which were reserved for signal preparation[18].

Claude Chappe had been a priest before the Revolution, which gave him sufficient income. He was interested in mechanics, physics and ways to transmit messages using static electricity. However, the Revolution ended his ecclesiastic income. In March 1792, he presented his invention to the Legislative Assembly: "A certain means of establishing correspondence, such that the Legislative Body can ensure its orders reach our borders and receive a response within the same session" (Gerspach 1860).

In March 1793, Charles-Gilbert Romme prepared a report on Chappe's telegraph system for the Committee of Public Education. Mistrustful of this, Chappe wrote to Lakanal. Due to Lakanal's report, the Convention appointed Claude Chappe to the position of Telegraph Engineer by decree and gave him exclusive rights to the telegraph system in France. He soon established the first lines[19] and had the monopoly on the system. The Paris-Lille telegraph line was functional from August 1794. Military and political history soon proved the advantages of the telegraph system. The news that the city of Condé had been won back from the Austrians was transmitted on the very day of the Convention. The deputies applauded this victory and the new invention. They sent the victorious army their congratulations and received a response before the Parliamentary session ended. Reinforced by

18 The grid was 92 × 92, instead of 98 × 98, in order to make space for service signals and transmission in alphabetic mode.

19 The Chappe telegraph system was inaugurated on September 1, 1794.

this success, the Chappe brothers expanded the telegraph network and regulated the work of the station operators[20].

From 1830 onwards, France, which had become a constitutional monarchy, started encouraging business. Since large companies required the telegraph system, the State developed an ambitious network[21] and introduced telegraphic correspondence (Law of 1837). Other European nations had not remained idle either. By the early 19th century, England, Russia, Prussia, Sweden and Spain had all acquired different optical telegraph systems. However, none of these countries had designed a semaphore system that performed as well as the Chappe system, nor had such a sophisticated code or such an organized network[22].

From 1838 onwards, an electric telegraph line operated along the London–Liverpool railway line. In France, the telegraph system remained entirely State controlled. In 1844, a royal decree finally authorized experimenting with an electric line along the Paris–Rouen railway line, and then the Paris–Lille line. It was only in 1851 that the electric telegraph system was fully adopted, allowing France to establish a network that fulfilled its ambitions.

2.2. Disparities in European technologies and standardization

By the middle of the 19th century, technological progress had transcended borders. It reduced distances and industry began to free itself from nation-State control. It was a period of scientific, industrial, economic and sociopolitical upheaval. With the advent of the railways, steamboats and the electric telegraph, the world seemed to have shrunk. Nations became increasingly aware of their interdependence on each other. Finally, industrialists and financiers traveled the world, offering their services to various parties – private clients as well as governments.

---

20 For enhanced confidentiality, the station operators who transmitted the messages in the semaphore towers were recruited from the illiterate populations.

21 Concentric lines led to lines radiating outwards from Paris. In 1844, the network was composed of 5,000 km of lines and 534 stations.

22 This lack of interest was due to strategic risks, unfavorable weather in the northern regions, and, quite soon, the desire to concentrate all efforts on an already operational electric telegraph system.

2.2.1. *Technological advances in Britain*

By the late 18th century, the distinction between the *sciences* and the *arts* (used here in the sense of the different crafts) varied between languages and between countries. Unlike in Continental Europe, in Great Britain there was no loss of prestige associated with a scholar looking into practical applications. The Royal Society of London for the Improvement of Natural Knowledge was less directly dependent on the Crown than its counterparts in Europe. It also rewarded innovation in many ways.

We must also highlight the importance of the highly eclectic circles of thinkers, especially the famous Lunar Society of Birmingham, whose members met every month on the day of the full moon (hence their name). During these meetings, the topics of discussion covered science, technology, politics, philosophy, art, economic theory and business, and also included morality and religion. Famous Lunar Society members[23] included Adam Smith, James Watt, Sir Richard Arkwright (creator of the first fully automatic spinning machines), the industrialist Matthew Boulton and the chemist–inventor–metallurgist John Roebuck, who pioneered the use of metallurgical coal. This was a major invention with a lasting impact on British industrial development.

Statistical comparisons between results from metallurgy using coke-fired furnaces and charcoal-fired furnaces are quite revealing. By the late 1770s, British metallurgy had completely abandoned the use of charcoal. However, Continental Europe only abandoned charcoal in the 1840s or 1850s. The resulting volume and quality of the iron, steels and cast-iron produced gave Great Britain a headstart of three to four decades over other European countries.

In France, the *Encyclopédie* by Diderot and d'Alembert (a general encyclopedia covering "sciences, arts and crafts") led to a rigid standardization in the arts and crafts. Nevertheless, it was followed by the *Encyclopédie méthodique*, also known as the *Encyclopédie Panckoucke*. This book consisted of over 50 scientific dictionaries, with the aim of offering a coherent and updated vision of science and technology. The man who compiled these, Panckoucke (1782–1832), aspired to improve and

23 Non-British luminaries included Benjamin Franklin, who attended multiple meetings, while Antoine Lavoisier carried on correspondence with them.

complement existing information. Many eminent scholars such as Condorcet, Laennec, Lamarck and Monge contributed to this encyclopedia. Several articles from Diderot and d'Alembert's *Encyclopédie* were updated and reprinted in this new publication.

Consequently, in 1814, a volume dedicated to metallurgy was published. The explanation on the first image in the book is eloquent. It reads: "Large furnace that the English use to convert iron into steel: this furnace is heated using coal". This is followed by multiple columns explaining the use of tall furnaces using black coal that is transformed into coke. However, it was only in the late 1830s that French metallurgists realized that the use of black coal was now non-negotiable.

The industrial age was comparable to a *New Iron Age*. This period saw greater distinctions between different kinds of iron (cast iron, iron, different grades of steel) as well as iron alloyed with non-ferrous metals. All these products were gradually chemically isolated, and the primary material (cast iron) was reworked with great precision to manufacture a variety of tools, machines, electrical components, industrial and urban installations, ships and railways. The development of *industrial standards for iron*[24] was a key factor in the rise of industrial standardization.

As in several other sectors, Great Britain had a considerable headstart in the development of metallurgy, steam-powered machines and railways. The first steam-powered machine may have been invented by French mathematician Denis Papin in 1690, but in 1712 Thomas Newcomen designed the atmospheric engine. This machine combined steam and atmospheric pressure to pump water at great depths (to remove water from mines or supply water to cities). In 1804, English engineer Richard Trevithick developed the first steam locomotive, which could move 10 tons of iron at 8 km/h. In 1830, George Stephenson built *The Rocket*, a revolutionary locomotive that used a cylindrical boiler and reused exhaust gases from the firebox to improve performance. He inaugurated the Manchester–Liverpool line and exported his locomotives across Europe.

The first entirely mechanized spinning device was developed by Richard Arkwright in 1771. It ran on his patented device, the *Spinning Frame*. This

24 Anticipating the development of institutional standards, which came later, notably to prevent risks or negative factors that could result from the use of competing standards.

machine was the first to solve a complex technical question: the fiber was stretched out through multiple rollers at different points, while simultaneously ensuring tenson and finally winding it around a bobbin. Another major refinement was that it integrated 128 bobbins on a single machine. The industrialist John Fielden makes a note of the surrounding social skepticism and the unabashed use of child labor:

> At a meeting in Manchester a man claimed that a child in one mill walked twenty-four miles a day. I was surprised by this statement, therefore, when I went home, I went into my own factory, and with a clock before me, I watched a child at work, and having watched her for some time, I then calculated the distance she had to go in a day, and to my surprise, I found it nothing short of twenty miles. (Fielden 1836)

It was only in the 20th century that the main standardization organization (ISA, ISO, IEC) and their domestic counterparts established safety norms[25].

2.2.2. *Monge: descriptive geometry and industrial design*

A core problem with standardization is descriptive geometry, which is integral to industrial design. It becomes an essential information system that is used to define certain technical norms.

Gaspard Monge (1746–1818) was a precocious figure: by 14, he had already designed an innovative fire pump. He soon became a highly regarded scholar, one of the founders of the École Polytechnique and a globally renowned descriptive geometry theoretician. In the preface to his book dedicated to this discipline, Monge clearly lays out his ambition for France and the world, as well as the industrial, technological and scientific aims of descriptive geometry, which he believed was an indispensable tool. He made note of the industrial progress in other countries, especially Great Britain, and defined the objective of descriptive geometry as being:

> Descriptive geometry has two objects in view: the first is to determine methods for representing on a sheet of paper which has only two dimensions, viz., length and breadth, the forms of

25 We will see in Chapter 4 that the American standardization organization played a pioneering role here.

> solid bodies which have three, length, breadth, and thickness, provided that these bodies can be rigorously defined.
>
> The second object is to determine methods for recognizing from an exact construction the forms of solid bodies, and thence to deduce all the truths resulting both from their forms and respective positions. (Monge 1820, p. XVI)

Monge was not really the inventor of descriptive geometry, as was widely believed. However, his global theoretical vision and pedagogic determination contributed significantly in assembling, unifying, codifying and standardizing the existing corpus in this domain (which was not widely shared at the time as it was a military secret). He put in place conventions, such as codes for shadows that made it possible to determine the relative positions of surfaces on a volume.

2.2.3. *The new media: photography, cinema*

While France may have been slow in catching up with industrial metallurgical progress, it outstripped other countries in photography and cinema. Other countries soon caught up, especially the United States. While these technologies were still too poorly developed to be standardized in the 19th century[26], they were the subject of the earliest standardization attempts in the 1930s under the aegis of the ISA (see Chapter 4). The 35 mm format became the gold standard.

Photography and cinema also transformed the scientific method[27] and certain technologies, like galvanoplasty, photoengraving and medical radiography. The impact of these innovations went beyond the scientific field: they transformed industry, the arts and daily life, as could be seen in the explosion of postcards and stereo imaging.

In parallel, printed periodicals shaped thoughts, including scientific and technical thinking. The limitations in the production of the daily press accelerated innovations in printing[28]. This led to the convergence of several

26 It was only at the end of the 19th century that the first films and photography equipment were industrially manufactured. It took even longer for the world of cinema.

27 For example, Marey and Muybridge's chronography.

28 Printing technologies are continuously being improved even today.

disciplines that would later be standardized through the ISA and then ISO: paper production, mechanics, photography, electromagnetic and, much later, information technology.

2.3. The post-1850 move toward international technical regulation

British advances led to de facto monopolies, especially for railways, where British firms enforced their standards for track gauges. But beyond this technological domination, their stable political traditions and institutional pragmatism encouraged negotiations and *gentlemen's agreements*, which were key elements in the standardization process.

In continental Europe, things were much more unstable due to the revolutions of 1848. In the second half of the 19th century, new technologies transformed lifestyles in a lasting manner. This impacted the privileged classes first and then those who aspired to enter these classes. With a population of around 80 million in 1850, Europe saw the emergence of regulations, especially in the field of pharmacopeia, while urban infrastructure was modernized (drainage systems, water and gas distribution across all floors in a building). However, industrial standardization was still dominated by industrialists who were always torn between collaboration (normative dynamic) and commercial differentiation (falling back on "in-house specifications"). Up to the end of the 19th century, the institutional standardization of technologies (apart from telecommunications and electricity) was underdeveloped at both the domestic and international levels[29].

2.4. The exemplary case of Standard Oil

John D. Rockefeller, who founded the Standard Oil Company in 1870, became an exemplary case in the war of standards. When he set up his company, he adopted a business model and industrial standards that were restrictive but highly favorable to himself:

– He recovered waste products which could then be refined to obtain sub-products while also reducing the pollution from his oil wells.

29 Except in Great Britain.

– He ensured consistent quality, making his petroleum safer and less malodorous, which was a huge advantage for petroleum-based lighting and heating, his major market at the time.

– With his team of high-level researchers, he soon understood the benefits of refining oil from poor-quality oilfields (notably those with highly acidic petroleum), which he acquired at low prices.

– He was therefore able to produce high-quality kerosene that was essential for lighting.

– He recovered sub-products that he used to make lubricating oil, tar, solvents, removers, etc.

– He developed fuels meant for combustion engines (a very promising technology at the time), especially for maritime use. His fortune soared with the democratization of the automobile.

Due to this self-imposed standardization, Rockefeller was seen as a philanthropist, a man who cared for the life and health of the users of his products. This image was further reinforced in 1913 when he established the Rockefeller Foundation, which served as a shield against criticism directed at him. *Standardized quality*, a feature reflected in the very name of this company, allowed himself to acquire a near monopoly. In 1911, the US Supreme Court upheld an antitrust ruling and Rockefeller was forced to divide his empire into 34 companies, including those that became part of the famous Seven Sisters, which still play a fundamental role in global petroleum geostrategy.

2.5. The Great Exhibitions – incubators for the ITU, BIPM and IEC

The Great Exhibition of 1851 in London was the first of its kind, an international and popular forum dedicated to technology. It was organized at Hyde Park, within a custom-built iron and glass structure called the Crystal Palace. The exhibition was an initiative undertaken by Prince Albert, the prince consort of Britain's Queen Victoria. This young Belgian-Bavarian prince with a pan-European exposure was a fervent advocate for modernity. For many years, he had presided over and organized commercial and industrial fairs within the United Kingdom. When the Great Exhibition was organized, inside its 92,000 m^2 glass house, the elite from all circles all over the world, politicians, intellectuals, scientists and industrialists, flocked to it.

From May 1 to October 15, 1851, 6 million visitors, from across all social classes (many making multiple visits), explored the scientific, industrial and artistic innovations displayed by over 14,000 exhibitors. Among the personalities who attended were Charles Darwin, Karl Marx, Michael Faraday (a member of the jury awarding medals), Charles Dickens, Lewis Carroll, George Eliot and Charlotte Brontë, as well as a number of European princes and Indian maharajas. The London exhibition promised the advent of a technological world with no borders. However, this progress could not grow without some regulation, whether technical or societal. Even the most ardent defendants of universalism had to agree that nothing could evolve completely independent of any power or market. For telegraphic, rail and electric networks, as well as urban infrastructure (gas, drains, water pipes), the State often played a key role as the primary investor as well as regulator.

The Great Exhibitions, which came to symbolize collective amazement at the miracles wrought by industry, were organized every 3–5 years, starting in the second half of the 19th century and considerably accelerated the process of globalization. These exhibitions were an important context within which formal and informal meetings occurred, promoting the organization of any number of specialized conferences on electricity, mechanics, metrology, railroads, telegraph systems, chemistry, statistics, etc. Some of these conferences resulted in the creation of the first international standardization organizations. These exhibitions offered an idealized vision of the relations that could exist between companies and the communities of governing forces around the world. They attracted a public that was keen to discover the benevolent uses of technology. The crowds numbered in the millions: 6 million visitors in London in 1851, 5 million in Paris in 1855, 6 million again in London in 1862, 15 million in Paris in 1867, 7 million in Vienna in 1873 and 10 million in Philadelphia in 1876 (an exhibition that saw the introduction of the telephone – and ketchup!). The impact did not fade over time: 16 million visitors attended the Paris exhibition in 1878, a record that was broken by double that number in 1899 (the exhibition for which the Eiffel Tower was built). The 1893 Chicago exhibition saw close to 28 million visitors come to admire the first fluorescent lights. In 1900, Paris welcomed 51 million visitors[30] who came to see the cinema, the escalators in the Grand and Petit Palais and the Olympic Games.

30 This record would remain unbroken for 70 years until the Exhibition in Osaka in 1970 (64 million visitors) and then in Shanghai in 2010 (73 million visitors).

The exhibition in Saint-Louis (USA) in 1904 celebrated 100 years of the purchase of Louisiana from France. The Olympic games were also organized here. The event drew 20 million visitors, representing 63 countries. The International Electrician's Congress was also organized as a part of the exhibition, leading to a collaboration that would result in the creation of the International Electrotechnical Commission (IEC), founded in London in 1906.

The Great Exhibitions thus proved to be the catalysts for the emergence of a global technical culture that was updated periodically. They were the symbol of a deep and unshakeable faith in universal and shared progress. They also played a direct role in the creation of three significant international standardization organizations:

– the ITU, founded in 1865;

– the BIPM, created in 1875;

– the IEC, formalized in 1906.

Questions around patents and intellectual property were also debated here, especially at the exhibitions in Vienna (1873) and Paris (1878). These discussions led to the signing of the Paris Convention in 1884. However, there were significant differences between national interests and industrial interests: legal approaches were still dominated by national traditions and continued to be applied according to the reigning legal principle in each country[31].

2.6. The invention and founding of standardization organizations

At the dawn of the industrial era, an early level of standardization emerged within companies, although this was not yet an institutionalized standardization. Companies developed production rules in order to sell goods that were homogeneous and likely to win customer loyalty. These clients had to be able to count on the finished or semi-finished products (pig

31 Although a few important principles are universally accepted, the debates over how to define international standards for intellectual property and innovation have not really provided any universally acceptable solution even today.

iron, metallic ingots, beams, screws, spare parts, etc.) as well as the raw materials or standardized bulk products (ores, cereals, cotton bales, etc.). This standardization was also applicable to complex equipment such as tools, steam engineers or mechanical textile manufacturing devices.

When a customer is also a producer of manufactured goods, they must be assured that the products they are using in their own manufacturing process have constant characteristics. This is because they, in turn, need to assure their customers of the quality, reliability and compatibility of spare parts[32] and primary materials. This interdependence between various crafts deepened significantly in the 19th century and became a major feature of the industrialized world. Large companies had extensive networks for solidarity and exchange: professional guilds (especially the powerful Ironmasters' Association in France), networks of former students of specialized schools, chambers of trade and regional chambers. In the domain of heavy industry, metallurgists (who were grouped together in these organizations) formed alliances to establish *centers for the sale of semi-finished* products. In France, this led to the creation of many *Comptoirs* (sale points or cartels), such as the Comptoir de Longwy (1876), the Comptoir for Springs (1892), the Comptoir for Beams (1896) and the Comptoir for the Export of Metallurgical Products (1904). Beyond the economic advantages they offered, these groups enforced de facto standardization in production. Clients were now able to choose their joists, screws and rivers from *common catalogues* and were thus guaranteed specific characteristic features for each product.

Standardization also fulfilled another need: that of States who wished to protect their citizens against risks related to technological innovations. Industrialization was accompanied by a rise in the use of steam engines, railroad networks, bridges and other metallic infrastructure. To prevent any risk, it was essential to guarantee the resistance of the materials being used. In this regard, the English scholar Thomas Young (1773–1829) was one of the first to put forward the fundamentals of a theory of *the modulus of elasticity in metallic beams and the resistance of cast-iron columns*[33]. In France, these problems were deeply studied by Navier, a graduate of the Ecole Polytechnique and Professor at the École Nationale des Ponts et

32 And that these will always be available.

33 A theory that he presented in his work *Lectures on Natural Philosophy* (Young 1807).

Chaussées (National School for Bridges and Roadways), who contributed to the development of methods for calculations related to metallic structures[34].

The Central Commission for the Navigation of the Rhine (CCNR) one of the first international standardization organizations

The IUT, founded in 1865, is often considered to be the first of the international standardization organizations. However, the Central Commission for the Navigation of the Rhine (CCNR) was created in 1815 at the end of the Vienna Congress. This commission extended a pre-existing treaty, signed between France and Austria in 1804, to nine riverine countries.

Until this point, it was common for States that shared a border to collaborate on technical issues. However, the CCNR was a truly international organization, bringing together multiple nations who would work together to manage navigation along the Rhine. In this respect, it is undoubtedly the oldest organization for technical and standardized cooperation in the world. Although it was not a universal body (its scope being geographically limited), the CCNR inspired other institutions. By setting up an international administrative body which was given the responsibility of collecting (and redistributing) taxes on shipping, to improve infrastructure, it introduced a model that would be replicated later by the ITU: *a permanent diplomatic conference,* responsible for regularly studying questions submitted for the approval of the member States. These rules related to various domains: technical, commercial, customs, environmental, security, administrative, etc. As we will see later, in the case of the postal and telegraph systems, it was quickly understood that prosperity in trade was ensured by standardized rules. Reducing dock feed (or even abandoning them altogether) allowed traffic to flow freely, and this traffic increased with technical progress and accelerated industrial exchanges. This logic was reinforced in 1868 with the Mannheim Convention, which laid the ground for free and non-discriminatory navigation on the Rhine.

Box 2.2. *In 1815, the CCNR pioneered standardization organizations*

The Industrial Age was thus characterized by an intimate alliance between science and technology, especially thanks to engineering schools. Companies did not stop at recruiting specialists: they also trained their

34 Theory developed in *Leçons sur l'application de la mécanique à l'établissement de la construction des machines* (Navier 1826).

workers, their foremen and their in-house engineers. As Gille (1978) highlights, any technological evolution required a corresponding cultural transformation. It was not enough for scholars to make discoveries – their inventions had to be integrated into industrial research and technical teaching for companies to use these inventions. Large civil engineering projects were a perfect illustration of this dynamic. Before construction could begin, investors had to be persuaded and political decision-makers had to be reassured that these structures would be reliable. Metallurgy, mechanics and architecture thus progressed rapidly, based on resistance tests, elasticity tests and rupture tests that grew increasingly more precise. Thus, in France:

> Bridge designers [had to] comply with increasingly detail regulations. The first, dated February 26, 1858, simply defined the test load. The regulation dated July 9, 1877, specified general computation methods and safety limits for metals. In 1891, a circular added recommendations on the resistances to adopt, the nature of the overloading, wind force, and deflection. Finally, the regulation dated March 1, 1903, also took into account the increased weight of locomotives and wagons. (Lemoine 1986)

As technological progress accelerated, it grew in complexity, and therefore different roles were involved in developing standards. The world witnessed a tripartite partnership, which became a fundamental feature of standardization:

– large industrialists (metallurgists, civil engineers, railroad companies), linked to capital and banks;

– the world of scholars (scholarly societies, large engineering schools), who aspired to rational progress;

– the States, jealously guarding their sovereignty and keen to preserve industrial competitiveness, especially for strategic and military reasons, while also ensuring the safety of their people vis-à-vis industrial risks.

2.6.1. *The 19th century: an era of networks*

The Industrial Age would only grow because it was able to establish the networks that could now be built upon. The railroads, telegraph systems, electricity and steam engines for travel were essential infrastructure that allowed Continental Europe to catch up with Great Britain. Railroads now transported large crowds as well as heavy goods (ores, coal, pig-iron, iron bars and plates, etc.), mail and publications. Due to steam engines, the duration of maritime journeys was no longer unpredictable, including on large rivers like the Rhine and Danube. While sailboats needed 2 months to make the journey to America, in 1838 the paddle steamer *HMS Sirius* traveled from Ireland to New York in 18 days. In 1863, *HMS Scotia* (now equipped with a propeller) made the journey in 8 days. Refrigeration techniques (CO_2 compression around 1890) revolutionized international agricultural trade.

All these developments were highly interdependent. The construction of factories and collective equipment in large cities required increasingly efficient transport and communication infrastructure: ports, canals, railroads, telegraph. The latter became essential in managing and controlling train traffic, as well as for all industrial and administrative activities, and commercial and private correspondence. By 1850, around 23,000 km of railroad tracks stretched across Europe. These networks developed with government support. In Anglo-American countries, competition and emulation between companies continued; however, governments granted privileges to railroad entrepreneurs. In Great Britain, for example, Parliament encouraged the signing of legislative acts that supported the development of the railways, such as the Angerstein Railway Act (1851), the Ambergate Railway Act (1854) or again the Alford Valley Railway Act (1856).

Across the British Empire, while India and Australia still struggled to develop coherent networks, the Canadian government adopted the Railway Guarantee Act in 1849. This law allowed railroad construction to be indirectly subsidized. In the United States, the federal Land Grant Act, passed in 1850, allocated more than 375 million acres (16 million km^2) to railroad companies. In Europe meanwhile, France, Prussia and Austria adopted more centralized policies, notably using "the expropriation of lands for public interest". In 1850, it was possible to travel by train between Paris, Berlin, Vienna and Warsaw, with no interruptions. And by this period, the United Kingdom was almost entirely crisscrossed by railroad tracks. By the end of the decade, almost all large cities in Europe were connected from north to south and east to west. Within one generation, the landscape had changed forever: viaducts, telegraph poles, tunnels, mine shafts, factories, cities and the countryside changed beyond recognition.

The electric telegraph proved a major cultural shock: it allowed the instant sharing of information from one end of Europe to another and from one end of the world to the other![35] States used the same facilities as for railroads and telegraph lines came up along roads, canals and, especially, railroad tracks, thus ensuring safety and traffic control. By 1850, the United States already had 50 telegraph companies. The New York Telegraph Act enforced regulations that were aimed at promoting competition while ensuring that public interest was served.

The telegraph networks in Europe were still in fledgling form in 1850, except in the British Isles. However, by 1855, the European telegraph network had become significantly denser in the region between the Belgium and Netherlands, extending down to the Gulf of Genoa. France, Prussia, Switzerland, Austria and Italy connected their main cities, and the telegraph system reached Madrid, Scandinavia, St. Petersburg, the Crimea and Istanbul.

The press was a major actor in these networks and social debate, playing a central role in globalization. It shaped public opinion and promoted the diffusion of learning and techniques. Newspaper advertisements became a mass phenomenon, considerably amplifying the growth of telecommunications. All through the 19th century, techniques related to composition, printing and paper manufacturing continued improving: continuous paper production from 1800, paper from wood pulp around 1850, the rotary press in 1811, mechanized steam-powered presses by 1840 and entirely mechanized rotary presses by 1850. Color printing appeared in 1889. The press needed to have information first and thus depended on the telegraph system. In 1835, Charles-Luis Havas created an agency of political papers using the telegraph system to share information. In 1846, the Associated Press was founded, and in 1855, David Edward Hughes invented the printing telegraph, allowing the dispatches to be sent directly to the

35 This was the same period in which photography transformed culture. Invented in the mid-1820s by Nicéphore Niépce, the technology was perfected through the work of Daguerre (hence, daguerreotypes) and Fox Talbot until it became almost *instantaneous* in 1850 with the use of wet collodion. It captured reality in a way that radically changed how the world was perceived and allowed everyone to explore images from around the world (postcards, stereo imaging, etc.). Professional photographers and talented amateurs could take portraits, giving even the poorest families a chance to preserve visual memories.

editor. In 1859, Havas and Reuters signed a cooperation agreement[36]. From the 1860s onwards, stock exchanges around the world were instantly informed of variations in stock prices.

2.6.2. *Undersea cables: an absolute need for standardization*

Finance was globalized, leading to the emergence of the first multinational corporations, especially to invest in high technology products like undersea telegraphy. These undersea cables furnished the missing link between continents (especially Great Britain and Europe) and also made it possible to directly connect countries without traveling through hostile territories. The first telegraph cables were stretched across rivers and sounds. From 1842 onwards, Samuel Morse worked with Samuel Colt to connect Manhattan and Brooklyn and then New Jersey on the telegraph lines. Colt, a well-known arms-maker, had developed cables that could trigger undersea mines from a distance, notably protecting the New York City port. It was this military technology that led to the development of the first undersea cables[37]. In 1850, the first trans-channel cable connected Dover to Calais. The attempt was a technical success but the cable soon became inoperative. A second attempt laid a cable that was stronger, better insulated and protected against molluscs boring through it. It became operational by late 1851 and marked the beginning of a new era: England was now connected to the continent.

From the 1860s onwards, many innovations improved underwater transmissions: amplifiers, multiplexing, phase-inversion[38] (limiting electric losses) and progress in the insulating material used (rubber, gutta-percha). Financiers soon understood that once it was laid, the cable was practically irreparable. Therefore, the entire process had to be carefully monitored from the design phase onwards. This requirement brought in a rigorous standardization of the process, both in the construction of the ships laying the cables, as well as in the manufacturing and installation of the cables themselves.

36 See Lefebure (1992).

37 For technical subjects addressed with the historical mentality of the 19th century, see the collection: *Les Merveilles de la science ou description populaire des inventions modernes* (Figuier 1867–1891), an invaluable source of information for the writing of this work.

38 Forerunners of future alternating current distributors, first imagined by Tesla, an inventor ruined by Edison's aggressive and mendaciously alarmist competitive practices.

In 1865, the ITU was created and this was the first step in the institutional standardization of global telegraph networks.

2.6.3. *The need for uniformity across electric telegraphy*

By the late 1830s, it seemed obvious to most countries (apart from France) that the day of aerial telegraphy was past. From 1838 onwards, Wheatstone had developed a proper telegraph network across England. In Russia, from 1833 onwards, Baron Pavel Schilling was experimenting with an eight-wire electromagnetic telegraph, which had caught the attention of the Tsar, Nicholas I. In that same year, Friedrich Gauss and Wilhelm Weber, two researchers at Göttingen University, installed a line over a kilometer long, connected across rooftops, so that their laboratories were connected to each other by a two-wire electromagnetic telegraph system. Other telegraph systems, based on the same principle, were experimented with and improved. In 1838, von Steinheil was put in charge of installing an 8-km-long telegraph line along a Bavarian railroad track and in doing so, discovered (or rediscovered) the essential principle underlying the "earth-return" system. He had initially tried to use the two rails for the circuit, but as they were poorly insulated from the ground, the transmission was inefficient. He then realized that it was possible to return the signal through a ground connection[39].

Although continental Europe was scientifically highly advanced in the study of telegraphy, it did not yet have a market that could finance the large-scale development of the telegraph. Across the Channel, however, the railway companies were the first to invest in a large-scale network in order to control traffic. The service slowly paid for itself as paths opened up to other uses, especially private correspondence. Despite a relative lag in the field of science, the industrial advances in Great Britain allowed it to become the first to set up a telegraph network.

The successive improvements to the Schilling process carried out by William Cook, in collaboration with Charles Wheatstone[40], deserve to be studied with particular attention. Their telegraph system had two objectives:

---

39 A technique that had already been experimented with by Harrison Gray (1805–1875) in Long Island in 1826: https://www.americansilversmiths.org/makers/silversmiths/211267.htm.

40 William Cooke was an inventor and former army officer, and Wheatstone was a researcher at King's College, London.

transmitting textual messages in English, while also guaranteeing a reliable transmission of 100% of the railway service communications, especially those concerning traffic around the stations and the garages of the convoys that were forming. Cooke and Wheatstone were thus the true inventors of a new telegraph system. They automated the first process. Hitherto, operators had had to interpret the needle deflections to decode the message. However, with Cooke and Wheatstone's system, the needle pointed directly to the letter of the alphabet. They also developed a system to manage railroad traffic along a single track, codifying the *block system* principle, which endured for the next 200 years[41]. The Cooke and Wheatstone telegraph continued to be refined and, because of improvements in the conducting wires and the insulating materials used for these, they soon required only two wires to transmit the messages. In 1845, this telegraph system made waves in England by enabling the arrest of a criminal, John Tawell, who was spotted in a train between Slough and Paddington. The system was also used to announce the birth of Queen Victoria's second daughter, with the news being published in the *Times* less than one hour after the royal birth. By 1852, England was crisscrossed by 6,500 km of Cooke and Wheatstone's telegraph lines.

We must also examine another point: given that Samuel Morse was a later entrant into the history of the electric telegraph, how did he manage to not only impose his code (which became the universal code) but also carve out a name for himself as the emblematic inventor of the electric telegraph system? All needle telegraphs required great dexterity to manipulate and interpret the systems at the terminal stations, and great skill in encoding and decoding the messages, which led to many errors.

Before the invention of the Cooke and Wheatstone telegraph, each letter or digit was transmitted and recognized because of the human interpretation of a series of deflections in one or more needles (deflected to the left, to the right, or vertical at rest). This system required learning a complex code that was based on the number of needles, their position and the origin of the signal in a given conducting wire. The Morse code offered several advantages: it was simple, ergonomic and made economic use of impulsion,

41 Cooke was undoubtedly inspired by military manoeuvres: this system of blocks remains the basis for the most modern standardized safety protocols for railroads. See especially Nguilla-Kooh and Doyen (2021). This article considers the normative and cybersecurity challenges related to the block system, as it exists, which is standardized even today in the European Railway Traffic Management System (ERTMS), and by CEN and ISO.

as it was based on the frequency of letters in English[42]. It thus became a veritable language in itself and operators could be easily trained to use it. It could be whistled, like the Bosun's whistle call[43], and would thereafter be adopted by Scouts, who learned the code at a young age (on a whistle, with a flashlight, or a simple mirror). Whether it was transmitted through sound, by blinking one's eyes or some other means, the Morse code soon became the universal code for emergencies and survival.

From the beginning, Morse and his associates developed a system to record the signals onto a strip of paper, reassuring to the telegraph companies. In 1837, however, Steinheil had already developed a similar system but had never been able to develop it on an industrial scale. Morse's system also prevailed because to develop a network in the United States, it was essential to be able to transmit information over very large distances. To meet this need, he had developed signal repeaters to amplify the signal, which were a key element in his invention.

It was on the basis of this invention that he claimed to be the true inventor of the telegraph, declaring in court:

> I do not propose to limit myself to the specific machinery or parts of machinery described in the foregoing specification and claims; the essence of my invention being the use of the motive power of the electric or galvanic current, which I call electromagnetism, however developed, for making or printing intelligible characters, signs or letters at any distances, being a new application of that power, of which I claim to be the first inventor or discoverer. (O'Reilly v. Morse, 56 U.S. 15 How. 62 (1853))

Due to these advantages, by the end of the 1840s, the Morse telegraph, with the Morse code and the signal repeaters, prevailed almost everywhere as the de facto standard, except in Great Britain and in France (which was experimenting with the Morse code in parallel to its existing Chappe network).

42 Developed by one of his two associates: Alfred Lewis Vail.

43 This mode of commanding through whistles was already in use in the English navy from the 17th century onwards. Its name is derived from the bosun (or "boatswain").

2.6.4. *The Germanic origins of a telegraphic union*

Except for the United Kingdom and the United States, where telegraph systems had been considered to be a free-market enterprise from the start, all other nations saw this as a State-run business. It was a technology that was often reserved on priority (or sometimes even exclusively) for government business and diplomatic dispatches. As mentioned before, because of their continued territorial expansion, the railroad companies were the first natural investors in this technology.

By the mid-19th century, the telegraph was becoming an essential aid to progress in all developed countries, but it required universal development. German-speaking countries were the first to concretize a nascent international telegraphic union by signing a succession of diplomatic alliances[44]. Thus, on October 3, 1849, Prussia and Austria signed a convention governing the installation and use of electromagnetic telegraphy to exchange State dispatches. This was the first sign of the need for an international framework for telecommunications.

From 1850 onwards, Saxony and Bavaria joined this initiative and signed the convention in Dresden to become part of the Austrian-German telegraphic union. These four central States quickly put in place the first international regulations applicable to their own internal traffic. Although it was not mandatory to adopt these rules, they were adopted naturally. This step led to a win-win principle, carried forward by standardization. The telegraph administrations in these early countries took on early experiments around traffic management, setting tariffs, checking the wires and equipment, as well as organizing stations and offices. Their thinking on these subjects was largely inspired by the postal procedures set in place after the invention of the postage stamp. The best practices were retained and adopted. From the beginning, the Union adopted the Morse system for its official equipment[45]. The Austrian–German telegraph union was thus a pioneer in the field, inventing and establishing a standardization framework, which was in marked contrast to the absence of any interoperability, security

---

44 The historical portal of the ITU, especially the list of various conferences, is an inexhaustible source of documentation. See: https://www.itu.int/en/history/Pages/home.aspx#/fr.

45 This would prevent the telegram being retranscribed at certain points as it crossed the border, as was done in the early years.

and international exchange capabilities. The scope[46] of the earliest common standards widened rapidly and grew more specific: transmission time quality and compliance; confidentiality of communications; maps, updated in real time, of the wires, offices and maintenance centers; the service being open to all, as long as they respected good manners; taxation computed based on the words and the distance traveled; the sharing of financial resources from international traffic, divided between member States on a pro-rata basis depending on the transmission pathways.

In 1851, the Union became the Austro-German Union (Vienna Conference), allowing all German states and countries with a German-speaking minorities to join the union. Wurtemberg and then Luxembourg joined the organization. A major volution then took place: the pricing was no longer only based on the distance traveled by the dispatches, but was replaced by a *zonal tariff*, involving a distribution of resources based on the telegraphic infrastructure in each member State.

In 1852, the Netherlands and Hanover joined the Union. From the start, the Union had established the principle of uniform standards with respect to transmission and pricing, applicable to official traffic and private dispatches. In 1852, during the Berlin Conference, France and Belgium, as well as the Submarine Telegraph Company, concluded a Germano-Franco-Belgian Convention. The rules of this body were adopted by Switzlerland and Sardinia (Berne, 1852), and then by Spain (Madrid, 1854). In parallel, Austria, representing the Austro-German Union, signed an almost identical convention in Turin (1853 and 1856). However, the administrative delays, disorder and diplomatic rivalry exasperated the people working toward the standardization of the European telegraphy technology. During the fifth telegraphy conference organized by the Union at Stuttgart in 1857, the delegates took certain fundamental decisions. There was a strict separation brought in between:

– diplomatic agreements between States, considered to be fixed;

– the professional principles adopted by consensus, considered to be intangible;

– the regulations or standards, which could be modified, appended to the Convention.

46 The *scope* or *field of application* is common jargon today, but was not yet formalized at this stage.

They also examined the relations between the Austro-German bloc and the Telegraph Union in Western Europe. For the sake of international telegraphy, it became essential to adopt a single set of regulations that would apply to all States on the continent. The Federal Swiss Council suggested organizing a conference to bring together the two blocs. Thus, in June 1858, Prussia, Belgium and France signed a diplomatic convention in Brussels. This was complemented by technical appendices, officialized in Berne in September 1858. However, this new convention did not completely succeed. Despite the progressive convergence between technical, procedural and diplomatic provisions, the two blocs (Austro-German and Western Europe) continued to exist separately. Until 1864, European telegraphy was governed by the 1858 conventions signed in Brussels and Berne.

During the conferences at La Haye (1861), and then Hanover (1863), the Austro-German Union implemented a two-layered decision-making model@ unanimous decisions for fundamental principles, majority-based decisions for secondary aspects. However, the slow pace of proceedings in both blocs prevented them from keeping up with technical advances, making it increasingly urgent to standardize procedures, especially between the Germanic and Western alliances.

1865: an attempt at monetary and international standardization, Latin Union

The question of money has long been associated with metrology. Contrary to the units of measurement, money did not need to be standardized internationally. However, there was an attempt made that is largely forgotten today: the *Latin Union,* a monetary union founded in 1865 and active until 1914 (and then, briefly, between 1918 and 1927).

It was based on the germinal Franc decimal unit and the basis was a bimetallic standard (silver and gold): 1 Franc = 4.5g of silver. The founding members of this Union were France, Belgium, Switzerland and Italy. Greece joined them in 1868. Many other States joined the Union (32 members in total, eventually), notably Austria, Russia, the Ottoman Empire and even the United States, which minted a special gold coin, the *Stella*, equivalent to 20 French francs (1879–1880). The Latin Union laid the foundations for an international monetary system, but its effectiveness was limited due to the absence of the United Kingdom and the German Empire.

Box 2.3. *The Latin Monetary Union*

2.7. 1865, the founding of the ITU following the Paris Convention

Napoleon III himself took the initiative of organizing a congress in Paris, in March 1865, to negotiate a general treaty not only for the countries that were already members of one of the two blocs, but for all European States. Only the United Kingdom and United States were not invited to this, as their telegraph networks were privately run by industrialists.

In 1865, however, technology became a key factor in discussions around international telegraph organizations. The major part of the telegraph industry, especially the manufacturing and laying of undersea cables, was dominated by British and American firms[47]. Medium-range undersea were already in service, although the transatlantic link was not yet operational. In 1858, Cyrus Field (1819–1892) was able to lay an undersea cable that allowed Queen Victora and the President of the United States to exchange wishes for universal peace. However, this was a short-lived connection: it became functional on August 5 but stopped working on September 5 of the same year. This partial failure spurred engineers on to improve the cables in terms of design, manufacturing, isolation and installation. Crucial questions such as prior checks on quality, transmission and signal amplification, and how to account for underwater relief and the risks of rupture in ocean trenches were all systematically studied and resolved.

All the States who were invited accepted the invitation. The French administration had prepared a draft project for the convention and the Vicomte Drouyn de Lhuys[48] presided over the Congress as the representative of the inviting power. The chosen method was to separate diplomatic discussions (in principle, ratification by the signatory States, negotiated between plenipotentiaries) from technical and procedural aspects, which were discussed in a commission on the basis of the French project. This approach allowed the work to progress much faster. The final agreement included, notably, the unification of tariffs, with zone-wise divisions rather than computations per kilometer. All the languages of all signatory countries

47 From 1860 onwards, England was connected to Ireland, Belgium and the Netherlands. France was connected to Corsica and Algeria. In 1865, telegraph professionals from around the world knew that Cyrus Field planned to lay a new cable over the summer. This major undertaking redistributed global diplomatic maps.

48 The Vicomte Drouyn de Lhuys was the man who had finally succeeded in killing the Foy-Breguet monster: a Morse telegraph system that reproduced Chappe signals!

were used, all figures were expressed in numbers, and a mechanism to verify transmissions was put in place. These provisions formed the basis for the early standards of the ITU[49]. The Paris Convention was signed by the plenipotentiaries of the 20 founding countries[50]. Appended to the Convention was a table of the terminal and transit taxes, as well as general regulations. It was also decided that periodic technical conferences would be organized in order to keep up with evolving technologies. The first of these was planned for Vienna in 1868. During this conference, the Hughes teleprinter device[51] was adopted, as well as the non-competition clause for transmission pathways (the forerunner of a digital mesh network). At the same Viennese conference, an International Bureau for Telegraph Administration was created. It was set up at Berne and had a budget of 40,000 francs, to which all contracting countries contributed. Other countries soon joined the convention: Persia and British India in 1869, the United Kingdom in 1871, the Dutch East Indies in 1872, Egypt in 1876, followed by Brazil in 1877 and New Zealand in 1878.

The telephone in 1876: a bolt from the blue

Alexander Graham Bell (1847–1922) had first studied the simultaneous, multiplex transmission of multiple messages along the same cable, an essential problem to which many telegraph industrialists had dedicated their research. In France, for example, between 1874 and 1882, Émile Baudot developed and perfected a five-path, sequential multiplex telegraph system

In parallel to this, several researchers were developing the telephone, notably Thomas Edison and Elisha Gray. This fierce competition led to many appeals against Bell's patent, submitted to the U.S. Patent Office in 1876. Bell's demonstration of his invention at the Centennial Exposition in Philadelphia in 1876, organized to celebrate the centennial of American Independence, cemented his status as the inventor. This event attracted 10 million visitors and 35 participating countries.

Box 2.4. *The telephone*

49 To simplify the text, we will refer to this as the ITU instead of the official French name (UIT).

50 The International Telegraphic Union thus brought together: Austria, Baden, Bavaria, Belgium, Denmark, Spain, France, Greece, Hanover, Italy, the Netherlands, Portugal, Prussia, Russia, Saxony, Sweden (also representing Norway), Switzerland, Turkey, and Württemberg.

51 Although the Hughes printing telegraph was four times faster than the Morse equipment, the latter was eventually chosen for the secondary lines.

2.7.1. *The delayed inclusion of the telephone by the ITU*

It was only in 1885, during the Berlin conference, that the ITU decided to frame *recommendations* (in reality, standards) around international telephony. The telephone had already been developed and quickly commercialized, independent of the ITU. Initially (in 1877 in the United States and around 1880 in Europe), its use was limited to intra-urban communications with a manual connection[52]. The recommendations made at Berlin allowed the rules to be harmonized and formalized practices (in use for many years) that ensured that the telephone and telegraph systems could coexist, often using the same lines. It was notably specified that:

– the contracting States could set up international telephonic communications by laying specific wires or by adapting existing infrastructure;

– these lines were centralized in telephone offices and connected to public cabins, houses or businesses;

– the administrations agreed on the choice of equipment and service modalities, as well as tariffication;

– the billing unit adopted was a five-minute conversation;

– the use of the telephone was regulated based on the order of requests.

> [...] In 1903, the ITU conference in London admitted the use of telegraphic terminals called "speakers". This method, which was faster and more effective than either Baudot's or Hughes' devices, gradually gained in acceptance until telegraphy was largely abandoned. In parallel, to avoid congestion along the lines, a regulatory framework was put in place to manage dedicated timings for inter-urban and international telephone services. The rapid evolution of technologies pushed the ITU to accept new rules taking into account innovations like photography and belinographs, sound recording, and telephony. The idea that multiplex telegraphy could allow the transmission

52 Interestingly, the first automatic telephone exchange was invented in the United States in 1891 by an undertaker, exasperated by a competitor who had allegedly bribed the manual operators to work to his advantage.

of a vocal signal was a key element in the later development of radiophony that was able to carry voices[53].

2.7.2. *The ITU and radiotelegraphy*

ITU standards could have saved lives on the *Titanic*

The sinking of the *Titanic* could have claimed fewer victims if the ITU had managed to frame norms earlier regarding radios on ships constantly on-duty. The earliest norms that were framed largely concerned communication protocols, frequencies and other rules: time restrictions, the competencies of specialized coastal operators, communications between these stations and ships at sea. They also defined an international distress call: SOS, *Save Our Sailors*[54] : • • • — — — • • •.

When the *Titanic* hit an iceberg and sank in 1912, the ITU had already put forward many *recommendations*. However, the requirement for radios on ships of a defined minimum tonnage to always be on had not yet been universally adopted. Further, several nearby ships could have rescued other passengers from the Titanic if they had been subject to this normative obligation. The First World War interrupted the work being carried out by the international radiotelegraphy conferences, and despite the shock caused by the sinking, these new measures were postponed to the post-war period[55].

Box 2.5. *Standardization could have rescued more lives on the Titanic*

One of the main challenges the ITU faced was ensuring communication between ships at sea. Cable telegraphy was not adequate and they had to turn to other techniques such as semaphore signals or various marine codes (flags, bosun's whistles, light signals, mirror signals, foghorns etc.). David

53 See: https://www.itu.int/en/history/Pages/home.aspx#/en.

54 Or Save Our Souls.

55 It would, however, be anachronistic to follow this reasoning. Radio technologies were still new, equipment was costly, and it was not always easy to employ competent radio operators. Many shipowners were also not equipped with these devices.

Edward Hughes, in the 1880s, and several other inventors in the 1890s[56], experimented with and perfected the first wireless telegraph signal transmitters and receivers. The urgent need to regulate these new technologies was felt at the radiotelegraphy conferences in Berlin, precipitated by a diplomatic incident.

In 1902, while returning on his yacht from a visit to the United States, Prince Henri of Prussia tried in vain to send a courtesy message to President Theodore Roosevelt. His message was refused, as the yacht's radioelectric equipment was incompatible with that of the American coastal station. This incident vexed the German government, which organized a preparatory radiocommunications conference in Berlin in 1903. This was followed, in 1906, by the first International Radiotelegraphy Conference, which led to the creation of a Department of Radiotelegraphy within the ITU. The earliest ITU radiotelegraphic conferences were held in Berlin (1903, 1906) and then at Lisbon in 1908. They formed the basis of the first recommendations: transmissions of time signals, the frequencies accepted by coastal stations and ships, competencies of radio operators, etc. During the 1908 ITU Convention in Lisbon, the International Bureau for Telegraph Administrations became the International Bureau of the Telegraph.

2.7.3. *The ITU, procedural standards and not technical standards*

Despite the rapid progress in telecommunications and the organization of radiotelegraphy conferences, the ITU restricted itself to standardizing *the uses of telecommunication technologies*. Despite being highly qualified, ITU experts did not define technical norms, leaving this task to manufacturers of electrical equipment, who would, of course, take into account the ITU's needs and recommendations. The founding of the IEC in 1906 reiterated this division of roles. There was no competition between the two organizations. The ITU retained a vast field of standardization, including transmission protocols, wavelength allocation, training of operators, pricing of services, requirements of telecommunication companies and conditions for restoring emergency services in case of a natural disaster (tornadoes, cyclones, earthquakes, etc.).

---

56 Nikola Tesla, Jagadish Chandra Bose, Alexander Stepanovich Popov and Guglielmo Marconi are among the giants who played a role in the development of radio transmissions.

Historically, the ITU was first set up as a standardization organization that brought together States, and then telegraph administrators and telecommunication companies, including undersea cable operators. The ITU thus stopped at making successive choices based on technological progress. Its scope was strictly oriented toward usage, although increasing technical expertise became indispensable. It was essential for the ITU to master tools that could construct coherent networks, equitably allocate frequencies and ensure user safety. However, the organization did not try to standardize the technologies themselves, although the boundary between "uses" and "technology" was sometimes blurred. The ITU remains faithful to this mission even today.

The Universal Postal Union

The Universal Postal Union was an international organization created to standardize postal traffic on a global scale. As with the ITU, this standardization encompassed the tariffs for international traffic, the material organization of international transits and the setting up of harmonized tariff zones as well as defining mail categories[57] and protocols (modalities for returning post in case the recipient is unavailable, postage due). These led to international standards, leading to similar de facto standardization for traffic within each Member State.

Although we may find it unremarkable today, the postage stamp was a major administrative innovation, revolutionizing the economic model of postal exchanges[58]. The adoption of the postage stamp radically reformed the British Post Office with the iconic Penny Black stamp of 1840, bearing the profile of Queen Victoria. However, stamping technique already existed: the revenue stamp had been in use since 1624 in the Netherlands, in Spain since 1637, in France since 1674 and in Great Britain since 1694. The fundamental innovation introduced in the postage stamp was not the invention of the stamp itself, but the inversion in the payment of the postage charges: *paid postage* replaced *postage due*. This evolution led to significant savings for the Post Office, which no longer had to bear the cost of letters refused by recipients. Rowland Hill is credited with the idea of paying postage for postal dispatches, while James

57 Ordinary letter, registered post with or without acknowledgement of receipt, postcard, postal parcel, money order, press distribution, mass mailing, etc.

58 The postage stamp simplified the organization of payments and readability of tariffs in a lasting manner.

Chalmers[59] is credited with the idea of the adhesive stamp being canceled by the administration in order to prevent the fraudulent misuse of stamps.

It is interesting to note that there are two distinct accounts regarding this invention. In the first, a romantic account, Rowland Hill is said to have offered to pay the postage due for a barmaid who was too poor to pay for and accept a letter from her fiancé. Touched by his solicitude, she reportedly confided in him that she regularly refused the letters as she and her lover communicated through discreet little symbols drawn onto the envelopes. The second version, which is more neutral, comes from a 1909 conference, shared by the Director of the Bureau of the International Telegraphic Union (Frey 1909). He relates a similar story, with the protagonist being a man with limited resources who communicated with his family through predefined signs on the envelope. This incident is said to have convinced Rowland Hill of the need to reform England's postal service.

From 1840 onwards, the reform was implemented in Great Britain and was an immediate success. Consequently, the use of stamps as well as prepaid postage spread rapidly around the world. Postal tariffs were standardized to a considerable extent, although significant differences continued to exist between countries. In 1842, the German economist Johann von Herrfeldt proposed the creation of a Universal Postal Union. In 1862, the director of the United States Post Office Department, with the support of Abraham Lincoln, invited nations to an international conference at Paris in 1863, but without any notable result. Finally, Heinrich von Stephan, the director of the Postal Service of the Confederation of North Germany, suggested the creation of an International Postal Union. A conference bringing together 21 countries[60] was held at Berne and resulted in the signing of the Berne Treaty on October 9, 1874, marking the foundation of the General Postal Union. Many other States quickly joined this and in 1878, during a congress in Paris, the organization became the Universal Postal Union (UPU). It is still located in Berne and today encompasses 192 Member States. The working language of the UPU was originally French, until English was added in 1994.

Box 2.6. *The Universal Postal Union and standardization*

59 James Chalmers (1782–1853) was a bookseller and printer who appears to have invented adhesive stickers. His son Patrick, associated with Rowland Hill in working for postal reform, sought to prove that his father was the inventor of the adhesive postage stamp.

60 The earliest countries included Germany, Argentina, Hungary, Belgium, Brazil, Denmark, Spain, the United States, France, Great Britain, Greece, Italy, the Netherlands, Peru, Portugal, Russia, Sweden, Norway (which shared a delegation), Switzerland, Turkey and Venezuela.

2.8. Paris 1875: the Metre Convention and the creation of the BIPM at Sèvres

Although France had neglected the metric system for three decades, the French origins of the system could not be disputed[61] and its success continued growing. The metric system was thus officially adopted by an increasing number of countries: it was authorized in England (Bill dated July 9, 1864) and introduced in Germany by Reichstag in 1868. During the Universal Exposition in Paris in 1867, there was an international meeting specifically dedicated to the metric system, which shed light on the challenges in adopting it. The persistence of non-metric measurements in many territories convinced delegates of the urgent need for uniformity. Further, nations that had already adopted the metric system raised other concerns. The French reference standards of measurement were technologically outdated. Thus, the "Archive Meter", an *end standard* consisting of a flat ruler that was 1 m long, raised some difficulties in carrying out precise comparisons for measurements to create secondary references. At this level of metrological use, it was impossible to ignore the risk of the wearing away of the ends of the bar through contact with the measuring devices. In 24 years, the comparison and verification techniques had also progressed considerably, and certain measurements revealed significant disparities between the *national standard references* that were "secondary" references (the original being in France). The scientific community, especially geodesists, complained of the difficulty in reconciling triangulations at the borders. In October 1867, during the International Geodesic Conference in Berlin, this was considered to be a worrying situation and two major resolutions were adopted:

– the construction of a "European meter prototype", which would be as faithful as possible to the "Archive Meter";

– the creation of an International European Bureau of Weights and Measurements.

The Bureau des Longitudes (Bureau of Longitudes) alerted the French government to the situation: there was an urgent need to manufacture a new European prototype for the meter, which would be a *line standard*

61 Especially the standard references for the units conserved in the Archives de France, and then at the French National Conservatoire des Arts et Métiers's Dépôt central des étalons et prototypes (Central Depot for Reference Standards and Prototypes).

henceforth instead of an *end standard*. In May 1869, the Academy of Sciences at St. Petersburg requested the creation of an international commission. The Academy of Sciences in Paris was worried upon reading the report from St. Petersburg. French scholars felt that France ran the risk of losing standard reference for the meter. In the meantime, many countries that had doubts about their *secondary national reference standard* had gone as far as to think of carrying out a fresh meridian arc measurement. The report was presented by Jean-Baptiste Dumas, the permanent Secretary of the Academy of Sciences of Paris, and a Russian speaker. His formal conclusion was:

> The government must do all it can to create a European prototype meter before the Russian scholars do. On the other hand, there can be no question of carrying out new geodesic measurements. For seventy years, the *meter* and *kilogram* at the Archives have represented, respectively, the fundamental unit of the metric system, and the unit of weight. They must be conserved as they are, with no modification. (Dumas 1869)

From the beginning, and especially in the 1860s, the community of metrologists, as well as geodesists, knew that the reference standard meter had been designed to correspond to one ten-millionth of the meridian through Paris from the North Pole to the Equator. However, this first reference standard had to remain intangible and could not be challenged as the universal reference without upending the whole of metrology and undoing all the advantages of uniformity brought in by the metric system. On September 1, 1869, a French Commission, appointed by official decree, was given the responsibility of manufacturing the standards that the international community was requesting. This commission represented France in a collective project and would go on to become the French Section of the International Meter Commission. The French government invited scholars from 24 countries as delegates to the first International Meter Commission in Paris. This commission began work on August 8, 1870. However, on July 19, 1870, war broke out between France and Prussia.

Despite this troubled context, the French section of the International Meter Commission was aware of the urgency of its task. They thus created the meter standard using a bar with an X-shaped cross-section as well as a kilogram measure in a platinum-iridium alloy. The International Meter Commission was re-assembled toward the end of 1872. The 51 delegates from 28 states approved the work carried out. Twelve members, co-opted from among the fifty-one, formed a permanent international committee. This committee requested the French government to organize a diplomatic conference in Paris, which was the Diplomatic Meter Conference and took place in 1875.

This Conference opened on March 1, 1875, at the Ministry of Foreign Affairs in Paris. During this meeting, the scholars involved demonstrated remarkable diplomatic skill and were able to create a permanent international organization, which was no longer dependent on periodic diplomatic conferences[62]: the BIPM. It was also decided that the manufacturing of the prototypes, already undertaken by the French section, must happen under the supervision of the scholarly community. From the foundation of the BIPM, experts in metrology have maintained their independence vis-à-vis States. This desire for autonomy was notably related to the memory of the Reign of Terror, during which Lavoisier and Condorcet, major actors in the implementation of the Metric System, paid with their lives for their scientific work. The entire community understood the importance of depending exclusively on an international and permanent structure, the only guarantee of the credibility of an international body. The BIPM was thus placed under the supervision of an International Committee on Weights and Measurements (CIPM), which itself depended on the General Conference on Weights and Measurements (CGPM)[63]. The funding was guaranteed by the signatory States. During the final signing of the treaty in 1875, France got the BIPM to be set up at the Pavillon de Breteuil in Sèvres, where it was granted *extraterritorial status*, similar to an embassy. The objective of this new standardization organization was strictly circumscribed: it would define, continuously improve and promote the three units that were already known: the meter, the kilogram and the second. A few countries opposed the creation of the BIPM, but did not reject the metric system, especially for scientific and technological uses. The United States

62 With respect to standardization, as in other domains (business, associations or government institutions), the creation of a permanent and long-lasting organization is what truly concretizes objectives. To ensure the sustainability of a universal metric system, a permanent establishment had to be set up. Thus, from being purely conceptual, this project became an institutional reality.

63 For ease of reading, the term BIPM (the only permanent body) will be used most often in the text as a generic term to designate all three bodies housed in the Pavillon de Breteuil in Sèvres: the BIPM, CIPM and CGPM (see section 2.8).

was among the founding countries of the BIPM, and the United Kingdom also joined it through its scientific institutions.

At the end of the conference, the French section knew that they had to complete the work quickly. Their staff increased from 9 to 15 members. Many technical questions were raised: the resistance of the platinum-iridium alloy, the creation of new reference standards for the meter and kilogram, as well as planning out the pavillon de Breteuil. In 1880, the section finally handed over two standard references for the meter and three standard references for the kilogram to the CIPM. An international committee of experts was formed: Jean-Baptiste Dumas (France), Jean Servais Stas (Belgium), Olle Jacob Broch (Norway) and Admiral Mouchiez (France). This commission carried out thousands of measurements for comparison and finally selected two original prototypes from among the five reference standards that were put forward.

Chronologically, the BIPM, as well as its associated institutions, the CIPM and CGPM, was the second universal standardization body founded in the late 19th century. From the time of its creation, it adopted a very specific method and mode of co-optation in order to prevent any national intrusion that could compromise the universality of the reference values of the metrological standards for which it was responsible. The BIPM, CIPM and CGPM were not limited to the creation of reference standards: they also established a rational and standardized description of the units. This included the invariable notations and conventional abbreviations for the three base units (meter, kilogram, second), as well as the primary units derived from these (velocity: v, expressed in m/s; area: A, expressed in m^2, etc.)[64].

But there was still a long way to go to scientifically unite the metric system. The founding members of the international team at the BIPM had the primary and single goal of defining the three base units (meter, kilogram and second) in physical terms and, above all, maintaining the corresponding prototypes. For over a century, the meter was initially defined with respect to the length of a second pendulum. However, given the difficulties in obtaining reliable measurements with a pendulum, it was decided that the

64 In 1960, during the 11th CGPM, a new hierarchy of multiples and sub-multiples of units was adopted, progressively replacing the older prefixes inherited from the French Revolution. This led to the formalization of new prefixes, such as *zetta* (10^{21}, Z), *yotta* (10^{24}, Y), *zepto* (10^{-21}, z) and *yocto* (10^{-24}, y).

meter would become the primary unit of the metric system and would be defined with respect to the Earth's meridian. From the beginning (1795), the scholarly community knew that the "Archive meter" was approximately measured with respect to the Earth's meridian. However, it was universally accepted and shared.

In 1862, the British Association for the Advancement of Science (BAAS) declared that "All men of science are agreed to use the second of mean solar time as the unit of time". In concrete, astronomical terms, the second was thus defined as 1/86,400 of a mean solar day. However, for a long time, the second was the weakest link among the three base units of the International System of Units (SI – Système international des unites). From the 1960s onwards, advances in technologies on atomic measurement allowed Louis Essen (United Kingdom) to propose a new definition of the second. This would no longer be 1/86,400 of a mean solar day, but the "duration of 9,192,631,770 periods of the radiation corresponding to the transition between the two hyperfine levels of the ground state of the caesium 133 atom". This new definition was adopted during the 13th CGPM Conference (1967–1968).

The example of the second illustrates how scientific paradigms in metrology evolve. Generations of experts who successively defined the second, over a long period, did not share the same scientific culture: initially rooted in classical physics, then in electrical physics, and finally in atomic physics. At the end of the 19th century, all members of the BIPM were mathematicians, astronomers and traditional physicists.

Due to a clear division of responsibility between the BIPM and the Congress of Electricians (which became the IEC in 1906), the reputation of both organizations has remained spotless. When it comes to standardization, the credibility of these institutions is primordial. In 1901, Giovanni Giorgi convinced the scientific community of electricians that it was possible to establish consistency between the three base units and electrical units. The development of electrical sciences and technology required, in parallel, the definition of specific units for electricity. From the pioneering work carried out on the Earth's magnetic field by Gauss (1832), followed by the work of Weber, Maxwell and Thomson (later Lord Kelvin), the principle of a coherent system of electrical units, the CGS system (centimeter, gram, second), was formalized in 1860. However, it was only in 1921 that the BIPM founded a committee in association with the IEC: the Consultative

Committee for Electricity. The IEC thus took charge of the effective development of electric and electromagnetic units. It took several decades to theoretically formalize and stabilize the standards for these base and derived units, stretching over 50 years.

Differentiating between scientific metrology and legal metrology: OIML

Historically, France and many other countries had a body of civil servants who were inspectors or verifiers of the weights and measurements of the metric system. In 1875, the French Section of the Meter Convention was also given the responsibility of ensuring legal metrology. This responsibility was fortunately retired later, as it would not have been desirable for the same body to be the judge and defendant. A sophisticated system of measurements must, indeed, have two distinct approaches:

– *Scientific* metrology, theoretical or symbolic, which must, if possible, remain a sovereign function (or even sacred). This is the most transcendental level – that of standard reference measurements that are shared and accepted through a civilization. In Ancient Rome, these standard reference measurements were kept in the temple of Juno in the Forum. This theoretical level is what the BIMP has essentially been in charge of since 1875.

– *Legal metrology*, whose goal is to facilitate commerce and industry, as well as establish metrological confidence in domains such as health and environment. This aims to harmonize consumer protection and the protection of citizens at a national and international level. This domain ensures the conformity of many types of measurements.

National bodies and the International Organization of Legal Metrology (OIML) collaborate with each other to study the different domains of application and establish specific standards that exhaustively cover measurement methods. Founded in Paris in 1955, the OIML is scientifically dependent on the international system of units (BIPM), which is the only authority empowered to verify the conformity of measurements. The OIML defines legal metrology as: *the application of legal requirements to measurements and measuring instruments.* While, on average, minor errors tend to cancel out over a large number of measurements, biased errors could lead to considerable financial losses for the final consumer. This is why it is essential to have legislation on measurements and measuring instruments. The OIML has 64 State members and 67 correspondent State members today.

Box 2.7. *Legal metrology for industry and consumers*

It was only in 1946 that the SI was officially defined by the BIPM with four base units: meter, kilogram, second and ampere. This was the MKSA system. In 1960, at the 11th General Conference on Weights and Measurements, six fundamental SI units were officialized: meter, kilogram, second, ampere, kelvin and candela. In 1971, the *mole* was added, as the final fundamental unit. In 2013, all the definitions were reviewed, taking into account not only the astronomical measures that were initially used as references for the MKSA units, but also electromagnetic measurements of the microcosm. Indirectly, the slow transformation of the fundamental methods of metrology allowed SI scholars and experts (BIPM, CGPM and CIPM) to progressively become independent of the member States. Indeed, the current definitions of the seven SI units are only truly comprehensible to experts in quantum theory and therefore only they can question these. This distancing from national contingencies allows the BIPM to clearly define its scope, limited to fundamental metrology related to the fundamental units and their standard references.

2.9. The founding of the IEC

The founding of the IEC was the concluding chapter in the second half of the 19th century, a period that saw the emergence of awareness of the need for standardization followed by the creation of the first large standardization organizations, strictly speaking. The establishment of the IEC, as a permanent international institution, was formally decided in 1904 at the Congress of Electricians at Saint-Louis, Missouri, during the Universal Exhibition and the Olympic Games that were held here. Following this, the Central Secretariat and the office were officially established in London in 1906. Everything related to the IEC is presented in Chapter 3.

3

The IEC, Inventor of Standards

Today, the IEC has brought together and federates the national standardization bodies of 89 countries[1] as well as other partners, especially industrial partners. Its scope is defined as “the international standards organization for the fields of electricity, electronics, electromagnetic compatibility, nanotechnology, and related technologies”. Founded in London in 1906, in 1948 the IEC joined the other standardization organizations located in Geneva. This allows it to work in close cooperation with the ITU and, above all, ISO, which is very closely associated with it. It also significantly contributed to the setting up of the ISO, as well as its forerunner, the International Standards Association (ISA).

As we have already mentioned, in the mid-19th century a core group of scholars was passionately interested in electricity and the new horizons of particulate physics, which had not been explored so far. A group of three friends distinguished themselves in this field: William Thomson[2] (1824–1907), James Prescott Joule (1818–1889) and Hermann von Helmholtz[3] (1821–1894). Beyond their exceptional scientific exchanges, these scholars wished to bring together science and industry. Thus, Joule found the theoretical study of work and energy to be a practical means of evaluating

1 Sixty-two full members and twenty-seven associate members (i.e. with limited voting rights).

2 William Thomson, the future Lord Kelvin who also became the first president of the IEC.

3 Helmholtz was a Prussian doctor who held the post of professor in several fields over his career, and who was deeply interested in the existence of a *vital force* (*Lebenskraft*) as well as in electricity, mathematics, acoustics and particle physics. He was Max Planck’s professor and, in 1888, became the president of the first German Bureau of Weights and Measurements.

the returns from the steam-run machine used in his family brewery in Manchester. Joule was also friends with William Sturgeon (1783–1850), who, along with Joseph Henry, invented one of the earliest usable electric engines in 1832[4]. William Thomson was a member of the Royal Society and the president of the society from 1890 to 1895. He soon became one of the leading actors working on standardization in Britain, especially within the British Association for the Advancement of Science.

Invention of a method: looking back from over a century away, it is fascinating to see how this group of scholars and electricity professionals, who first came together in international congresses[5] that were largely held on the margins of the Universal Exhibitions, were able to invent and establish an official and durable international standardization organization, which was rigorously independent of any country, although it was recognized and supported by all its member States. The British tradition of a gentleman's agreement and scientific institutions being closely linked to industrial pragmatism played a major role in allowing these pioneers to imagine creating completely original standards, which had to simultaneously be independent of the diplomatic alliances between States (like the ITU), take into account the diversity of industrial solutions in synergy with scientific and economic rationale, and also retain the confidence of the member States in a new global technological diplomacy. These innovative standardizers became the promoters and guarantors of this new kind of diplomacy.

The nascent field of electrical sciences and the knowledge emerging from electrical scientists promoted this desire for unity beyond companies and competition between states, and also a desire to sidestep pointless rivalries among the community of scholars. The use of electricity was a field that was full of promise, but only partially explored, being difficult to control or even dangerous. An alliance between all parties was essential for progress within this highly awaited technology.

4 Joule and Sturgeon also originated the concept of *economic work*, from which followed the concept of a socioeconomic duty, which is still an active field of study at the University of Manchester: https://www.resolvepoverty.org/what-is-the-socio-economic-duty.

5 The first International Congress of Electricity, which was held in Paris in 1881 and was followed by about ten others, was part of a larger context involving many other scientific and technical congresses (metrology, statistics, astronomy, chemistry, etc.), which were also held on the sidelines of world's fairs, ideal meeting places to bring these congress participants together and publicize their work.

This initial group of visionaries who wanted to develop electric and electromechanical standards soon grew into a global community of electricians. But it benefited from the early institutional support of:

– the Royal Society, more specifically the British Association for the Advancement of Science (the BAAS, later the BSA), which had already been involved in developing national norms for two decades;

– highly powerful associations of American and British engineers, the ancestors of today's Institute of Electrical and Electronics Engineers (IEEE).

This was the institutional foundation upon which the pioneers in the development of electrical standards built the durable structure of the IEC.

Over the following decades, this organization continued to improve its methodologies, especially by refining the collegial atmosphere that was so essential to the discussion and controlled framing of the standards. It followed the model of science and industry, and the IEC was hierarchical (grouping experts by specialization and sub-specialization)[6], while also following geographic divisions, which were necessarily interdisciplinary, corresponding to the actual communities of experts present in each member State[7].

Since the development of standards was distributed across an international context as well as a national one, from 1927 onwards, the IEC supported the federation of generalist national standardization organizations (across all activities) within the ISA and then the ISO. These federated organizations were created through the dynamic of progress that was established and induced by the two world wars.

The development of standards also has another feature. Like the scientists who inspired the standardizers, the IEC's ontological principle is to never encroach on another expert group's competency, whether within the IEC itself or in other standardization organizations. This was another area where the IEC was a pioneer: the development of mixed committees or collaborations promoting the interoperability of standards in an interdisciplinary manner and supporting the convergence of techniques.

6 Both scientists as well as industrialists. This would give rise to the TC, SC and WG.

7 That is, national organizations for standardizing technology related to electrical technologies.

The IEC was also able to define a universally adopted method for technical terminologies, notably because of the exceptional expertise of Egen Wüster.

3.1. Metrological consensus at the Congress of Electricians in 1881

In 1881, the first International Congress of Electricians was held as part of the Great Exhibition in Paris. This exhibition, and especially the Congress of Electricians, may be considered as the point of origin for what would become the IEC a quarter of a century later. It was in Paris again, during the Congress of Electricians that took place on the sidelines of the Great Exhibition of 1900, that the decision was taken to establish the IEC. This decision would come into effect in 1904, during the Congress at Saint-Louis[8] 1906. Among the electrical innovations introduced at the Paris Exhibition of 1881, there was, notably, the *electric car* developed by Gustave Trouvé and propelled by a Siemens motor, electric bulbs from Thomas Edison, an electric tramway developed by Werner von Siems, a dynamo by Zénobe Gramme, the telephone by Alexander Graham Bell, electricity distribution networks, and various applications of electricity: galvanoplasty, medicine, electrochemistry, etc.

In the mid-19th century, electricians quickly understood the urgent need to define units of measurement. From 1831, the British Association for the Advancement of Science (the BA and later the BSA) existed in Great Britain. Since 1863, this organization has developed a system of units based on the decimal metric system. A single variant was proposed in 1873 by William Thomson to study electrical and magnetic phenomena, preferring the centimeter to the meter and gram to kilogram[9]. British electricians had defined a system with three practical electrician units: the *ohm*, which was a *unit of resistance* (R), the *volt*, which measured *electromotive force* (E), and the *weber* to measure *intensity* (I). These units were related through the formula: $I = E/R$, established by Ohm[10]. One *weber* thus corresponds to the intensity of the current flowing across a resistance of 1 ohm due to the action of an electromotive force of 1 V.

8 Definitively approved by the members of the Congress of Electricians in 1908.

9 This system was known as the CGS system (centimeter, gram, second) and was different from the official metric system which was the MKS system (meter, kilogram, second).

10 Georg Ohm (1789–1854), German physicist who developed Ohm's law.

This theoretical choice was resolutely based on the coherence between the metric system and practical units, that is, units that could directly be used by industrialists and the consumers of their goods. The actual creation of standard references for electrical measurements soon became a contentious issue internationally. France had developed another standard measurement for *resistance*: the Bréguet company[11] established the kilometer resistance, originally designed for telegraphists. The reference standard for this was "the resistance of a telegraph wire with a diameter of 4 mm and 1 km in length".

Germany used the *siemens* (symbol: US for *unit siemens*). This electric resistance is: the resistance of a 1-m long column of mercury with a cross-section of 1 mm^2. This is approximately equal to 0.9536 ohms. The British used the *volt* as the unit for electromotive force, with 1 V being equivalent to 108 CGS units. In practice, this corresponded to the electromotive force of the Daniell battery[12], which was also the practical standard reference for the volt in Germany and France.

The British defined the *weber*[13] as the unit for electrical intensity. The Germans used the *siemens* and their unit of intensity was equivalent to 1.16 webers. The French made use of both of these systems. There was thus an urgent need to define a *universal system of electrical units* so that science and industrial development could progress and fulfill the promise of the electrical marvels introduced during the earliest Great Exhibitions.

The first International Congress of Electricians in Paris in 1881[14] was a highly anticipated event. An international community of scholars, engineers, industrialists and civil servants were eager to attend, and a total of 250

11 Founded by the same Louis Breguet who had built the Chappe-Morse telegraph. It was a company that was renowned for its innovations in telegraphy.

12 The Daniell battery, invented in 1836 by John Daniell, remained the primary source for a stable current, especially for the telegraph, for a long time.

13 It was equal to the intensity of a current that passed through a 1 ohm resistance with an electromotive force of 1 V between its ends.

14 This entire section is based on the Ampère website (CRHST/CNRS 2013), as well as the editions of *La Nature* from 1881 to 1900 (La Nature 1881, p. 282) and many documents in the online historical archives of the IEC (see: https://www.iec.ch) and the BIPM (see: https://www.bipm.org).

participants from 28 countries registered for it[15]. Sessions were themed around three major areas of work:

– First group: electrical units and measurements[16], physics of the globe, atmospheric electricity and terrestrial magnetism, lightning rods and electrophysiology.

– Second group: international telegraphy, telegraphs, telephones, railway signals.

– Third group: applications like electric lighting, transmission of force through electricity, distribution of electricity, watchmaking and chronography, recorders, precision instruments, electrometallurgy (especially aluminum).

The congress was held over only four days, with three days of effective work[17]; however, the task carried out by the founding congress was an edifying one. This is a testament to the competence of the international community of electricians, being able to finalize *performative resolutions*, notably for the normalization of electrical units. However, the congress had to contend with the strong opposition from the British scholars, who stuck to the CGS system and insisted that the units remain coherent with the three metric units, as well as from the German engineers who wanted practical reference standards (in reality, they sought to impose the use of the siemens standards).

Discussions outside the Congress were essential to arrive at the necessary consensus that allowed the industrial community of electricians to grow at an international level with no hindrances. The French physicist Éleuthère Mascar, the secretary of the congress, recorded this in an account narrating the behind-the-scenes action[18]. After two long days of work, the Commission for Electrical Units seemed to be at an impasse. The German electricians did not want to give up the siemens, which was problematic as it was arbitrary, that is, not coherent with the metric units. Mascart was invited to dinner at the Chatham hotel, where he found himself in the company of Lord Kelvin

15 Participants included William Thomson, Helmholtz, Siemens, Crookes, Gramme, Henry Rowland, Becquerel and Lord Rayleigh.

16 The order of the program indicates the importance of defining the units.

17 There was a period of mourning for the American President James Abram Garfield, who had died from an infected gunshot wound 2 months after an attempted assassination.

18 This is a summary of Mascart's account, published on the Ampère CRHST/CNRS website.

and Sir William Siemens for Britain and von Helmholtz[19], Clausius[20], Kirchhoff[21], Wiedemann[22] and Werner Siemens for the German delegates[23]. They all agreed to the condition that the electrical units should remain coherent with the metric units. However, Werner Siemens could not bring himself to give up the siemens unit, even though he knew it was arbitrary. He was finally reconciled to this by his younger brother, Sir William Siemens, who was at the dinner and who had been born Wilhem Siemens in Hanover in 1832. Before he emigrated, or rather built the company Siemens in England, his older brother Werner had helped him complete his theoretical and practical education. On this evening, fraternal reasoning carried the day and his honor was satisfied. It must be noted that von Helmholtz, another guest, was not only a Prussian but a close friend of Sir Kelvin[24].

As with trade deals and in many other spheres of activity, a strategically planned dinner conversation is indispensable when formulating conditions for an agreement. Standardization is no different: mutual friendship and appreciation; long-term, medium-term and short-term vision of a technological discipline; being multilingual; having diplomatic skills; while also carrying scientific or industrial celebrity status are all essential qualities to be an effective actor in standardization, and Sir Kelvin met all these criteria!

The Congress concluded the following seven points:

1) The CGS system was adopted[25]. This satisfied the British Association for the Advancement of Sciences.

---

19 Von Helmholtz, Prussian physiologist and physicist (1821–1894).

20 Rudolf Julius Emmanuel Clausius (1822–1888), Prussian physicist, renowned for his major contributions to thermodynamics.

21 Gustav Kirchhoff, German physicist (1824–1887): electrodynamics, radiation physics and mathematical theory of elasticity.

22 Gustav Heinrich Wiedemann, German physicist specializing in electricity (1826–1899).

23 Werner Siemens (1816–1892), German industrialist, older brother of Sir William, born Carl Wilhelm.

24 They had worked together in Germany for four months on the calculation and experimental development of discharge from spark-gap transmitters (one of the foundations of future Hertz waves). Sir Kelvin invited Helmholtz to England multiple times to attend meetings of the British Association. It is certain that his presence at this dinner facilitated unanimity by balancing nationalities.

25 It will be seen that this detail regarding the scale of decimal values (CGS vs. MKS) is scientifically unimportant (see section 3.2.1 on the *Giorgi system*).

2) The unit of resistance would be called the *ohm*, with a value of 109 CGS units. The unit for electromotive force, or voltage, would be the *volt*, which would have a value of 108 CGS units.

3) The practical unit of resistance (the *ohm*) would be defined as a column of mercury with a cross-section of 1 mm^2 at 0°C. The German delegates were thus satisfied. Their system of measurement, based on a column of mercury, was very reliable and easy to implement. It was thus retained to serve as the standard reference. On the other hand, the name for the standard unit of measurement would be *ohm* and not *siemens*[26].

4) An international commission would be tasked with determining the length of the mercury column representing the ohm.

5) The unit for current intensity would be the *ampere*, which would be the intensity of a current "produced by one volt in one ohm".

6) The unit for the quantity of electricity would be the *coulomb*, which would be the "quantity of electricity transported by 1 A in 1 s".

7) The unit for capacitance would be the *farad*, defined as "1 coulomb per volt". Ampère and Coulomb, citizens of the host country, were given the honor of having the units for current intensity and charge named after them.

The major achievement of the first congress in Paris in 1881 was the bringing together of international luminaries from the world of industry and science, who managed to finalize a *coherent set of electrical units*. This "club of electricians" spotted what drew them together and they now planned periodic congresses that would allow them to arbitrate *shared recommendations* (i.e. norms) to establish future industrial techno-industrial standards. The implacable competition between electricians was proof of how rich and full of promise this emerging industry was. However, as with any sport, there had to be universally accepted rules and, therefore, a *Club House* where arbitration could take place. The 1881 congress in Paris was followed by other editions, interspersed with themed conferences to continue the work of building this international commune of electricians.

26 A column of mercury with a cross-section of 1 mm^2, whose height was yet to be defined to avoid retaining the height corresponding to the *siemens*.

3.2. The impossibility of giving the BIPM the electrical units

There was a visible chasm between traditional physicists and electricians. The latter carried the certainty of laying the foundations of new electrical and particle physics[27], which mechanical physicists and astronomers (who then made up the BIPM) did not understand. This had consequences on the relations between the IEC (and the earlier Congress of Electricians) and the BIPM, as they were supposed to share the units of the metric system. During the 1889 Congress of Electricians, it had to be acknowledged that the metrological physicists of the BIPM were outdated. The *joule* and *watt* were confirmed to be the units of energy and power. The *kilowatt* was retained in place of *horsepower* to measure the power of electric engines.

3.3. The stages in the founding of the IEC: 1881, 1904, 1906, 1908

The invention and then founding of the IEC were the fruit of a long process of reflection during the Congress of Electricians. However, this was not the only institution to be involved. There was a constellation of personalities and professional, scientific, national and even international institutions working together to arrive at results after 25 years of debates. Three major institutional actors we must name were as follows: (1) the British Association for Science Advancement, more specifically its committee in charge of norms and standards, especially with regard to electricity; (2) the American Institute of Electrical Engineers (AIEE); and (3) the Great Exhibitions.

This was the network, largely Anglo-American but resolutely international, upon which the IEC was founded:

– The British Association for Science Advancement (the BA, founded in 1831, later the BSA) was a pioneer in the field of theoretical definitions as well as technological standardization within Great Britain. In the 1860s, this institution worked to define norms, for wires first, and then for electrical units and undersea cables[28]. During the long gestation of the IEC, the BA

27 In 1865, Loschmidt (Austrian physicist, 1821–1895) proposed the first principles of the structure of molecules. In 1870, Lord Kelvin proposed the vortex theory of the atom.

28 A series of standards for screw threads from 0.25 to 6 mm (called BA), defined in 1882. These screws are manufactured as per the same standards even today, and used for miniature and scientific instruments.

constantly worked to support the theoretical study and effective implementation of universal standards for technology and science.

– British and American associations of engineers can be thought of as being the same as the BA, institutional supports for the future IEC. The modern-day IEEE already existed in the United States and in Great Britain. It would take too long to present their complex history here and the extreme diversity of disciplines and domestic commissions that these organizations encompassed. The IEE in Great Britain (Society of Telegraph Engineers and Electricians, and Institution of Electrical Engineers) was founded in 1871. In the United States, the AIEE was founded in 1884[29]. When the IEC was set up in London, the British IEE and BA helped its organizational setup by making available a general secretariat for all administrative and technical work. Practically, the two associations implemented the future principle of shared contributions from all member countries.

– The Great Exhibitions became the natural venues for many meetings and especially for the Congress of Electricians: at the exhibition in Paris in 1889 (marking a century since the Revolution); in 1893 at the Chicago Exhibition, when the units for electric measurements, including the Clark battery, were discussed and defined; in 1900 and Paris again, where the conferences led to the creation of the Commission électrotechnique internationale (CEI-IEC); and finally, the Congress at the 1904 exhibition in Saint-Louis (Missouri, United States) when the IEC was finally created. The London office was subsequently set up in 1906 and officially began functioning in 1908.

3.3.1. *The key personalities involved in founding the IEC*

There were hundreds of companies, institutions and personalities (scholars, engineers, entrepreneurs, financiers and senior civil servants) who collectively set up the IEC[30], but a few key individuals stand out. William Thomson, later Lord Kelvin, was clearly the primary creator of the organization. On the other hand, Colonel Crompton was the quiet authority

29 Both these institutions would come together in the 1960s to become the international organization IEEE with 160 member countries and 400,000 members.

30 The history of the organization, compiled on the occasion of its 50th anniversary in 1956 (Ruppert 1956), as well as the IEC's online archive (see: https://www.iec.ch) proved excellent resources.

who made it a reality and created a durable organization. Charles Le Maistre was the organizational spirit. Born in 1874, he was the secretary general of the organization from 1906 until his death in 1953. Unlike Kelvin, Crompton or Le Maistre, who address the whole gamut of questions before the IEC, the Italian engineer and scientist Giovanni Giorgi, a member of the *Associazione Elettrotecnica Italiana* (AEI), fulfilled a more specific, but fundamental role. He had the clearest vision of a coherent system of units that would bring together the BIPM and IEC points of view. It must be noted that he was born in 1871 and died in 1950 and was therefore the same generation as Le Maistre, while Crompton (1845–1940) was almost of Lord Kelvin's generation. This quartet of founders, equally matched in their skill but from different generations and distributed across different roles, was undoubtedly a determining factor in the success and enduring nature of the IEC.

Lord Kelvin Thomson was a scholar of great renown and one of the major discoverers of the new atomic physics of particles. He was exceptionally talented and had already published a much discussed dissertation at the age of 17. He was also a humanist, Latinist, Hellenist and a polylingual traveler. At the age of 26, he had already published around 50 articles. In June 1847, he published a founding article for the Cambridge Philosophical Society. He was an internationally renowned scientist, an inventor, a passionate navigator, a shrewd entrepreneur[31] and the undisputed leader of the founders of the future IEC. In 1866, Queen Victoria knighted him for his work on the transatlantic cable, and in 1892, he entered the peerage, becoming Baron Kelvin of Largs. In 1906, he was elected as the first president of the IEC. He died in 1907 and was buried at Westminster Abbey, close to Newton.

Colonel Crompton was a key figure in the effective establishment of the IEC. During the Saint-Louis Congress of 1904, it was Crompton who

31 His first dissertation at university bore the title *The Uniform Motion of Heat in Homogeneous Solid Bodies, and its Connection with the Mathematical Theory of Electricity*. He then published *On an Absolute Thermometric Scale Founded on Carnot's Theory of the Motive Power of Heat, and Calculated from Regnault's Observations*. He used his knowledge of the sea and of electricity and became a global authority on the theoretical study, manufacture and laying of undersea cables. He developed special probes, perfected mechanisms for unrolling cables, etc. He filed tens of patents: navigation devices, deep-sea probes, tidal predictors and also a cross-winding process for engines.

implemented the decision to create the IEC, proposed at the 1900 Congress in Paris. He was an industrialist working with electricity, and an orderly and organized man, a colonel in the Royal Engineers. As an industrialist, he believed it was essential to have a common terminology to describe electrical phenomena. His association with the creation of the IEC was almost accidental. His discussion was noted and he was invited to study the creation of a permanent international commission for electrical standardization. As the secretary general of the forerunner of the IEC, Crompton asked Charles Le Maistre[32] to support him and then succeed him to become the first secretary general of the IEC itself.

Charles Le Maistre was only 26 years old when he was appointed as joint secretary for electricity in the British Engineering Standards Committee (BESC[33]). The institution had just been founded to generalize, rationalize and centralize the standardization work carried out by the British Association for Science Advancement (the BA standards) and, as it happened, its subcommittee, the British Association of Standards of Electrical Resistance. Colonel Crompton saw a fantastic opportunity in this young man, all of 26 years old, a member of the IEE division of the Central Technical College in South Kensington, who had already gained 6 years of experience working in the electricity department of the Thames Ironworks Company. Charles Le Maistre's talent was employed in Saint-Louis and then in London. Almost 30 years his senior, Crompton appreciated his organizational ability, his qualities as a man of action and his fine knowledge of electricity and saw in him a shared passion for standardization. As the first permanent secretary general of the IEC, Charles Le Maistre had to initially define the statutes, regulations and mission, not just for the organization itself but also for its central headquarters in London. He soon surpassed all the expectations of the core founders of the IEC. For over 50 years, his main focus was on organizing, studying, assessing, promoting and encouraging the development of standards.

32 Then the joint secretary for electricity in the British Engineering Standards Committee (BESC).

33 The BESC was indeed the first national institution for generalist technical standardization in the world. In 1918, it became the British Engineering Standards Association, and, after having been granted a Royal charter in 1929, it became the British Standards Institution (BSI) in 1931, the name by which it is still known today.

While he may not have been the first professional in the world of standardization, he was undoubtedly the most talented inventor in the creation of standards. Not only was he responsible for the details on methodology and rules governing modern-day standardization institutions (especially the ISO and IEC), but he also directly brought about the foundation of the ISA and, later, the ISO, after the Second World War. It was Le Maistre again who promoted the emergence of many national standardization organizations. He was able to grasp, from the beginning, that standards could only be valid if they were produced within sector-wise committees that defined their scope[34] in a rigorous and invariant manner. The IEC had to preserve its sectorial specificity and for this reason, he soon foresaw that the electric standards in the metric system must eventually return to the BIPM.

With Giovanni Giorgi, this re-allocation of responsibilities could take place more subtly, and Le Maistre was wise enough to wait. As is usually the case, an organization's secretary general determines the continuity and durability of the organization, while the Presidents in charge of driving the production of standards are there to provide a vision of new horizons, to assess and finalize existing standards, or even identify those that must be removed. The post of president of the IEC had a tenure of 3–4 years. Thirty-seven presidents have succeeded Lord Kelvin, while there have only been seven secretaries general, with Le Maistre's tenure being the longest, at 47 years. Other secretaries general held the post for between 8 and 18 years. Charles Le Maistre, often called the Father of International Standards, truly deserved this honor.

In 1901, at the Congress of the AEI in Rome, Giovanni Giorgi, the Italian scientist and engineer, showed that it was possible to construct a coherent system of units by adding an electrical unit to the three mechanical units (centimeter, gram and second) in the existing CGS system. This fundamental electrical unit could be either the *ohm* or the *ampere*, as the other units of electricity could be derived from this basic unit. He proposed shifting from a three-dimensional system to a four-dimensional metric system. This radical

34 The specific use of the term "scope" in standardization jargon goes hand in hand with the precise formalization of the process of developing standards and the institutions that make up the "Institutional Standards Factory": each standard or preparatory work is defined by a scope; and each committee, commission, subcommittee, or working group must also define its scope.

change to the conceptualized units persists even today, despite the addition of other fundamental units.

Giorgi's suggestion made it possible to rationally derive all the electric units, except for the ampere. This was subsequently chosen as the fundamental unit, joining the first three MKS units, rather than the CGS units, as Giorgio felt that using the CGS units added unnecessary complications to the harmonization of the metric system as the scales of magnitude for the metric reference standards were not appropriate for effectively working on electrical phenomena. Indeed, when the last three units (*kelvin, mole* and *candela*) were added, and when the units were later redefined using atomic frequencies, there was thankfully no question of revisiting other multiples of the historical fundamental units, as they could not match the scale of particular phenomena!

Giovanni Giorgi's suggestion was a revolution on a Copernican scale in the metric system! However, at the time it was proposed, only the scientific and electrical engineering elites understood it – chief among these being Lord Kelvin and Oliver Heaviside[35]. It was therefore too early for this to become a unanimous decision, even within the IEC, let alone the BIPM. Nevertheless, the upcoming generation of researchers and electrical engineers adopted the "Giorgi system". From 1935 to 1938, Giorgi led the Italian delegation at the IEC conferences. It was in 1935 that Charles Le Maistre suggested that the "Giorgi system" be adopted by the IEC. However, the BIPM would only go on to adopt it after the Second World War.

3.3.2. *The final steps in the creation of the IEC*

In 1904, in Saint-Louis, the International Standardization Committee of the International Congress on Electricity unanimously concluded on the need to create "representative committees tasked with studying the question of unification of nomenclature and the classification of electrical equipment and machines". The congress also recommended that this work be carried out by correspondence and that the proposed secretary general (Charles Le Maistre) be given the responsibility of organizing and maintaining the

35 Oliver Heaviside (1850–1925), a British mathematician and physicist who is sadly not well-known enough today. He made many innovations across scientific domains, notably in telegraphy, but did not demonstrate his discoveries nor patent his processes. He was supported by Lord Kelvin but died isolated and unknown.

archives. In 1906, a preliminary meeting for the foundation of the Bureau in London was organized in London and attended by 16 countries. The American Institute of Electrical Engineers and the British Institution of Electrical Engineers (a division of the BESC), led by Le Maistre, had prepared the statutes. It was during this meeting that the name *Commission Électrotechnique Internationale* was proposed and Lord Kelvin was elected president. It was confirmed that Le Maistre would oversee the functioning of the London office. Two years later, in 1908, the IEC became a legal entity. Lord Balfour welcomed the new organization in a highly programmatic manner:

> As I comprehend it, the chief desire of the commission is to so arrange, by international agreement, the tests which are to be applied to different kinds of electrical machinery, so to describe the qualities of different machines that whilst the man who buys and the man who sells will know exactly what each, respectively, is doing, there will yet be the freest initiative left to both: to the man who desires machinery to be constructed to carry out some particular design of his own, and to constructors of machinery on their side, who desire to take advantage of the ever-increasing changes which growth in knowledge and increasing invention enable mankind to turn into account. (Balfour 1956)

In 1904, 10 national committees had been constituted, and six others were being created[36]. The statutes of the IEC granted one vote to each country (National Body). In 1914, the IEC had already published: a list of international letter symbols for quantities and abbreviations for the names of units; a series of definitions for hydraulic turbines, rotating machines, electrical machines and equipment; and international specifications for copper-type[37] (the preferred material for conducting wires). Four study groups were already working on nomenclature, symbols, the classification of electrical machines and primary motors (current generators).

However, the First World War brutally interrupted the work carried out by the IEC as well as the IUT and BIPM. Nonetheless, it strongly reinforced

36 These made up the first fledgling national standardization organizations which may or may not have specialized in electricity. Today, they are called *national bodies* (NBs).

37 The future TC.

the mobilization of scientists and engineers within their national electricity bodies and in many cases, these organizations were transformed into generalist, national standardization bodies before the war ended or very soon after. The war intensified the need for standardization. Electrical installations on board warships had to be interchangeable, as did the telephonic installations along the front, which had to be installed rapidly, sometimes under fire! Similarly, you could not have multiple standards for wireless telegraphy tube fittings, as is still the case today for light bulbs.

The normative standardization of military tubes by the IEC could be considered the major trigger for radio's rise as a mass entertainment device in the 1920s, as well as promoting the amateur practice of wireless telegraphy. In 1919, delegations from 20 countries met in London for a plenary meeting of the IEC. The war had led to intense advances in electrical technologies, especially in the field of radio, in both warring groups. The pre-war experts were delighted to be able to resume their projects. The IEC intensified the division of its organization into various sub-disciplines. In 1923, the standardization projects were distributed across 10 technical committees (TCs) that worked in parallel. The production of standards increased exponentially, year on year. The permanent headquarters in London found that its workload had increased considerably. "The Council decided to create a seven-member action committee to execute the Council's decisions, seconding the work of the central Office and coordinating the work of the National Bodies (NB) and Technical Committees (TC)"[38].

3.4. New York, 1926: decentralization of the IEC and creation of the ISA

The IEC plenary session in New York in 1926 marked a turning point for an organization that had come into its own. Note that 22 years after the decision taken in St. Louis, the IEC met in United States once again. This event, the most important event in the IEC's history, brought together 120 delegates from 19 countries who were welcomed at the White House by President Calvin Coolidge. For Charles Le Maistre (secretary general), Guido Semenza (president) and the directorate of the IEC, this meeting was one where significant decisions would be taken.

38 See: https://www.iec.ch/history.

From this point onwards, most industrialized nations had their own solid and responsible generalist, national standardization organizations (all disciplines together). At the IEC, everyone agreed on the need for building specialized structures for sub-domains, coordinated at the local, national, and international level. The challenge was to ensure that there was space for global discussions in order to harmonize electrical standards while ensuring that the London office was not flooded with excess work and information. It became essential to redefine the distribution of roles. The goal was to reinforce the initiative of the National Bodies while preserving the heritage of the pioneers of standardization. The standards had to cover theoretical aspects as well as specific features of the disciplines involving electricity.

Charles Le Maistre planned to carry out essential reforms in collaboration with the leaders of the TCs and national standardization organizations. The priority was to revisit the procedures for drafting standards that were to be published. There seemed to be an urgent need to make National Bodies responsible for the effective development of standards to ease the load on the central office in London and to stimulate local initiatives. This reform would allow the IEC to focus more sharply on final editorial control, governance and global strategy. To enhance the efficacy of the national bodies, they had to work closely with generalist national standardization bodies. This led to the idea, proposed in New York, of an international federation of national standardization organizations, which resulted in the creation of the ISA. Thanks to Charles Le Maistre's shrewd planning, the IEC plenary meeting coincided with the meeting of secretaries general of the national standardization bodies. The formal and informal exchanges that followed quickly led to the establishment of the ISA, itself the forerunner of the modern-day ISO (see Chapter 4).

With regard to the decentralization itself, a key decision was taken in New York in 1926: the secretary of each TC was put in charge of a national body (NB) and was responsible for overseeing the financing of this body, the management of standardization projects and the pre-publishing of the standards. The TC remained international committees, with the national bodies carrying out coordination and working in collaboration with other national bodies. Experts in each country continued to meet during the plenary sessions of the IEC and, if required, would correspond with each other or meet during specific meetings. This decentralization had some immediate and major impacts:

– lightening the load on the central office in London, which could resume focusing on the coherence and rigor in standards;

– enhanced financing, allowing the IEC to pursue its own development;

– the same method was adopted by the ISA (and inherited by the ISO), allowing for remarkable efficacy despite a significant publishing load.

From 1926 onwards, standardization was based on the distribution of skills between international actors, companies and research centers. This model promoted technology transfers and scientific collaborations. While some companies were wary about their industrial secrets, they understood that the standards simply laid a foundation that did not threaten competition but instead ensured interoperability without hampering innovation. Companies retained the freedom to go beyond the existing standards as long as they respected a minimum compatibility with an existing set of norms. This dynamic could, however, lead to modification or, in some cases, a complete recreation of the standards. Let us look at one example of this: as we said before, the First World War enforced the use of identical caps for wireless telegraphy lamps. The IEC standardized these characteristics, leading to the development of radiophonic applications. However, the technological advances that followed led to a diversification of tubes (diodes, triodes, tetrodes, pentodes, octodes, nonodes, etc.), thereby increasing the number of lamps per radio unit, which was a commercial argument at the time. Gradually, tubes that integrated several functions and frequencies into a single component were developed. All these initially retained the same cap diameter, but as circuits grew smaller, there was a need to add pins and standardize their positioning. The arrival of transistors completely transformed the architecture of electronic circuits, requiring new standards to be developed.

The IEC played a key role in many sectors, but its most significant success is undoubtedly the development of *weak currents*[39]. Up to 1939, this field was of modest importance within the IEC; however, between 1950 and 1960, it expanded spectacularly, leading to the multiplication of new work items (NWIs) and the creation of new, dedicated TCs and SCs. This rise in significance coincided with the rise of transistors, printed circuit boards

39 While outdated today, this was the terminology at the time. It is still relevant today in differentiating between the various professions involved in installing various networks in buildings.

(PCBs) and electronic components. After the Second World War, the IEC established various institutional standards that defined the characteristics of these components. Because of this standardization, Moore's law[40], formulated in the 1960s, remains valid even today. The rigorous interoperability of modular components led to the rise of a structure market, while standardization significantly lowered costs. At the same time, there was continued improvement in performance (power, memory, speed, miniaturization) at a constant price.

3.4.1. *The IEC's first technical committees*

From the first Congress of Electricians in 1881 to the last one, in St. Louis before the IEC was founded, the schedules for the working sessions clearly demonstrate the diversity of scientific and industrial concerns across several themes. In 1904, before the central office of the IEC was set up in London, the pioneering experts had to adopt a pragmatic approach. As discussed earlier, they decided to focus on three areas of study: nomenclature, symbols and the classification of electrical machines. Beyond these three areas, the preliminary standardization work could be carried out by informal groups, associations of engineers such as the AIEE or IEE, or in the form of national standards established by existing, stable organizations. However, with a few exceptions (such as conducting copper), the other areas of study did not fall within the ambit of these first three TCs in the IEC.

Nomenclature (TC 1) and *symbols* (TC 3) posed major challenges. In 1914, the IEC finalized an initial list of terms and definitions for electrical machines and equipment, as well as a list of international symbols for electrical units (W, V, A, Ω, etc.), also including the graphical representation of the different components, states or flows within the circuits and machines. On the methodological front, the work carried out by TC 1 and TC 3 also governed the advances in future standards and facilitated theoretical progress in electromagnetic physics. It made it possible to write equations, draw electric schematic diagrams univocally and establish a common language beyond the vocabulary used by different languages. This theoretical formalization proved to be a fundamental tool for communication between engineers, as well as entrepreneurs and stakeholders throughout the field of

---

40 Gordon E. Moore predicted in 1965 that the number of transistors on microchips would double roughly every two years while costs decrease.

electricity. Furthermore, it simplified the publishing of norms and the regulations that ensured the safety of users and professionals.

3.4.2. *Eugen Wüster's contributions and nomenclature*

Where scientists are concerned, establishing a typology of concepts and the elements studied and preparing end-pages with indices or glossaries is a practice almost as old as writing itself. Ancient Babylonian tablets contain lists of objects, people or gods. With the advent of the codex, this practice became a generalized one, made easier by the ability to flip through volumes and access a table of contents or index. Later, different academies designed different systems of classification, especially in zoology, botany and chemistry, for example, the systems of Linnaeus, Leibniz and Buffon.

In the second half of the 19th century, the question of nomenclature was raised in almost every scientific and industrial congress. Engineers in the 19th and 20th centuries were given homogeneous training in this discipline. As for industrialists, when they delivered a product (and a fortiori machines or complex installations), they had to provide an index in addition to user manuals, information on maintenance, and other contractual documents. The pioneers of electrical standardization were often trilingual (English, French and German). From the 1880s onwards (or even earlier in a few cases), these experts worked in close collaboration, and it was observed that to arrive at a consensus, they had to absolutely ensure that they were discussing the same objects, concepts and phenomena, independent of their respective mother tongues.

Regardless of whether it was called terminology, vocabulary, lexicon or nomenclature (the term retained for TC no. 1: IEC/TC 1), the objective was the same: guarantee a rigorously univocal reference for components, circuits and machines. This practice had already been established among technical designers and consisted of using letters or numbers as identifiers. These identifiers, independent of language, could be made up of a series of numbers or letters (whether or not they meant anything), and the essential point was that they had to be unique and unambiguous. These identifiers could also be associated with the symbols defined by TC 3. The nomenclature committee had to invent its own methods. In 1927, they established a system of classifications into groups and sections, as well as a numbering code for terms and their definitions.

Eugen Wüster's entry into the IEC/TC 1 was a key point in the development of this terminology. An Austrian, and an engineer by training, he had inherited a family firm comprising an electric power plant, a cold rolling mill and a manufacturing unit for saws and woodworking tools. A large part of his wealth went into financing his passions[41], linguistics applied to technical terminology, as well as lexicography and the standardization of technologies, especially in the field of electricity. What set Wüster apart was his ability to bring engineering rigor to lexicography, interlinguistics and terminology. He was the founder of linguistic engineering. Based notably on the concept of *onomasiology*, proposed in 1902 by Austrian linguist Adolf Zauner (Zauner 1902), and on the older concept of *semasiology*[42], Wüster was the first to theorize both these approaches and reveal their underlying mechanics. He highlighted their fundamental difference:

– The *semasiological* approach, adopted by philologists and lexicographers, consisted of collecting words in a language and listing their different meanings in one or more languages.

– The *onomasiologic*[43] approach, which worked in the opposite way, is the approach used for terminology. This approach starts from ideas and concepts, or even concrete objects, with the aim of organizing them into a coherent system.

Wüster made significant theoretical and practical contributions to TC 1 in the IEC. Thanks to his dynamism, the first edition *International Electrotechnical Vocabulary* (IEV), was published in 1938 with exemplary scientific rigor and in six languages. In parallel, in 1936, Wüster promoted the creation of TC 37 within the ISA, dedicated to the "standardization of the principles in the formation of terms and the development of terminologies and dictionaries". After World War Two, this ISA committee became ISO/TC 37: Terminology (principles and coordination).

---

41 Involved early on in the Esperanto movement, Wüster (1923) was the principal author of the Esperanto-German encyclopedic dictionary. This work served as the basis for his dissertation on philology, which is still considered a fundamental reference work for modern terminology.

42 *Semasiology,* the science of signs (from the Greek σημείο (sign) and λογία (logia, study)), denotes the analysis of the meaning of words; *onomasiology* is also derived from Ancient Greek: ὀνομασία (denote by a name) and the same λογία (logia, study).

43 This approach must be prioritized by standardization experts.

He became the secretary of this TC in 1951, under the aegis of the Austrian Standardization Institute (ASI). In 1951, he also founded the *Österreichische Gesellschaft für Dokumentation und Information*, before creating Infoterm in 1971, which was a terminological documentation center[44]. Eugen Wüster died in 1977 and sadly was not able to witness the advances made possible by the standardization of linguistic engineering, the documentation associated with network computing and, more recently, artificial intelligence.

However, he did live long enough to observe the progress of data processing and then the information sciences. *Terminotics* had emerged as a separate discipline. His biggest legacy, however, was the International Electrotechnical Vocabulary (IEV), terminology that was unique to electrotechnology, electronics and communications, born out of the work of IEC/TC 1. The IEV[45] has evolved with conceptual and technological advances in linguistic engineering. From 1927 onwards, EIC/TC 1 experts adopted a system of classification of terms, dividing them into groups and sections, along with a number code for the terms and their definitions. This model continues to evolve with the needs of the IEC. This hierarchical organization, founded on unique identifiers, is still in use today. The IEV is structured into nine broad categories:

- Class 1: General concepts.
- Class 2: Materials.
- Class 3: Measurement, automatic control.
- Class 4: Electric equipment.
- Class 5: Electronic equipment.
- Class 6: Generation, transmission and distribution of energy.
- Class 7: Information and communication technologies.
- Class 8: Particular applications.
- Class 9: Standardization and related activities.

44 For more details on this question, see Humbley (2007, pp. 82–91).

45 Just as we chose to retain IEC rather than CEI, we use IEV rather than the French version, VEI.

In 2025, the IEC had over 115 TCs, 113 subcommittees (SCs) and 776 working groups (WGs) and had published over 10,000 standards. The IEV (published by the IEC) lists over 20,000 entries spanning 80 domains and facilitates exchanges between the TCs and SCs. The terms in the IEV are defined in French and in English, and their equivalents are provided in multiple languages including Arabic, Chinese, Spanish, Japanese and Russian. A free, online version of the IEV, Electropedia[46], has been available since 2007 and has become an essential reference and serves as the model for many other terminological bases. It has largely been adopted by professionals in the electrotechnical sector.

3.4.3. *The creation of mixed committees within the IEC*

In its early days, the IEC only collaborated with a limited number of standardization organizations, maintaining close relations with the ITU and Consultative Committee of the BIPM, notably. The First World War provoked major technological advances in the domains of electricity and telecommunications. Further, the reconstruction of industrial and urban infrastructure led to systematic electrification, reinforcing the role of standardization. The different kinds of progress led to an increase in generalist national standardization organizations (the NBs), federated within the ISA as well as the IEC, and also to the emergence of many networks and sectorial federations. The IEC thus had to adapt to these changes. Among the chief organizations created at this time, there were, notably:

– the International Council on Large Electric Systems (CIGRE), 1921;

– the World Energy Conference, 1924;

– the International Consultative Committee on Long-Distance Telephony (CCIF), 1924;

– the International Union of Producers and Distributors of Electrical (UNIPEDE), 1925.

To coordinate these collaborations, mixed TCs[47] were created such as the International Mixed Committee on the Electric Traction Equipment and the Special International Committee on Radio Interference (CISPR). Putting in

46 See: https://www.electropedia.org, which is also the site for the IEV.

47 The forerunners of the Joint-TC; for example, the ISO/IEC JTC 1 (see Chapter 5).

place formal liaisons and the establishment of mixed committees was a major advance in the methods used to produce standards.

3.4.4. *The increase in the number of TCs and the requirement for SCs*

During the 1881 Paris Congress, three sub-domains of electricity were clearly identified (see section 3.1), which served as the basis for the creation of the first TCs in the IEC. However, as the number of TCs increased, the technical management and decision-making in plenary sessions became too complex. The IEC council remedied this by appointing an Action Committee[48] made up of seven members, who were given the responsibility of optimizing the organization of the projects. Many experts did not have enough knowledge of all the items studied by a TC, and the largest TCs thus began to swarm out into more specialized bodies.

This "swarming out" was quite literal. While each TC had a secretariat and a president, it was necessary to replicate this mode of governance within each subcommittee (SC). This ensured a sufficient level of governance, competence management and that developing standards matched increasingly specific applications. The experts, who could continue dominating the meta-sub-profession and meta-sub-discipline, were thus able to concentrate on coordination between these TCs that were divided into multiple SCs. The new methods that had been introduced in the 1926 plenary session in New York to decentralize the publishing responsibilities of TCs in different countries (NBs) applied *mutatis mutandis* to the hierarchy of the SCs. The same would happen with the ISO.

3.5. IEC diplomacy in the decade from 1940 to 1950

The Second World War led to significant upheavals in the international functioning of the IEC. Based in London, the organization was able to survive, unlike the ISA, but its activities were almost completely suspended. However, during the war years there were considerable advances in electrotechnology and the standardization bodies among the Allies played a key role in these.

48 Today the Standardization Management Bureau, the equivalent of the TMB in the ISO.

The rise of the *weak current* transformed an essential sector in the IEC: information and communication, including information sciences, television and new media. In the 1960s, this evolution led to a close-knit collaboration with the ISO on information technology and communication, leading to the creation of a specific mixed committee: ISO/IEC JTC 1 (see Chapter 5).

In 1948, the IEC handed back responsibility for electrical units to the BIPM.

The same year, under secretary general Charles Le Maistre, the organization was shifted to Geneva, a strategic move that reinforced its role on the international scene.

During its creation in 1947, the ISO adopted the same method of governance as the IEC (as its predecessor, the ISA, had also done). This governance was based on rigorous procedures and a democratic voting method (one NB = one vote), like the UN system. The methodology followed resulted from the scientific and professional nature of the electrotechnical domain, which could be described as *chemically and physically pure*. IEC experts used clear and unambiguous terminology, limiting the risk of misinterpretations. Although the increasing level of specialization made it difficult to gain overall mastery of the disciplines, the international scientific and industrial community of electricians spoke in a single voice.

Another key factor is that electricity and electronics constitute a relatively young field, developing and expanding over less than two centuries. Their rapid progress is still continuing with the arrival of quantum technologies and biodigital innovations. Given these evolutions, the electrical and electronics world recognizes the need for standards which, when adopted in a timely manner, offer a major economic advantage (as illustrated by Moore's law). Conversely, the ISO covers a much larger and more heterogeneous field of standardization, which limits the uniform application of the IEC model. However, this approach has remained an essential reference for all actors in the field of standardization, as we analyze in Chapter 4.

4

From the ISA to the ISO

> What would other countries think of a place where 100 centiliters were provided for a liter, or where an anchor bolt guaranteed to resist 15 tons did not shear under a load of 15,000 kilos? Fortunately, the relevant professions, with government support, played a significant part in creating nothings, and they were designed in such a way that it took years to decrypt them. As soon as that happened, they entered a process of revisions. (Vian 2022)[1]

Today, the ISO has become the global institute in charge of standardization of products and services. Along with ITU and IEC, which also shifted to Geneva after the Second World War, the ISO is now the international reference center for standardization. In this chapter, we will focus on the ISO, its predecessor, the ISA (1927 to 1939), and its federated generalist national standardization bodies (NBs). Most of these national bodies were founded in the period following the end of the First World War and in the 1920s. Thanks to the EIC, the ISA was founded in 1927. Although it remained a very modest institution (one or two full-time positions) until it was dissolved in 1939, it would prove to be significant for the generalization of standardization at an international level, across several professions. In just 12 years, over 60 technological branches were standardized through as many TCs.

---

1 From 1942 to 1946, Boris Vian, who had trained as engineer at the École Centrale, a premier engineering school in France, worked with AFNOR. He conceived of a *roman à clef* (a novel that fictionalizes real facts and people) that captured his vision of standardization: *Vercoquin and the Plankton*.

The Second World War again showed that standardization played a key role in military victory. And Charles Le Maistre, who had previously been the crucial man in the founding of the ISA, was again the person who facilitated the founding of the ISO from the ISA. Many significant issues that came up arose out of a complex and interconnected world. The objectives of standardization would become increasingly interdisciplinary. The ISO had to consider a growing number of subjects that were not technological (social and environmental), which required standards. Since 1947, the number of TCs increased from 70 to 350 (as of 2025) and if the TCs and SCs are added together, we have over 800 committees. This raises questions about technical governance as well as how to manage a much larger number of experts. This increase in TCs is a result of the diversification of standardization needs and has resulted in a much larger global corpus of standards. It also poses problems with respect to access and distribution. Although flashbacks are inevitable throughout book, required to explore all questions, this chapter places particular focus on the historical dimension. We begin with the emergence of national organizations. A few pages will suffice for the ISA and how it came about (already covered in part in Chapter 3), and we then move on to the ISO, the central subject in this chapter.

4.1. Generalist national standardization bodies

In the 1860s, the scientific and technical community in Great Britain realized that they needed institutions that allowed them to develop national standards, especially for mechanical industries. In 1901, Sir John Wolfe-Barry (the architect-engineer who designed Tower Bridge in London) proposed creating a committee to standardize the cross-sections of iron and steel: the Engineering Standards Committee. The BAAS committees associated themselves with this body as they had been publishing standards for over two decades[2]. This was thus the forerunner of the future British Standards Institution (BSI), although this name was only given to the institution in 1931.

There was spectacular progress following standardization within the metallurgical industry in Britain. In 1903, the British Standard Mark was

2 It must be recalled that Le Maistre was made secretary of a sub-section for electricity within the same institution.

created (today known as the *Kitemark*®). This national certification soon motivated industrial buyers to demand standardized semi-finished products, which drastically reduced the range of products that metallurgists could sell. Thus, the range of cross-sections of steel came down from 175 to 113, and the number of possible track gauges reduced from 75 to 5. Standardization soon spread through all British dominions. The British Engineering Standards Association was founded in 1918, and the Engineering Standards Committee was awarded a royal charter in 1929. In 1931, its name changed to the British Standards Institution.

Apart from Britain, however, generalist national standardization bodies in other countries only emerged toward the end of the First World War. In 1916, the Netherlands, which was neutral, created the Royal Netherlands Standardization Institute (NEN). In 1917, in the middle of the First World War, Germany founded the national standardization body, the Deutsches Institut für Normung (DIN). In 1918, the United States founded the American Engineering Standards Committee (AESC), which became the American Standards Association (ASA) in 1928, and then became the American National Standards Institute (ANSI) when it became a part of the ISO in 1946[3]. In 1918, France created the Comité Permanent de Standardisation (Permanent Committee for Standardization), the predecessor of AFNOR, which was founded in 1926.[4] In 1919, Switzerland created the Schweizerischer Normalien-Bund (SNB, Swiss Standards Association), which later became the SNV. In 920, Austria founded the Österreichischer Norme-nausschuss für Industrie und Gewerb (Austrian Standards Committee for Industry and Commerce).[5]

3 In 1912, the American Institute of Electrical Engineers (AIEE) had invited its sister organizations (the American Society of Mechanical Engineers (ASME), American Society of Civil Engineers (ASCE), American Institute of Mining and Metallurgical Engineers (AIMME) and the American Society for Testing Materials (ASTM)) to establish a national organization for the definition of common industrial standards. This was the foundation upon which the AESC was created in 1918, with the decisive support of the Department of War, the Marines and the Department of Trade.

4 Since this complex series of events relates largely to French history, we will not explore it here.

5 In 1932, this became the Österreichischer Normenausschuss. Following the Anschluss or Nazi annexation of Austria in 1938, it became a branch of the DIN. However, it returned to its original identity as the Österreichischer Normenausschuss after the Second World War and, later, became Austrian Standards Institute.

In 1921, the Italian Association for Mechanical Professionals founded the Mechanical Standardization Institution (UNIM), which later became UNI in 1928, expanding to include other sectors of industry. The Hungarian Standardization Institute, and then the Hungarian Standardization Bureau, was created in 1921[6]. In the same year, the Japanese government founded the Japanese Engineering Standards Committee (JESC). In 1949, this became the Japanese Industrial Standards Committee (JISC), which was organized as a State-run body, but worked in conjunction with experts from industrial firms. The Swedish Institute of Standards (or Svenska Institutet för Standarder (SIS))[7] was founded in 1922. The Czech Electrotechnical Association was set up in 1919 (an NB under the IEC) and the Czech Standardization Association was set up in 1922. The nation's history from 1938 onwards (joining the Third Reich as Czechoslovakia, coming under the Soviet sphere of influence, and then the division into Czechia and Slovakia) resulted in great upheavals within these institutions. In 1951, standardization became associated with legal metrology. This situation still continues in the UNMZ, the Czech office for standardization, metrology and testing, which was set up in 1968. In Poland, a non-governmental body, the (Polish Committee for Standardization (PKN), was set up in 1923[8].

In 1923, the Norwegian Standardization Association (Norges Standardiseringsforbund) was founded. Since 2003, this has been a private organization, Standards Norway (SN). As in Sweden, this body does not cover the electrical and telecommunications sector. In 1924, a private, not-for-profit organization, Suomen Standardisoimisliitto, was established in

---

6 The German occupation, followed by the Soviet period, threw Hungarian standardization into disarray. In 1995, the Hungarian standardization institute (MSZT) has became a non-government, not-for-profit, public benefit organization.

7 It worked in conjunction with the Svenska Informations -och Telekommunikations-Standardiseringen (ITS) and Svensk Elstandard (SEK) for all standards related to electrical and electronic technology.

8 After the German occupation ended, and then following its position as a satellite state of the USSR, standardization here was associated with legal metrology, as in Hungary. The committee, which was reconstituted in 1945, became a public sector body and the standards were mandatory. In 1972, it became the Polish Committee for Standardization and Measures, and then in 1979, it became the Polish Committee for Standardization, Measures and Quality Control (PKNMiJ). In 1993, the PKNMiJ was dissolved and the Polish Committee for Standardization (PKN) from 1923 was re-established; however, this time it was governed by the public budget and was a public body. Metrology has since been in charge of a distinct body: the Central Office of Measures.

Finland. Electrical and telecommunication standards came under two distinct organizations here: SESKO and TRAFICOM. In 1925, the Soviet state established an interdisciplinary standardization committee whose standards had to be mandatorily adopted. The committee also had prerogatives in the field of metrology, hence its name (until 2004): the State Committee of the Russian Federation for Standardization and Metrology. After 2004, the name was changed to the Federal Agency for Technical Regulation and Metrology (GOST-R) and the standards ceased to be mandatory.

4.1.1. *Preference for NBs to be independent of States*

This brief overview of the historical outcomes of these early national standardization bodies created prior to 1926[9] shows how difficult it was to establish dialogue between all these national and generalist standardization bodies, which were organized so differently in different countries. And yet, the ISA persevered and managed to do this, and the ISO continues this today. This ability to ensure smooth cooperation comes from the fact that the IEC, then the ISA, and then the ISO, all emphasized that the NBs must be as independent of the State as possible, while being officially recognized by the State. The founding vision of the IEC was the spirit of universality in regulation technology, and its primary objectives were (1) optimizing technological progress as allowed by the science; (2) regulating counterproductive competition to allow global prosperity within a professional branch; (3) going beyond this, both at the national and international level, regulating possible competition between professional branches to promote synergistic cooperation leading to technical convergence, which would enhance global prosperity (again, at the national as well as international level).

These objectives for standardization were not created out of thin air. In 1926, like today, the secretaries of the national standardization bodies were all people with wide-ranging technical and scientific knowledge and were also exceptionally talented in synthesis and consensus building. These secretaries general were co-opted as they were the best representatives of the global spirit of standardization. In 1926, the overwhelming majority of the 18 bodies invited were independent and non-governmental bodies.

9 This was the year that the plenary session of the IEC took place in New York at the same time as tens of secretaries from generalist national bodies, who would go on to form the ISA.

At the time, only Japan and the USSR had government-run NBs. However, the situation changed radically in Europe, first with the Nazis and then the Soviet governments. This desire for NBs to be independent of their respective governments (which is not a formal requirement) was not developed on a whim within the IEC (nor the ISA or later the ISO). In 1906, when the IEC was founded, this question of independent NBs had already been raised, especially by American and British delegates who had spent many years discussing questions related to technology in general, and standardization specifically, within their respective bodies (the AIEE and IEE). The early leaders within the IEC could clearly observe that the contributions from representatives sent by non-autonomous NBs struck a false note in the overall smoothly orchestrated open debates that led to the development and publishing of standards[10]. In the case of war, when the entire economy and industrial set-up were mobilized for the military industry, standardization clearly became a State affair, or rather, a joint concern between the allied States in each camp. However, at these times international standardization was interrupted and constrained by military standards.

4.1.2. *The founding of the ISA and its contributions: 1927–1939*

As we saw in section 3.3, the IEC played a large role in the creation of the ISA. The fact that the plenary sessions of the IEC and the meeting of the secretaries of the generalist national standardization bodies from around the world both took place in New York in 1926 was the key moment in the creation of the ISA. Among the national organizations, the American Engineering Standards Committee (AESC), the predecessor of the ANSI, was the national body that expressed the most support for an international federation of generalist NBs. The statutes of the ISA were discussed in London in late 1926 and the association was officially founded in Prague in 1928. The Association Française de Normalisation (AFNOR) or the French

10 The macroeconomic and microtechnological vision handed to officers in non-autonomous organizations contradicts the diverse points of view from scientific and industrial experts, which produce solutions to complex standardization problems. On the other hand, when associating with others, the experts appointed by ministries or the standardization engineers who are often delegated by national bodies that are independent of the States make significant contributions to the discussions by reiterating the microtechnological requirements and macroeconomic aspirations of the concerned countries. This last point is crucial to mitigate the (sometimes harmful) influence of some multinationals.

Standardization Association also played a key role here. Following the proposal made by the French body, the ISA adopted the first international standard that was finalized based on normal numbers[11]. The new organization used the same methods as the IEC, especially with respect to the decentralization of the effective development of standards within the various NBs. For the ISA, this was an essential condition for viability. It was understandable, however, that the European industrial community, which was deeply divided by nationalist tensions, was not keen on making large investments in an international generalist standardization bureau:

> The ISA was run by a Mr. Huber-Ruf, a Swiss engineer who administered the organization virtually single-handedly, handling the drafting, translation and reproduction of documents with the help of his family from his home in Basle. He attempted to keep the ISA going when the war broke out in 1939, but as international communication broke down, the ISA president mothballed the organization. The secretariat was closed and the stewardship of the ISA was entrusted to Switzerland. (Kuert 1997)

Looking back now, we can see that it was almost a miracle that a single man was able to run an international organization and maintain such a high level of ambition, including in the last few troubled years. Thanks to active participation from the industrial world, Huber-Ruf had been able to establish around 60 categories of standards. Formally federated with the ISA, but wishing to remain separate from the increasingly authoritarian European political world, many NBs, especially Anglo-American ones, led isolated standardization projects.

Thus, in the United States, individual and workplace health and safety became a major concern. In 1919, standards were published for industrial conveyor belts; in 1920, the American standardization organization coordinated the implementation of new national safety codes, which would replace the older rules and regulations, which were often inadequate in preventing accidents. All the early American safety standards date to the interwar period: they ensured protection for the eyes and heads of industrial workers. In its first 6 years, therefore, the AESC developed standards for mines, electricity, mechanical engineering, the construction of roadways and

11 Created by ISA/TC 19, which was re-formed in 1947 as ISO/TC 19: Standard numbers.

road traffic. In the 1930s, many standards and best practice guidelines were published to prevent industrial hazards and also developed for household technologies.

Standardization was a key factor in Germany's industrial growth. The DIN thus became a label that certified the excellence of German industrial products. Of course, the DIN's standardization went on to be used by the Nazis for military production, and also in forcing occupied territories to build the Atlantic Wall as part of the brutal "Organisation Todt".

However, beyond the National Socialists' grim and notorious uses of the DIN, there are three examples of standardization developed in Germany when the ISA existed that were long-lived and, in at least one case, globally renowned: (1) the "normograph", a stenciling tool that was widely used until the 1980s by industrial designers and graphic artists around the world, although it is largely forgotten today; (2) the logical series used for paper formats: A0, A1, A2, A3, A4, etc.; and (3) the ISA index for the sensitivity of photographic equipment.[12]

The normograph was created around 1909 *by* Georg Bahr, a teacher in Berlin. This was originally a metal ruler, perforated with cutouts that allowed the user to draw letters and numbers using a technical drawing pen. The Bahrscher Normograph, which was industrially manufactured in plastic, became widespread in the industrial, administrative, and commercial work even before the First World War. In their research, Soudanne and Maupetit (2016) believe that it is possible to conclude (thanks to marginal notes in the original standard) that the characters prescribed in the ISA standard "Technical Documentation of Products"[13] use the same font (Minerva) as that proposed by the DIN. This standard was submitted to the ISA under the number DIN 16-1451. Until the 1980s, this pocket-stencil, still known as the normograph, allowed architects and industrial designers to trace letters to label plans or to write a text so cleanly that it looked printed. Before printers became so common, the normograph was a ubiquitous office tool for all design professionals, although it is entirely forgotten today.

12 Points 1 and 2 in this section are taken from the work of Soudanne and Maupetit (2016).

13 Today, the international standard ISO 3098-1-2015, standardized within ISO/TC 10.

The paper formats, on the other hand, are still in use around the world:

> Standardized formats [for paper] correspond to older formats for which standards had already been drawn up in France at the time of the Revolution, but never applied: the *grand registre* format (today A2), the *moyen papier* format (today A3), and then the *grand papier, petit papier* and *half-sheet* (approximately our modern-day B3, B4, and B5). The dimensions were not the same as would be applied [by DIN] but the proportions of the format had been codified and concretized during the 20th century [based on] the work of the German engineer Walter Porstmann. [In 1922, as a part of the DIN, he] developed the DIN 476 format and defined the A format as the standard reference. (Soudanne and Maupetit 2016)

ISA/TC6 "Papers, cardboard and pulps" was one of the first TCs to have been established in the ISA, set up in 1927. It was reconstituted in 1947 by the ISO.

The DIN also created standards for the general organization of human work in an office. In their thesis, Julie Soudanne and Léa Maupetit also describe the "Normung bringt Ordnung" ("Standards Bring Order") exhibition, organized in 1932 in Leipzig as part of a Salon organized by the DIN, which:

> highlighted the economic gain from a unified format as well as everything else that followed from this: filing cabinets, drawers, bureau, etc. In fact, all movements that an individual could make were analyzed for design purposes, from the desk to the chair, to the windows, so as to obtain an ideal form. The body thus became an element of industrial productivity and made it possible to define new needs. This theory was later laid out in Ernst Neufert's work *Bauentwurfslehre* (Architects' Data in English), first published in 1936 in Germany. In this book, he established the fundamental principles concerning design, execution, form, and the required space and also discussed rules for the measurement of structures, sites and furniture. He demonstrated great precision, basing the work on existing standards and units of measurements, including the DIN format, and used this to define what he judged to be ideal dimensions. (Soudanne and Maupetit 2016)

These ideal dimensions for designing workplaces for humans were standardized by DIN. However, Albert Speer later appropriated these concepts to construct the barracks of the Nazi concentration camps.

In this period, Germany was also at the cutting edge of the photographic and cinematographic industry. Thus, DIN standards were defined to define a sensitivity index for photographic equipment: standardized units that reflected the competitive clash between Germany and the United States. For several decades, two standardized scales to measure photographic and film sensitivity coexisted. They were developed separately in Germany (the standardized units were called the DIN scale) and in the United States, called the ASA scale. The DIN, or Deutsches Institut für Normung, scale, was a logarithmic scale, while the ISO scale (formerly known as the ASA or American Standards Association scale) was based on a linear scale. Both these ways of measuring sensitivity were incompatible with each other; however, a conversion yielded approximate results. Today, the DIN unit has disappeared, but practically speaking, so has photography and film that use chemical equipment.

4.2. Standardization before and after the Second World War

The Third Reich soon saw the advantages in taking over the DIN and developing standards not only for their war effort, but also to standardize the processes used to construct the Atlantic Wall and the concentration camps. As a result, standardization institutions in all countries under German occupation or domination had to bend to Nazi diktats and AFNOR, whose statutes were modified by the Vichy government, had to submit, although they faced opposition from the Resistance. Yvan Delemontey has a clear analysis of this period:

> The 1940 defeat and its dramatic consequences led to the Pétain government paying close attention to this question, which was seen to play an essential role in the economic recovery of the country. The liberal interwar regime that oversaw the creation of the Association Française de Normalisation (AFNOR) in 1926 was succeeded by an authoritarian and centralized regime that enforced strict discipline through statutes that were laid out in the law dated 24 May 1941, marking a revolution in the history of French standardization. The establishment of standards was now almost mandatory in all domains and placed

> under the authority of a standardization commissaire with wide-ranging powers. New standardization subcommittees were created (which came under the new organization committees that regulated professions in a corporate manner) with the purpose of carrying out the preliminary work for establishing norms in each branch. (Delemontey 2020, pp. 137–150)[14]

4.2.1. *1945, founding of the ISO by the Allies, continuing the work with the ISA*

Two organizations can be thought of as having given rise to the ISO: the UNSCC and ISA. Building upon the standardization of industries during the war, in 1944 the Allies founded the United Nations Standardization Coordination Committee (UNSCC). During the Second World, the BSI had immediately stopped developing standards that were not useful to the war effort. *War emergency standards* were developed and the British government declared that the BSI was the only body that could publish national standards: over 400 war emergency standards were designed and published between 1939 and 1945. The ISO was founded at the end of the war. Charles Le Maistre took on the post of secretary general of the UNSCC in addition to serving in the IEC (also situated in London) and in 1926, in New York, he had also been the initiator of the ISA. Willy Kuert (the secretary of the Swiss Standardization Association (SNV)) gives us a firsthand account of the process:

> The problem Le Maistre had to solve at the end of the war was how to create a new global international standardizing body. In October 1945, UNSCC delegates assembled in New York to discuss the future of international standardization. Delegates agreed that the UNSCC should approach the ISA with a view to forming an organization which they provisionally called the

14 This steering group in AFNOR, which would become the Standardization Coordination and Steering Committee (CCPN), today coordinates 11 strategic committees (COSs). It was the forerunner of the ISO's Technical Management Bureau (TMB) – see section 4.4.1. It must also be emphasized that historian Yvan Delemontey's words resonate strangely with those penned by Boris Vian (cited at the beginning of this chapter), who worked in AFNOR in 1942.

> "International Standards Coordinating Association" […] According to its constitution, the ISA had lapsed out of existence. [After multiple strategically planned parallel meetings between the UNSCC and the ISA in Paris], it was resolved to convene a conference of all member countries belonging to the UNSCC and ISA three months later in London […] Twenty-five countries were represented by 65 delegates. […] When Le Maistre gave a report of this meeting to the ISA members at the conference, they reacted by deciding to liquidate the ISA at once. The conference between the UNSCC and the ISA was therefore abandoned on its first morning, but was immediately reconvened as a conference of the UNSCC and various other national standards associations. Thereafter, the conference was plain sailing. (Kuert 1997)

In his interview, Willy Kuert described the urgent creation of new ISO/TCs based on the former ISA/TCs. He recounted the various negotiations carried out to define the constitution of the ISO, the name of the future organization, the planning of its headquarters and its central secretariat, the official languages adopted, etc. The UNSCC and ISA ceased working when the ISO became operational. The ISA is dead, long live the ISO!

Professions and technologies changed dramatically with the war. With various branches coming together, industrialists had a growing need for standardization. The ISO was set up in Geneva, followed by the IEC, which was in the same building. The IEC became the ISO Electrotechnical Committee but retained its original abbreviation and remained autonomous. Several questions were resolved during the preliminary meetings for the founding of the ISO: financial contributions (which took into account the population and commercial power of each member state) and membership rights (all countries, including those who had lost the war, were given one vote).

Due to its extreme slightness, the ISA had produced only a relatively small number of international standards. However, it had succeeded in establishing around 60 TCs, whose secretaries and chairpersons were divided between various NBs. It was indisputably a European standardization club, but the method was the right one and the ISO inherited a structure that was in a position to be reactivated (which was not immediately obvious after 6 years of war), as well as a significant corpus of international standards that had to be updated to account for technical progress.

Henry Saint Leger was appointed the new secretary general of the ISO, an appointment that was very deliberately made. In the final weeks of the war and even after the fighting ceased, the Russians and Americans each took their share of the engineers and scientists who had been involved in Hitler's new weapons programs. In the Far-East Military Tribunal, as in the Nuremberg trials, the industrial leaders who had contributed to crimes against humanity received little or no condemnation. To re-stabilize the economy, everything had to be forgotten, at least formally. And yet, the ISO's secretary general, Henry Saint Leger, had been a member of the American delegation at the Nuremberg trials. The message sent out to industrialists, scientists and politicians from different standardization organizations in the defeated countries was loud and clear. All these countries were invited to participate in the standardization of the technological progress taking place, a gauge of renewed prosperity in the world. At the same time, the organizations in the defeated countries, and the experts there, were under close surveillance.

Charles Le Maistre supported and helped the new secretary general. In the words of Roger Maréchal, the deputy secretary general of the ISO:

> But Mr. St. Leger didn't appreciate this help. They weren't on good terms. Mr. Le Maistre, who was not always in Geneva [he was in charge of the liaison with London], asked his assistant, his executive secretary Mr. Ruppert, to be of help to St. Leger. But again sparks flew! (Maréchal 1997)

Even in Switzerland, in this new period immediately following the war, it was not easy to manage this new organization:

> The early years were difficult, five people in all, very little money, and yet the organization had to become known to all, as the UN demanded, and develop international standards, which was difficult given the organization's limited resources. In 1957, the central secretariat had only 15 employees: mail was typed out on mechanical writing machines and documents were reproduced using stencils and a Gestetner machine. At the time, the final recommendations were printed externally [...] Of

course, we only produced about twenty recommendations[15] per year. (Barchetto 1997)

4.2.2. *The ISO and social and technical changes*

The need for the ISO to grow and be restructured, with respect to the growing importance of standardization (which was so evident during the Second World War), was a tricky problem. It would take 20 years. The third secretary general of the ISO, the Swede Olle Sturen, headed the ISO from 1969 to 1986. In an interview, he gives a clear analysis of the ISO during this pivotal moment[16]. He emphasized his desire to respond to the demand of the growing ISO and the new needs, more societal in nature, resulting from the ISO becoming a part of the collective of international organizations in Geneva. Whatever the challenges faced by Olle Sturen, as with almost all the senior leadership in the ISO or IEC, as well as most of the leadership in the NBs, he was constantly aware of the fact that these were associative and not-for-profit bodies. It was therefore imperative for them to ensure that the contributions of Member states[17] were spent in a rational manner.

Over the two decades in which Olle Sturen headed the ISO, 58 new technical committees were founded, among other TCs dedicated to social and environmental problems, for example, air quality (TC 146); water quality (TC 147); solar energy (TC 180); geothermal energy (TC 182); lifts, escalators and moving walks (TC 146); ergonomics (TC 146); surgical implants (TC 150); the safety of toys (TC 181); etc. The global corpus of standards would grow sixfold during Olle Sturen's tenure. DEVCO, a special program for developing countries, had already been created in 1961 (before his tenure); however, in 1970, he supported the creation of CASCO to ensure consumer safety through tests and certification, and in 1978, the creation of COPOLCO to standardize consumer interests.

The question of how to structure documentation was essential to allow access to standards and ensure they were compatible with each other. This

15 Which would only be called *international standards* from 1970 onwards.

16 This section draws heavily from Olle Sturen's interview. Before his role as secretary general in the ISO, he was director of the Swedish Institute for Standards (SIS) in 1957 (Sturen 1997).

17 With respect to the member countries (NBs), this referred to contributions from participants, essentially companies.

was taken into account through the creation of ISONET. In 1968, after his tenure as secretary general was extended, the Technical Management Board (TMB) was ready to be established. This was a college of 15 experts delegated by an equal number of NBs, which met every year with the vice-president of the ISO to examine the creation, dissolution or redistribution of certain TCs. The TMB also had other responsibilities: it was in charge of appointing the different presidents or secretaries of the TCs and SCs, and it also assessed and supervised their work.

The creation of the TMB[18] was an essential step in the international technical governance of standardization. In 1968, Olle Sturen was thus able to pass on to his successors an organization whose governance had been modernized and rationalized without being bureaucratized. In two decades, he had only doubled the number of full-time employees. Further, most of the senior leadership was provided from the most active NBs. Most notable of all, Olle Sturen modernized the ISO's information system to make it more efficient and better adapted with respect to documentation. He also ensured that the productivity of the information system, and thus the costs of developing standards, did not lead to an increase in contributions from industrialists and member states. His Executive Secretary, Roseline Barchietto, was full of praise for the transformations that he implemented:

> Appointed in 1968 as the new secretary general, the Swede Olle Sturen radically transformed the ISO. He introduced the Telex machine, and he decided to have all the standards printed in an in-house printing center, without using external printers. Immediately after International Standard ISO 8879 on Standard Generalized Markup Language (SGML) was published in 1986, the secretariat introduced an experimental publication system based on IBM 9370 software. (Barchietto 1997)

Another leading figure who must be named here to fully understand the ISO's improved competencies is Raymond Frontard, who entered AFNOR in 1945 and went on to become AFNOR's director general. He was also president of the CEN and was a long-time member of the ISO council. He was, above all, the key figure responsible for the documentation of

18 The IEC has a comparable structure, the Standardization Management Board (SMB). Most of the large NBs also have committees that mirror the TMB and SMB. Thus, AFNOR has put in place 15 strategic committees (COSs) for each market or per theme.

standards. He was first chair of the ISO/TC 46, dedicated to documentation, and he designed an efficient documentary system for AFNOR that he then introduced to ISO. This was the ISONET network, implemented in 1977, and he was the founding chairman of the ISONET Management Board (Frontard 1997, pp. 19–27).

Vince Grey's role in standardizing containers and the creation of JTC 1

The history of standardization is marked by people with a passion for their work, and Vince Grey is a perfect example of this[19]. A former marine engineer officer, he discovered standardization in 1952 during an American Standards Association (ASA) meeting. He then joined the organization and oversaw several technical committees. In 1956, he developed an interest in the standardization of goods containers, a key challenge in international transport. He proposed the creation of ISO/TC 104 "Freight containers" and became the chairman of this committee. This initiative was undertaken to harmonize the different standards, which were complicating the transshipment of containers between Europe and the United States. The challenges involved included the standardization of *corner fittings*, essential for handling containers, and the unification of dimensions. After many discussions between the Europeans, Russians and Americans, as well as between the transnational companies handling road transport, railway transport and shipping, the ISO adopted the 1 series of TC 104 as the *international standard*, ensuring that it was widely adopted by the industry and facilitating the rise of intermodal transport that was getting globalized.

Later, between 1960 and 1980, Vince Grey played a key role in the merging of ISO/TC 95 (office machines) and ISO/TC 97 (calculator and information processing), a project carried out along with the IEC, which resulted in the creation of ISO/IEC JTC 1, a basic joint committee for standardizing information technologies.

Box 4.1. *Standardization of freight containers*

4.2.3. *DEVCO, CASCO and COPOLCO*

DEVCO, a committee for issues related to developing countries, was founded in 1961. By construction, it is open for all ISO members to participate in as full members, observers or correspondents. The DEVCO Chair's Advisory Group (CAG) meets twice a year and helps DEVCO track

19 The information here is from Vince Grey's interview, "Setting Standards" (Grey 1997).

the implementation of action plans for developing countries. It has eleven members, eight of whom are from developing countries and three of whom are from developed countries. DEVCO's role is even more important given that ISO's structure clearly favors the establishment of standards by developed countries at the cost of developing countries. It is true that the statuses of "Observer Member" and, to a lesser degree, "Correspondent Member" allow developing countries to be passive participants in ISO work; however, a subscription membership only allows them to remain informed (see section 4.3). Nonetheless, in many cases, standardization offered them protection against the deleterious effects of certain unregulated technologies; for example, fertilizers, food containing dangerous ingredients, pollution-emitting machines or vehicles which may also have few (or no) safety features. DEVCO can support these countries in adopting key technologies to better protect themselves against the harmful effects of products sold by unscrupulous corporates. Thus, a few experts who are well trained through workshops organized by DEVCO can help local decision-makers in finalizing calls for tender that integrate protective standards.

The Committee on Conformity Assessment (CASCO) was founded in 1970. The aim of this body is to develop international standards for assessing conformity. In order to do this, CASCO must:

– identify and analyze emerging trends;

– be a site of information exchange;

– give opinions and submit recommendations to the ISO council regarding new or revised actions and policies;

– evaluate existing or emerging methods to assess conformity, as well as any related standards;

– advise and supervise the different TCs, in both the ISO and IEC, in order to define their requirements in terms of conformity.

CASCO has since become an essential cog in the system to ensure that standardization directly benefits both individual consumers and companies and institutions, whose purchases must be more carefully guided since these products will be reintroduced into other products and services.

The Committee on Consumer Policy (COPOLCO) was founded in 1978. Like CASCO and DEVCO, it is a group of experts who directly advise ISO leadership. This committee proposes resources meant to help consumers benefit from standardization. COPOLCO also encourages consumers to participate (directly, or more often, indirectly through Consumer Associations) in national projects, regional projects (such as CEN) and international projects (ISO, IEC, even ITU forums). COPOLCO is a space where information can be exchanged on the experience of consumer participation in the development and application of standards. It is closely linked to CASCO's actions and complements and extends CASCO's work. It helps the ISO council propose new standardization initiatives for consumers and in training teachers and managers within companies.

4.3. The ISO and IEC: a shared model of governance and unique methodology

The ISO and IEC, as well as their joint committees (JTC 1, *Information technologies*; JTC 3, *Quantum technologies*; JSyC BDC, *Biodigital convergence;* as well as the newest body, JTC 4, *Smart and sustainable cities and communities*), have a shared methodology and common system of governance, with very few differences. This methodological harmonization is also seen in the ITU (although there are more marked differences here) and the three organizations coordinate together as part of the World Standards Cooperation, a common working group founded in 2001.

The ISO is a non-governmental organization under Swiss law, made up of 175 members (as of 2025), which are national standardization organizations (one per country). These NBs meet once a year in a general assembly in order to develop a common policy and define strategic objectives.

There are three member categories:

– *NBs who are full members*: these members influence the development of ISO standards and ISO's strategy by actively participating and voting during technical and political meetings. They can sell and adopt ISO standards in their countries.

– *NBs who are correspondent members:* these members attend the ISO's technical and policy meetings as observers and can also sell and adopt ISO standards at a national level.

– *Subscription members*: these members are informed of ISO projects but cannot participate in them. These members are not allowed to sell ISO standards nor officially adopt them in their countries[20].

On an administrative level, *the secretary general runs the ISO office*. As with the IEC, they guarantee the continuity of the institution. Their mandate (through a 5-year tenure that can be renewed) is to direct the permanent team based in Geneva and to coordinate the decentralized production of standards within the NBs.

As of 2026, the secretary general of the ISO is Sergio Mujica (Chile), whose tenure runs till 2027. He joined the central headquarters of the ISO as secretary general in 2017. The ISO's *Strategy 2030* was developed under his leadership.

Since the creation of the organization, this function has been successively occupied by an American, a Swiss, a Frenchman, a Canadian-New Zealander, a Canadian, another Swiss, and since 2017, the Chilean Sergio Mujica. The ISO also has a President, Sung Hwan Cho (South Korea); a former senior executive and research engineer within the automobile industry, he was elected as president for a 2-year term in 2024. He is assisted by three vice-presidents[21] as well as a treasurer. The presidential committee coordinates the group's policy[22].

The ISO council meets three times a year. It includes 20 member committees (whose composition keeps changing to ensure there is a balanced representation of member States), the ISO leadership, the presidents of the ISO committees in charge of developing policy guidelines (CASCO, COPOLCO, DEVCO) and other committees that come directly under the

20 It must be emphasized that when NBs participate in a TC or SC, they are divided into two categories: Participant Member or Observer Member. These are distinct from the general status of "member of the ISO", which confers all the rights and obligations of membership upon a country, especially with respect to the general assembly. Thus, although the ANSI (United States) is a full member of the ISO, it may only be an Observer Member, or not even participate, in certain TCs or SCs.

21 The first vice-president oversees policy questions, the second oversees technical management (they manage the TMB and supervise the overall strategy of various TCs and SCs, as well as liaisons) and the third oversees finances.

22 The president's committee puts out advisory opinions on strategy questions.

council[23]. The Geneva office of the ISO might appear to be a very formal administrative structure, but in reality the member countries delegate their most competent and experienced experts to this office. Thus, the Geneva office is more of a humming beehive where the fundamentals of the standardization processes are built.

4.3.1. *The Technical Management Board, convergence regulator*

The Technical Management Board (TMB) plays a central role in managing the diversity and complexity of the interdisciplinary standardization processes. The full board meets three times a year and its members, designated by NBs, are appointed for three years, a tenure that can be renewed multiple times. The TMB supervises technical projects and is the major body involved in evaluating the ISO's technological decisions. It oversees all TCs and SCs in charge of developing standards. The 15 members chiefly represent the countries that make significant contributions to the production of standards, especially because of their involvement in a large number of secretariats of the TCs or SCs, thereby bringing international expertise to the management of these committees and the publishing of standards. The TMB also plays a crucial role in ensuring continuous coordination between the ISO central office and the production of standards within the TCs and SCs in the NBs.

The ISO, IEC and JTC 1 share a common method for producing standards, with just a few differences in details. Experts debate and develop standards within the structured frameworks of the TCs and SCs. From its inception onwards, a TC or an SC must define its structure and set up a precise program of work, which is summarized in its scope and, if required, in the scope of its sub-structures (SC, WG or other special groups). In concrete terms, each TC or SC distributes its tasks among the experts within their specialized WGs so that they can cover all aspects of the standardization project. A newly formed TC or SC generally starts with two

23 Four permanent advisory committees are, respectively, in charge of finances (CSC/FIN), strategy and policy (CSC/SP), applications for governance posts (CSC/NOM) and overseeing governance practices within the organization (CSC/OVE). There are additionally two advisory groups: one dedicated to the ISO's commercial policy (CPAG) and the other to information technology (ITSAG).

or three WGs[24]. This mode of functioning goes back to the founding principles of the IEC.

4.3.2. *Integration of TCs and SCs: the example of ISO/TC 37*

All committees (TCs or SCs) have historical stratification as well as increasingly complex interactions between technological branches, due to their multiple sites of convergence.

The development of standards in a sector rarely follows a simple hierarchical structure where the experts are divided between a few WGs. In most cases, the TC adopts a mixed structure, combining WGs (directly led and managed by the TC) and half-a-dozen SCs, each run by their own secretary and chairperson. These SCs are themselves further divided into several WGs and most often managed by other NBs from their parent TC. ISO/TC 37 is here used as an example to illustrate this complexity through an overview of its different groups and sub-groups.

The goal is to highlight the complexity of the structure using just one of the 200 TCs in the ISO as an example. The aim is not to look at all the WGs in detail, nor study their various liaisons[25]. What is important, in terms of the method for manufacturing standards, is how the experts divide the designing of standards for each branch.

ISO/TC 37 "Language and terminology" was officially founded within the ISO in 1947[26]. However, as with many other historical TCs, this committee had initially been created under the aegis of the ISA in 1937.

24 There are more specific and cross-disciplinary groups (AG: advisory group; AHG: ad hoc group; CG: strategic coordination group; JWG: joint working group), which advise the leaders of a TC or an SC. They produce internal non-normative documents: exploratory reports, prospective studies, or communication supports.

25 As of early 2026, ISO TC 37 has 86 liaisons with TCs and SCs (ISO, IEC, ITU), in addition to many institutions.

26 It can be recalled (see Chapter 3) that in 1936, Eugen Würster had proposed creating ISA/TC 37, dedicated to terminology standardization. After the Second World War, this TC became ISO/TC 37: "Terminology (principles and coordination)" and Austria took on its secretariat in 1951, under the Austrian Standards Institution (ASI).

From 2016 to 2024, ISO/TC 37 was presided over by Laurent Romary (France, INRIA) who was succeeded by Alex Chengyu Fang (CityU Hong Kong), while the secretariat is run by the SAC (China). Its current scope is: <Standardization of descriptions, resources, technologies and services related to terminology, translation, interpreting and other language-based activities in the multilingual information society.>

Its working structure is made up of five subcommittees:

– SC 1: Principles and methods.

– SC 2: Terminology workflow and language coding.

– SC 3: Management of terminology resources.

– SC 4: Language resource management.

– SC 5: Translation, interpreting and related technology.

Apart from the management committees in TC 37, there are also three WGs:

– TC 37/WG 10: Technical communication.

– TC 37/WG 11: Plain language.

– TC 37/WG 12: Translation-oriented writing.

Finally, a mixed working group was created with JTC 1/SC 42: ISO/IEC JTC 1/SC 42/JWG 5: Natural language processing systems[27].

4.3.2.1. *ISO/TC 37/SC 1: Principles and methods*

The scope of this subcommittee is: <Standardization of principles and methods related to terminology, terminology policies and the ordering of knowledge.>

Its secretariat is Chinese and it has a Spanish chairperson. There are three WGs in this SC:

– WG 3: Principles, methods and vocabulary.

– WG 4: Socioterminology.

– WG 5: Modeling concepts in terminological work.

27 JTC 1, the first partner in this joint committee, manages this entire liaison, which gives it an overview of the five SCs under ISO/TC 37.

4.3.2.2. *ISO/TC 37/SC 2: Terminology workflow and language coding*

The scope of this Subcommittee is: <Standardization of terminological methods and applications for language and linguistic content.>

Its secretariat is Canadian and the chair is currently vacant. It has a specific maintenance agency and three WGs:

– ISO/TC 37/SC 2/MA 1: Authority to update ISO 639 (language codes);

– SC 2/WG 1: Language varieties;

– SC 2/WG 2: Terminography;

– SC 2/WG 9: Presentation/representation of entries in dictionaries and revision.

4.3.2.3. *ISO/TC 37/SC 3: Management of terminology resources*

This subcommittee has a German secretariat. Its scope is: <Standardization of the specification, design and interoperability of terminological resources.> It has four WGs (not described here).

4.3.2.4. *ISO/TC 37/SC 4: Management of terminology resources*

The secretariat is currently the Korean Agency for Technology and Standards (KATS, South Korea). Its scope is: <Standardization of the modelling, specification, design, documentation and encoding of digital language resources to enable integration, interchange and replicability.> This has five WGs (not described here).

4.3.2.5. *ISO/TC 37/SC 5: Translation, interpreting and related technology*

This subcommittee has a German secretariat. Its scope is: <Standardization in the field of translation, interpretation and associated technologies, as well as technical writing, content management, localization, globalization and internationalization.> It has five WGs (not described here).

This brief presentation of the structure of ISO/TC 37 demonstrates the complexity within the organization of just one of the 200 TCs in the ISO. In terms of the methodology used to manufacture standards, what is important is how experts structure the work of designing standards in each field of activity. What may appear formal at first glance is, in reality, an organization that is essential for the rigor required for standardization. We must recognize that behind this formalism there is the collective wisdom of experts, who must ensure that each standard meets a precisely defined requirement, while also complementing other aspects of a profession, a group of professions or a cross-disciplinary problem.

4.3.3. *The steps involved in manufacturing standards*

The development of a standard follows a process that is similar to many other projects: there are alternating phases of discussion, reviewing of comments and internal votes in order to establish consensus (in plenary meetings or within WGs). Next, the reports and writers–publishers of standards draw up intermediary documents, which are centralized and distributed among national standardization bodies (NBs) by the country in charge of the secretariat of that technical committee (TC) or subcommittee (SC). Within each participating NB, the national technical mirror committee of the concerned TC or SC examines these documents. The documents may then be (1) approved, with or without comments; (2) approved subject to some reasoned modifications; and (3) rejected, on the condition that the refusal is supported by comments.

This process illustrates the rigorous application of consensus-building, which is a fundamental principle of standardization. Indeed, it is impossible to reject a proposal without offering rational arguments to support your rejection. Rationality is the prerequisite for all steps in the standardization process. This methodology, inherited from the scientific world, as well as from companies and institutions, ensures that each phase of discussion begins with an analysis of the comments submitted during the preceding steps. The goal is to respond to these in an inclusive manner by bringing in customized solutions. These remarks often relate to technical details, cultural, linguistic or even religious specificities, which may limit the universality of the standard. The majority of these comments relate to technical elements, the viability of a technological solution, the proposal or an alternative method, making it possible to enhance the coherence and pertinence of the standard.

When the NB in a country decides to take on the management of a TC or an SC, it is a major responsibility. The chair is also generally selected from the same NB[28]. In conjunction with the chairperson, the secretariat of the TC or SC verifies all the documents produced by the experts involved, ensures that they are distributed and supervises the different voting phases, the enforcement of deadlines and interoperability. For every standard or official document, during the initial stages and in the three final stages, the concerned secretariat regularly interacts with the Geneva office. Notably, they collaborate with the TMB to carry out qualitative control. An ISO engineer acts as the interface between the secretariat of the TC or SC and the TMB. Finally, the editorial consistency of the standard, especially in the final stages, is validated with the publishing head of the ISO for the concerned domain. The seven phases involved in developing standards[29] are as follows:

1) *Preliminary phase and preliminary work item (PWI)*: Earlier called a new work item, the PWI denotes the initial proposal of a standard document, which could evolve into a standard, an expert report, or an associated document. This proposal may come from various actors within the ISO (NB, liaisons, IEC, etc.) and must be formalized as a preliminary project with detailed objectives. The TC or SC fixes a deadline for this phase. The PWI must respond to the needs of certain experts and, ideally, to market requirements.

2) *New proposal (NP)*: The NP mentions the experts and NB who support the proposal. The TC or SC makes a decision based on a simple majority among its participant members. If the NP only leads to an expert report that will be given to the TC, the procedure followed is relatively simple. This could also be a diplomatic way to refuse the creation of a standard. If the proposal is validated, a working group must be constituted to oversee the examination of the future standard, with a designated editor to oversee its publication.

3) *Preparation of a working draft (WD) and then a committee draft (CD)*: The WD is the first draft of the standard, whose outline is already defined. The quality of the WD reflects on the reputation of the project team and the WG that is working on the standard. This document largely circulates within the TC or SC and receives several critiques and suggestions before being transformed into a CD. This CD is then submitted to the NBs, who vote and comment on it.

28 This rule applies to the IEC but is not binding on ISO.

29 A standard may also go through an accelerated Fast Track procedure.

4) *Assessment and approval*: The standard then undergoes a test phase and successive experimental versions[30]:

– *Draft international standard (DIS)*: The advanced stage of the standard submitted to the NB. This is an experimental standard, allowing certain companies to anticipate market changes;

– *Final draft international standard (FDIS)*: The final version before publication. At this stage, the adoption of the final standard is almost certain.

– *International standard (IS)*: The final standard, published and integrated into the ISO catalogue.

5) *Publication and adoption*: The standard is then published as an official ISO standard and included in the national catalogues of the NBs who have approved it.

6) *Translation and adaptation*: We must differentiate between the *bilingual co-production* of a standard and the simple *translation* of a standard. The ISO is accountable for a standard that is jointly published in English and French (or Russian). On the other hand, if an NB carries out the translation of a standard, only the NB is accountable for it. Some NBs may get the ISO to append translations to the standard, especially China, Japan and Korea.

7) *Revision of the standards*: Standards must be revised, amended or removed at least every 5 years. A revision is initiated if at least 50% of the NBs are in favor of this.

30 In all of these stages, the NBs test the standard with industrialists and users. In order to be validated, a DIS and then an FDIS must have at least two-thirds positive votes and less than a quarter negative votes. Any negative vote must be supported by technical reasons, but positive votes can be simply cast with no remarks, or submitted with comments.

5

JTC 1: Convergence Catalyst

By construction, advanced technologies are born out of multiple and complex cross-cultures between different technical branches. For example, wine presses were adapted for the printing press; sewing machine mechanisms were used to develop devices, within cameras and cinematographic projects, to advance the film at a steady rate, just like the bobbin moved to release thread at precise intervals. Photography made cinema possible, and the standardized 35-mm film used in cinema, in turn, led to further advances within photography. Convergence in information and communication technology (ICT) is therefore a natural phenomenon that continues today at an unprecedented rate of progress. Because of this accelerated cross-disciplinary growth, standardization organizations have had to mobilize and take up the full spectrum of challenges related to ICTs.

In the 1950s, the IEC saw a significant rise in the need for standards within the field of weak currents. The 1970s saw the earliest computing languages and micro-computing. The latter, which was readily adopted by companies and institutions, soon overtook the older data centers in convenience and processing power. In the 1990s, personal computers became more and more portable and connected within networks. A growing number of people in developed countries began using these new tools. Before the advent of the Internet, or rather, concurrently with the Internet, networks were the focus of convergence, bringing together various disciplines and professions. Thus, Integrated Services Digital Networks (ISDNs) bring together voice, data, video and all other applications or services, while guaranteeing end-to-end digital connection[1]. There are two important features that differentiate ISDNs from traditional telephone networks: the connections are digital from one end to the other and are continuous, and they are not billed by duration, unlike modem connections.

The vision of JTC 1 in 2020

In 2020, the chair of JTC 1 clearly summarized the key convergence question facing both suppliers and consumers of ICTs:

> Convergence is occurring in two dimensions:
>
> (I) The three basic technologies: (1) information technology; (2) consumer electronics and (3) telecommunications – converge in the sense that the same fundamental technologies are applied in all three areas. This can be termed horizontal convergence; the resulting technology is often called ICT. The advent of ICT demands a closer overall cooperation, in the standardization arena, among the three key international standards organizations: the ISO, IEC and ITU.
>
> (II) Simultaneously, ICT progresses into all aspects of life (business, industry, home, administration, education, charity, etc.), with conventional processes and applications now exploiting the capabilities offered by ICT. This may be termed vertical convergence. New ICT applications are characterized by the involvement of different technologies and high complexity; in general, they cannot be covered by a single standard, but are of an interdisciplinary nature. This demands a closer cooperation between technology-oriented and application-oriented experts, both in product and in standards development.

Who can be considered the primary actor in the progress of ICTs? This is an unproductive question. The innovations created within laboratories around the world put out little rootlets that can only take hold and flourish within a global market on the appropriate scale; JTC 1 is a unique forum that meets the multifactorial challenges posed by ICTs and where a large variety of technologies are integrated into usable standards. Convergent technologies have become ubiquitous in all aspects of modern life[2].

Box 5.1. *The prospective vision of JTC 1*

1 ISDNs simultaneously manage data transmission, network management and billing services, as well as commercial or free exchanges, to carry out the services offered by the network.

2 See: https://www.iso.org/committee/45020.html.

In order to achieve this, ISDNs defined a set of interface protocols between users and the public network. At the same time, the Internet (of which the general public had long been unaware) became more generalized with the World Wide Web, which popularized the markup language that is specific to the Web today: HTML. The first decade of the 21st century was characterized by the emergence of the mobile phone. This is also an all-digital age, wiping away every last trace of analog information and communication, especially with respect to television. Smartphones have become the focal point of this convergence with highly sophisticated personal and professional uses: telephony, photography, writing, learning, translation, purchases, navigation, calculations, managing one's schedule, browsing the Internet, messaging services and social networks. Hyperconvergence is racing ahead even beyond this omnipresent smartphone technological revolution.

5.1. 1960–1987: the predecessors and establishment of JTC 1

At the end of the Second World War, the sector that would become the computing sector was a highly promising field. To some creative researchers and industrialists, it was clear that this burgeoning discipline would revolutionize how we thought, how we handled machine tools electronically and how we shared information and documentation. This industrial transformation first took place within military industries but was destined to be generalized. Large, developed States, who wished to profit from this prosperous new sector, had to accelerate standards production in order to have a framework within which electronic industries could cooperate to achieve their desired ambitions. In the three or four decades following the War, experts from the IEC, ITU (especially the CCITT) and the ISO gradually formalized standards, defining a theoretical, conceptual and practical framework to similarly facilitate the widespread use of this electronic and technological world[3]. Manufacturers of electric and electronic equipment from the IEC were fully aware of the advantage this gave them.

However, this was not always the case with other professions and branches within the ISO: mechanics and metallurgy, health, transport, food, stationery, cinema, photography, finances, watchmaking, etc. All these

3 CCITT: Comité consultatif international télégraphique et téléphonique (Consultative Committee for International Telegraphy and Telephony). A committee in the ITU, whose abbreviated form works equally well in French and English.

professional disciplines would become electro-technological (the term "digitized" would soon be used) in production (production and marketing processes) and the products and services for the end user were also digitized. For example, the European watch-making industrialists[4] did not understand early enough how convergence would change the technology in their field (liquid crystal displays, electric motors). Prestige brands could sidestep the crises, but entire swathes of mass consumption brands disappeared within the European watch-making industry[5]. In the United States, Kodak took too long to transition to digital photography (ISO/TC 42). On the other hand, the field of cinema (ISO/TC 42) was digitized later, and it was able to profit from lessons in going digital from its sister technology, that is, television.

At the IEC, the intensification of convergence among multiple professions, activities and uses seemed an obvious fact. The ITU had largely developed its own user standards, with increasingly specific details on the technical aspects of telecommunications. However, as an institution, it could not produce industrial standards, which remained the responsibility of the IEC or the ISO. Nonetheless, the scope of the standardization of uses of electronics became more and more fluid. Who would take charge of engineering and software standards? The ISO or the IEC? Should actors in the IT and audiovisual fields be left to their own devices, to develop information storage, without offering them an institutional and universal standardization framework that would allow them to periodically reach consensus on the technological fundamentals of their respective industries and activities? These are precisely the questions that the ISO and IEC are working together to address through ISO/IEC JTC 1.

Following on the use of mechanical calculators, which were still part of office equipment until the 1960s, states and large companies began investing in the first generation of computers, which were also heavy. The digital computing of that era required its early users to have complete theoretical and technical knowledge of the calculator: the various functions of the electronic circuit as well as the theory of programming, where coding could only be carried out line-by-line.

Of course, the concept of computing evolved over time and its theoretical basics were stabilized. In 1936, the Turing machine was a purely abstract

4 Unlike in Japan.

5 The case of Lip, in France, was a tragic example of poor anticipation of technological convergence.

concept. However, its designer, Alan Turing, was asked to realize his theories for the British Secret Service, leading to the creation of the *Colossus* machine and the British version of the Polish code-breaking machines, *bomba*, called Bombe in English. This advance finally allowed the allies to break the *Enigma* code. In the Axis group, the Germans had developed the Z3 computer (designed in 1938 and destroyed in 1943 in the Allied bombing of Berlin). In the United States, the US military built the ENIAC. Norbert Wiener, who headed a highly interdisciplinary team between 1942 and 1948, invented cybernetics, which was at the heart of the science of control and communication. He also participated in important operational work on aiming control and firing calculation (the basis for the development of computer graphics). Shannon, who had originally worked in the field of telephony, proposed a signal theory. In 1940, von Neumann designed the first theoretical plans for what he called a "computer"[6] while working in the US army's Ballistic Research Laboratory.

The war also led to advances in all sectors of media. Radar, which gathered information from radiowaves over a large range of frequencies (Ampex project), led to the earliest patents for rotating magnetic heads, which were later used in magnetoscopes. Military walkie-talkies eventually trickled down to civilian uses that are forgotten today (radiotaxis, pagers for emergency workers), which acted as transition technologies and were the predecessors of digital mobile phones.

Television was a highly promising market for large electronics companies: one TV per household! This was the product taken up by advertisers and policy heads, even more so than the radio. Television formats are constantly changing, which makes standardization difficult. However, this standardization is essential for the ITU to allocate Hertzian frequencies[7]. Color television accelerated standardization over large geographical regions: NTSC and PAL[8], with SECAM forming a French exception[9]. A TV for

6 In France, Philippe Dreyfus called this "*informatique*" (information technology) in an article in *Le Monde* dated May 2, 1962, a concept that was submitted to IBM France and which would soon enter common parlance.

7 The number finally stabilized in the late 1950s: 525 or 625 scan lines.

8 Which depends on power frequencies of 50 or 60 Hz depending on the continent.

9 In the short term, this justified setting up a French electronics market to support de Gaulle's "Plan Calcul", which aimed to develop France into a nuclear power.

everyone became an inexorable dynamic. The development of heavy video production equipment, as well as terrestrial Hertzian broadcast networks made up several markets (often State-run markets, supported by national standards). Producers of electronic components (printed circuits and transistors) found a fabulous consumer market for television receivers.

While standardization generally rationalized and accelerated progress, especially in the electrotechnological sector, it was also true that standardization (national or international) is an excellent way of momentarily slowing down progress in certain sectors by carrying out standardization in successive steps. This allows time for the development of other sectors that experts know have to grow further to allow for convergence. This then gives rise to transition technologies, which can nonetheless offer interesting market opportunities. We must be wary about labelling these "dishonest" practices. Just like the economy has an invisible hand guiding it, standardization can provide scheduled, voluntary periods of inertia during which different convergent branches can synchronize how they come together.

Thus, video transmission standards depended on the older standards of alternating current at 50 or 60 periods, which led to cascading standardization problems. The broad television standards of 60 Hz NTSC, on the one hand, and 50 Hz PAL and SECAM, on the other hand, led to decades of distinct markets and separate hubs of innovations. The equipment is highly specific: screens, recording systems, transmitters and receivers. Computer technology, which developed almost exclusively in America, adopted the 60 Hz frequency, and as multimedia emerged, these inconveniences grew, especially with regard to video composition.

Computer monitors found it difficult to compose interactive videos in PAL and, even more so, the SECAM format. Because of this, interactive video discs (a transition technology) developed somewhat later in Europe. Applications developed in one zone could not easily be transferred from one continent to another. This also had consequences on the standardization of cinema recording and projection (24 frames/s). In the United States and 60 Hz zone, films were projected at their original speed, with certain frames being digitally ignored. In the 50 Hz zone, the projectors simply took 24 images to 25. This led to a saving of 3.5 min over a film of 1.5 h, which was just the time needed for an advertising break.

Incentives from the State, exciting future prospects and incentivizing actions over three decades of transition

All large, developed nations put in place incentives for the greater spread of a new culture of information and communication, both within companies and in society as a whole. In this context, large developed countries wished to structure their national market and plan infrastructure purchases. This required in-depth studies to support national industries (notably, of course, the military) and for the spread of ICT culture within the general population.

Japan put in place the Jacudi plan (Japan Computer Usage Development Institute), which was a plan for a computerized society, proposed in the mid-1960s as a goal for the year 2000. In the United States, *Porat's Report*[10] (Porat 1977) described a new global information society. In France, the *Rapport Nora-Minc sur l'informatisation de la société* (Nora-Minc Report on the Digitization of Society), published in December 1977 by Simon Nora and Alain Minc (Nora and Minc 1977), discussed the concept of telematics (the increasing interconnection between computers and telecommunications) and made the concrete proposal of the Minitel network. This was initially a digital alternative to the telephone directory and was meant to save on the cost of paper; however, it became a means for society to adopt the use of information technology. There were many other actions taken throughout the world: Europe set up large projects to support industrial development and research. Military research, especially in the United States, promoted the industrial development of electronics and information technology: ARPA (Arpanet, 1969), when combined with university networks and the TCP-IP protocol, would lead to the development of the Internet. These projects were in line with the problem of publishing voluminous, complex and interactive technical documentation, which led to the development of the first major standard for markup languages: IBM's Generalized Markup Language (GML, 1969). This was the point of origin for SGML, in the Machine-readable Cataloging (MARC) format in libraries[11] and then led to HTML (and thus the Web), finally producing XML.

Box 5.2. *Jacudi, Porat and Nora-Minc*

10 Marc Uri Porat, author of a report that proposed the concept of the *information economy* and measured its effects.

11 Notably, the Library of Congress in Washington, which was where MARC was first developed in 1968.

The creation of community TV networks in the 1970s led to citizens producing and broadcasting content themselves over cable networks. Pedagogic experimentation with interactive technologies, especially the use of videotapes and then video discs, became a non-negligible *niche market.* Applications related to electronic commerce and financial applications were developed in parallel, especially chip-based cards[12]. On the global scale, the interconnection of financial circuits and national stock markets became a considerable market. The World Information Technology and Human Resource Center (1981–1986) was founded by Jean-Jacques Servan-Schreiber. This was run by Nicholas Negroponte and Seymour Papert[13] who developed the *Logo* language, an educational programming language. This original, experimental institution induced interesting transatlantic technological transfers. Teletext, which was simultaneously developed in many countries in the early 1970s, allowed information to be delivered in the form of text and animation, interwoven into television broadcast signals: Antiope (FR), Ceefax (United Kingdom). This would lead to the European standard: *World System Teletext* (WST).

5.1.1. *Technical committees that led to JTC 1*

In 1960, technical committee ISO/TC 97 (information technology) was founded following the creation of a standardization committee in the United States that is known today as the InterNational Committee for Information Technology Standard (INCITS). ANSI (United States) was in charge of the secretariat and presidency of ISO/TC 97 and its scope was expanded to include computers, peripherals and information systems. On the other hand, ISO/TC 95 was created for office machines, which were relatively distinct from computers at the time this committee was established.

In 1981, ISO/TC 95 was merged with ISO/TC 97. In 1983, there was a larger integration of committees when two subcommittees in ISO/TC 97, TC 97/SC 8 (numerical control of machines) and TC 97/SC 9 (programming languages for numerical control), merged to create a new

12 Roland Moreno (1945–2012) was the inventor of the chip-based card (1974).

13 Jean-Jacques Servan-Schreiber (1924–2006), journalist, French politician and passionate about the future; Nicholas Negroponte, founder of the MIT Media Lab; Seymour Papert (1928–2016), creator of the research group on epistemology and learning within MIT. Notably, they invented the LOGO programming language and the new mathematics field of Turtle Geometry.

TC, ISO/TC 184: Industrial automation systems. In 1984, ISO/TC 97 was reorganized so it could more effectively respond to the needs of the IT sector. Its scope was modified to: <Standardization, including terminology, in the field of information processing systems including, but not limited to, personal computers and office equipment>. The various committees in TC 97 were reorganized, and an effort was made to bring together similar activities, led by three vice-presidents. These three groups were:

– *Application elements*: composed of ISO/TC 97/SC 1 (vocabulary); ISO/TC 97/SC 7 (software and systems); ISO/TC 97/SC 14 (data elements) and ISO/TC 97/SC 22 (programming languages).

– *Equipment and media*: ISO/TC 97/SC 10 (magnetic discs); ISO/TC 97/SC 11 (flexible magnetic media (diskettes); ISO/TC 97/SC 13 (interconnection of equipment); ISO/TC 97/SC 15 (file labeling and structuring); ISO/TC 97/SC 17 (person identification cards); and ISO/TC/97 SC 19 and ISO/TC 97/SC 23 (digital optical media for storage and exchange).

– *Systems*: ISO/TC 97/SC 2 (coded characters); ISO/TC 97/SC 6 (teleinformation); ISO/TC 97/SC 18 (text preparation and interchange); ISO/TC 97/SC 20 (cryptographic techniques); and ISO/TC 97/SC 21 (upper layers of OSI).

JTC 1 was eventually created in 1987, as a joint committee, between the ISO and IEC[14]. JTC 1 was thus born out of the merging of ISO/TC 97 (information technology, dissolved when JTC 1 was created) and IEC/TC 83 (information technology equipment, also dissolved upon JTC 1's creation). IEC/SC 47B (microprocessor systems) was also later merged into JTC 1.

Most of the standardization working groups (WGs) dedicated to applications, equipment, media and systems were integrated into the newly formed JTC 1. At this time, the standardization of Open Systems Interconnection (OSI) seemed to be of the highest priority. OSI proposed standardizing a seven-layer model, supported by significant actors in the market (governments, large clients and IT system manufacturers). JTC 1

14 A designation that was undoubtedly preferred to "mixed committee" to emphasize the collaborative nature of the standardization efforts.

responded perfectly to the expectations of its parent organizations, the ISO and IEC. It soon became the committee for convergent ICT, an entity that was autonomous enough to be able to define its own technology standardization policy and respond to the challenges posed by digitization, multimedia and telematics.

Over almost four decades, there were four successive rounds of SCs that were formed: the first round of SCs was from 1964 (formally 1987) to 1991, the second group was from 1996 to 2002, a third group was formed from 2009 to 2013 and finally a fourth round, which only includes the creation of three SCs, from 2017 onwards. The last SC in this group was set up in 2024.

The first round began in 1964, then in 1984 there was the creation of the first SCs under ISO/TC 97, which was the precursor to JTC 1. It laid the technological foundation for JTC and was divided into five sub-groups:

1) Numerical coding of information: SC 2 (alphanumeric characters), SC 24 (computer graphics, especially geographic) and SC 29 (digital audiovisual).

2) Teleinformatics: SC 6 (teleinformatics) and SC 25 (interconnection between information processing devices).

3) Physical media and components: SC 17 (personal identification cards and security devices) and SC 23 (digitally recorded media for information interchange and storage).

4) Software: SC 7 (software and systems engineering) and SC 22 (programming languages, environment and software system interfaces).

5) Interdisciplinary problems: SC 27 (safety) and SC 28 (office IT peripherals).

Five years elapsed before the second round of SCs (1996–2002)[15], marked by the founding of two new sub-groups:

15 From 1996 to 1998, the first three SCs from this round of creation produced standards that would reinforce, specify, or transform the fundamental standards of the first standardization base. There were also reorganizations and dissolutions at this time. In 1997, JTC 1/SC 30 "open exchange of electronic data" was dissolved (considered to be a duplication of effort). SC 33 "distributed application services" was re-allocated to SCs 6 and 7. As of 2025, these were the last SCs to have been dissolved.

1) Data exchange and identification: SC 31 (automatic identification techniques and data entry), SC 32 (data exchange and management) and SC 34 (document description and processing languages).

2) Technology for users: SC 35 (user interfaces, with an ergonomic approach for users), SC 36 (information technology for learning, education and training) and SC 37 (biometrics).

Seven years passed before the third round of new sub-groups (2009–2013), in which four new SCs were created:

1) SC 38: distributed application platforms and services (the Cloud).

2) SC 39: environmental impact of information technologies and data centers (Big Data).

3) SC 40: IT service management and IT governance.

4) SC 41: Internet of Things and related technologies (IoT).

Apart from SC 39's specific focus on environment and sustainability, this round of SC creation was marked by JTC 1's desire to standardize Internet applications[16].

The fourth round (2017–2025) saw the creation of three SCs, created at longer intervals:

1) SC 42 (2017): artificial intelligence.

2) SC 43 (2022): brain–machine interfaces.

3) SC 44 (2025): privacy by design.

If JTC 1 no longer dissolves SCs and creates very few new ones, it is because it has reached a stage of maturity. Its higher levels (president, secretariat, council), as well as its annual plenary assembly, only decide to create new SCs after ample reflection. Quantum technologies, for example, were first studied in a WG that was directly attached to JTC 1's central bureau, and not in the form of an SC, as would probably have been the case in the early 2000s. Nevertheless, in 2024, the ISO and IEC, in conjunction with JTC 1, had already created ISO/ECT JTC 3 (quantum technologies) as

16 For example, the standardization of automatic steering applications in vehicles or telemedicine. These applications had to be rigorously reliable and could not depend on opaque GAFAM+ networks.

well as JSyC BDC (biodigital convergence). This was followed, in late 2025, by JTC 4: Smart and sustainable cities and communities.

These three domains require joint standardized study between the ISO and IEC and will mobilize communities of experts that are different from, but also complementary to, those in JTC 1.

Let us briefly review each of the SCs under JTC 1. However, we will take the liberty of developing some of these SCs (of which the author has direct experience) in greater detail than others.

5.1.2. *The first round of SC creation began with JTC 1/SC 2*

JTC 1/SC 2 was founded in 1987[17]. Its current scope is: <Standardization of graphic character sets and their characteristics, including string ordering, associated control functions, their coded representation for information interchange and code extension techniques. Excluded: audio and picture coding.>

JTC 1/SC 2 was not only the first SC[18] created under JTC 1, but it was also the most ambitious. This SC has allowed JTC 1 to demonstrate its ability to respond to an essential challenge that had seemed an unattainable dream until this point: writing in all languages[19]. In the period leading up to the creation of JTC 1, the experts within ISO/TC 97 had long considered the question of creating a single SC that would be in charge of the overall standardization of numerical coding of information. From a purely information technology point of view, the question was clearly a single, unique problem. The industrialists who were pioneers in the imaging field were already making use of the similar multi-channel RGB (red, green, blue) and this was a similar process of using “multiple channels” for coding characters.

Specialists in coded representation of writing had to take up the considerable difficulty of arriving at a unified manner of coding the large families of alphabetic Western writing systems over a single 8-bit byte.

17 An official date that does not take into account the previous existence of ISO/TC 97/SC 2.

18 If we exclude SC 1, which was dissolved and which was dedicated to the vocabulary of JTC 1.

19 In synergy with the Unicode Consortium.

Computer graphics, which was an emerging field at the time, posed other coding problems. Digital audiovisual media also had its own specific requirements. This was what was officialized and, until the 1990s, JTC 1/SC 2/WG 8 (the coded representation of audio, image, multimedia, and hypermedia information) continued to exist. However, it was decided that several SCs would be created: SC 2 for coding written characters (soon limited to the first, monumental problem of exclusively standardizing the codification of characters[20]), a second SC (SC 24) for computer graphics and a third for audiovisual information (SC 29).

Standardizing binary alphanumeric coding was (and has remained, for over a century and a half) the founding principle of information technology and digital communication. The entire code that is used for ICT, and especially for letters and digits, is based on binary coding. This long history (which we simplify here) begins with the Baudot code (1874) and saw its first modern results in ASCII in the early 1960s. Given that digital globalization was already highly developed in the 1980s, it was impossible for industrialists to think of developing a global IT market limited to just a single system of writing: the Roman script without any diacritics and Western Arabic numerals. Other languages that could be written in the Roman script could be accommodated, but this came at the cost of ruling out a number of new and emerging uses, especially word processing and publishing. Other alphabetic, non-Latin languages had developed some clumsy workarounds, but the ideographic scripts of South east Asia, for example, needed a definite alternative. The Japanese had already begun developing and standardizing, at a national level, 16-bit applications rather than the 8-bit extended ASCII. The universal standardization of characters was a project that had to succeed at all costs – or risk having the IT industry disintegrate into separate, continental markets.

ASCII code, which appeared in 1963, provisionally finalized the successive evolution of telegraph code. By going digital, text coding was released from the difficulties associated with mechanical writing systems. Interpreting the selection of an item on the keyboard as a letter, digit or punctuation mark now depended on a calculation carried out by the computer.

20 However, the problem of organizing text was something that Unicode, which was being created at the time, could address.

In 1960, computers processed 8-bit information[21]. ASCII (American Standard Code for Information Interchange), often called 7-bit ASCII, would become the standard for the earliest information technology calculators. ASCII was standardized by ANSI. Today, the standard ISO/IEC 646 defines 128 characters numbered from 0 to 127 and coded in binary code from 0000000 to 1111111. However, while 127 coding possibilities (from which we must subtract digits, arithmetic operations and digital command codes) are enough to encode non-accentuated Roman script (essentially English and Latin), the standard in its state at the time was unusable for processing texts in other writing systems that used the Roman script with additional accents and diacritic signs. It was also essential to meet the requirements of markets with other alphabetic but non-Roman writing systems (Cyrillic, Greek, Arabic, Hebrew, and various writing systems of Indian languages). The development of basic technical solutions (processing memory, system software) that allowed the manufacture of successive generations of computers (with processing memory that could compute over 8, 16, 32 or 64 bits) took place over several decades. Meanwhile, IT industrialists were constrained to respond separately to two large markets: those with alphabetic writing, and those with East Asian writing systems, where, for a long period, only Japan was able to meet their requirements.

The gradual development of solutions for around tens of families of alphabetic scripts posed a problem, even if it was apparent to everyone that these were transition technologies. The inclusion of East Asian languages was difficult, but a major challenge that had to be undertaken. The Japanese had developed 16-bit solutions that met the basic needs of not only Japanese but also Chinese and Korean, and which also allowed alphabetic writing to be integrated. These were solutions standardized by the JIS: the Japanese Industrial Standards Committee.

Western industrialists had proposed several solutions to extend ASCII: (1) the industrial standard EBCDIC (Extended Binary-Coded Decimal Interchange Code) which was put forth by IBM, and VT200 by DEC; (2) in 1973, the standard ISO 2022; (3) in 1978, 8-bit codes for Romance languages, the UKPO standard for videotex; (4) in 1979, the standard ISO 4873, ISO 8-bit code for information interchange. None of these standards were truly satisfactory. However, working and communicating in the script of one's own mother tongue, or at the very least in your everyday link

21 Seven actually, as one bit was reserved for control and command codes.

language, was a fundamental requirement, and one that the IT market of the 1980s had to fulfill for the digitization of society and the global networks that had begun to form.

At the time, no multinational could claim to have single-handedly developed a satisfactory solution. It became increasingly urgent and essential to standardize common, non-competitive bases for a universal coded representation of writing. JTC 1/SC 2 put forth 16 standards, ISO/IEC 8859-n (sometimes called extended ASCII), to meet the requirements for alphabetic scripts. These 16 standards met immediate user requirements for Roman scripts with accents or diacritical marks, as well as other alphabetic scripts (especially Arabic, Cyrillic, Thai and Greek). This series of standards was organized such that it was possible to code each family of scripts as many different registers. This made it possible to shift from one script to another in the same text through *escape sequences*[22]. For example, allowing a scientific article in French to quote passages in Greek, Arabic or Hebrew, or the directory in a multilingual library[23].

However, the challenges taken up by JTC 1/SC 2 were more ambitious and fundamental. As is often the case in standardization, two tasks had to be separately defined: one was preparing a catalogue of characters, the other was using these characters to compose pages of unilingual or mixed writing, or even carrying out complex sorting within mixed corpora (such as library catalogues). The Unicode consortium (see section 6.1) was already working on the second question, and this reinforced the decision to limit SC 2's scope to the catalogue of characters[24]. This limited, but essential, project soon revealed the magnitude of the task: tackling around 200 known languages with writing systems. In 1990, SC 2 developed the first version of the standard ISO/IEC 10646, coding characters over 4 octets (32 bits) (Universal Multiple Octet Coded Character Set). The objective of this "universal directory of character codes" was to provide a single response to the circulation or digital processing of all characters in all writing systems in the

22 As with the Baudot code, which constantly oscillated between four registers of code materialized by a series of five holes or the absence of holes within the telegraph strip.

23 This example is deliberately used: while it is indeed possible to publish a library catalogue, it is impossible to digitally process (carry out computations over) this whole catalogue: sort alphabetically, find a name or a word.

24 All writing systems in the world, including ancient writing systems, musical notations, mathematical symbols, emoticons, etc.

whole world. To use the jargon from the olden days of typographic printing using lead types, the task was to significantly increase the capacities of a *virtual type case*[25], going from 128 to 258 "compartments" in much larger cases (2^{16} or 65,536 theoretical positions). First, there was the Basic Multilingual Plane (BMP), and then as 32-bit systems were developed, as many planes as needed were added, since 2^{32} allowed the construction of a theoretical virtual case with over 4 billion compartments (coding points).

In 1992, the Unicode consortium proposed a method for a hexadecimal numbering system, which was shared with JTC 1/SC 2 (see Chapter 6). In concrete terms, JTC 1/SC 2 was given the responsibility of identifying each character from every writing system in the world and giving each a unique name. This was carried out in progressive steps. For example: A, a capital letter in the Roman script (Unicode code 0041); Ã (A tilde), a capital letter in the Roman script (C3); β, Greek symbol (03D0); ç (c with cedilla), a lowercase letter in the Roman script (00E7)[26];], left square bracket (005D); $, dollar sign (0024); =, sign for equality, (003D); ⚕, Staff of Aesculapius (2695); 1/9, ordinary fraction denoting a ninth (2151); Ḭ, capital I with tilde below, capital letter in the Roman script (1E2C); 2F14 ⼔, Chinese radical for spoon, versus Japanese radical 21 in Kanji = 5315; 2F4A ⽊, Chinese radical for tree, versus Japanese radical 75 in Kanji = 6728 木; etc.

This task, completed in less than three decades by the experts in JTC 1/SC 2, was a truly Herculean effort. The experts had to first create a shared directory of characters and summarize their characteristics: their form[27] along with more complex and disparate questions (ligatures; bigrams, trigrams; change in form when in initial, median, or final position, etc.). They had to ensure that the new standards were compatible with the earlier standards (ASCII and extended ASCII). It was a mammoth undertaking, but working together with Unicode, the experts in the field were eventually able to succeed.

---

25 A type case was a wooden box, meant to hold lead characters within the same font type. It was divided into compartments called *cassetins*.

26 This number is a hexadecimal code that makes it possible to access all characters.

27 A fundamental methodological position, but it would be beyond our scope here to explore this in detail. These are *theoretical glyphs* independent of their multiple cultural or esthetic variants.

Concurrently, in 1978 the Japanese had developed the standard JIS X0201, "Coding characters over 16 bits", allowing word-processing systems to function using two syllabaries (the two *kana*: *hiragana* and *katakana*), while also allowing them to use the most common *kanji* (ideograms). The Japanese standard over 16 bits opened up the possibility of coding not only Japanese, Chinese and the Korean *hangul,* but also coding primary alphabetic writing systems from around the world – Roman, Greek, Cyrillic, Arabic, Indian scripts, etc. – without being constrained by escape sequences, like those used in the standards ISO/IEC 8859-n. This question, which Western industrialists had neglected for too long, became a burning issue to avoid losing out on the global control of information technologies[28].

It must be noted that the specific requirements of ideographic writing had posed many bureaucratic problems in the field of linguistics. Typewriters for these languages were practically non-existent until the first word processors appeared. Using a keyboard to type ideographic characters was a problem that was only fully resolved with the advent of AI. The printing of texts required heavy industrial equipment that was difficult to adapt for office use. The Japanese (as well as the Taiwanese and Hong Kong) electronic industry had to meet (or sometimes circumvent) these challenges, for example, through the rise of photocopying, the use of high-definition digital screens to display the essential details in the ideograms, and, of course, the development of 16-bit computing, at a time when the West was still working with 8 bits.

Furthermore, ideographic writing systems, especially Japanese, were naturally predisposed for the easier development of AI. This is because with ideograms, writing *directly encodes symbols for ideas*, unlike alphabetic languages where the writing depicts *the sound of the pronunciation of the words, which symbolize the concepts or ideas*. Additionally, in Japanese, the writing encodes statements in two distinctive functional ways: (1) the *vocabulary*, including proper names in Japanese (national patronyms, Japanese toponyms, foreign toponyms and brand names), which is symbolized by the *kanji*, which is a collection of ideograms that are almost identical (in semantic terms) to Chinese ideograms; (2) whatever is not part of the lexicon, that is, the *syntactic glue* (written in *hiragana*), in addition to

28 See, notably, Lucas (2002, pp. 183–198) or Hudrisier and Lucas (1991, pp. 44–46).

onomatopeia, transliteration of foreign words, proper nouns in foreign languages and recent technical terms (which are written in *katakana*[29]).

This specific feature of Japanese writing gives it an additional cognitive advantage over Chinese. In fact, beyond the coding of ideas, a page of writing in Japanese (read diagonally) allows the reader to easily distinguish the functional zone in a text (concepts and proper nouns written in *kanji*[30]) from those areas that tie the concepts together grammatically, and also identify zones with transcribed text (especially most technical words written in *kana*). An American, Joe Becker, tried to overcome this challenge in the early 1980s through a specific project at the Xerox research center in Palo Alto. This was a project for the universal coding of what were already known as "Unicode characters".

At this time, the combined participation of the Japanese, Chinese and Koreans in JTC 1/SC 2 as well as the Unicode project significantly accelerated progress, while also posing certain difficulties in terms of methods. Many experts were not multilingual and did not have a grasp of English and East Asian languages. This is why the register of East Asian characters appeared separately, though concurrently, in the registers for the standard ISO-IEC 10646 and in Unicode: this was denoted by CJK for Chinese, Japanese and Korean[31]. It must be noted that CJK, which is a specific block in the directory of unified characters from around the world, was determined through mutual agreement between experts delegated by the national bodies of these three related languages. They had to urgently arrive at a consensus in order to code all characters within a zone in the register of codes that was necessarily limited. This was facilitated by coding over 16 bits and then, subsequently, over 32 bits.

29 These are generally called the *kana*, in plural, as there are two writing systems (*hiragana*, women's writing; *katakana,* the writing of monks) versus a single syllabary of 51 signs.

30 Visually distinct from the syllabary as they generally have more complex writing forms.

31 In reality, and despite their appearance, the *hanguls* in Korean writing are a syllabary. However, ancient Korean texts are often a mixture of ideograms and *hanguls*, especially poetry and traditional medicine texts. We sometimes use the term CJKV (V for Vietnamese), adding an ancient form of writing Vietnamese, the *chữ nôm:* a system of ideophonograms that were in use until the early 20th century, and which must not be confused with the *quốc ngữ*, which are Romanized characters invented in the 17th century by a Jesuit, Alexander of Rhodes.

We must acknowledge how important JTC 1/SC 2 must have been from its inception to be able to set the tone for a new culture of technology standards within JTC 1, being able to bring together diverse professionals (typographers, computer scientists) within the same WGs with industrialists and social science researchers in applied or exact sciences (ethnolinguists, researchers working on IT, historians of writing systems and computers, library scientists, musicologists, paleographists, etc.) from regions all across the world.

It is indisputable that JTC 1/SC 2 played a significant role in the "vision of JTC 1" and, specifically, was able to give the IEC and ISO a new way of thinking of standards and developing new methods for standard production.

5.2. The first round of SCs created in JTC 1: 1964–1991

This first round of SC formation in JTC 1 began with the essential question of codifying writing (SC 2), which would then be complemented by SC 24 (coding computer graphics) and then SC 29 (coding audiovisual information). SC 29, set up in 1991, was the last SC set up in this phase. This period also saw the creation of many other SCs, notably, SC 6, SC 7, SC 17, SC 22, SC 23, SC 25, SC 27 and SC 29.

JTC 1/SC 6, telecommunications and information exchange between systems, was the cornerstone of JTC 1. Just as with the standardization of the coding of alphanumeric information (SC 2), teleinformatics was an area of interest common to the ISO, IEC and the ITU-CCITT in the 1960s. Its original structure closely reproduced the OSI seven-layer model. Today, in the digital age and with the advent of cybercrime, we must distinguish between two categories of teleinformatics in order to limit the risk of intrusion and contamination:

– standards for secure intranet, for which SC 6 continues to develop standards reflecting current realities;

– standards for an extranet, allowing companies and organizations to safely exchange information with collaborators.

Its current scope reflects its history and importance: <Since SC6 was established in 1964, SC6 has worked on standardization in the field of telecommunications dealing with the exchange of information between open

systems, including system functions, procedures, parameters as well as the conditions for their use. This standardization encompasses protocols and services of lower layers including physical, data link, network, and transport as well as those of upper layers including but not limited to Directory and ASN.1: MFAN, NFC, PLC, Future Networks and OID>.

JTC 1/SC 7, Software and system engineering, was founded in 1987[32].

Its current scope is defined as: <Standardization of processes, supporting tools and supporting technologies for the engineering of software products and systems.

Note: The processes, tools and technologies are within the scope of JTC 1 terms of references and exclude specific tools and technologies that have been assigned by JTC 1 to other of its SCs.>

SC 7 does not work in isolation. Along with SC 22 (dedicated to programming languages), it standardizes both the development and use of software. This standardization also complements the work of other SCs created in this period, dedicated to the coding of three broad categories of documents:

– writing (SC 2, 1987);

– computer graphics and geographic information (SC 24, 1987);

– audiovisual coding (SC 29, 1991).

JTC 1/SC 17, Cards and security devices for personal identification, was also created in 1987[33]. This is a historic SC within JTC 1, which works on essential technologies within various domains: bank cards, travel documents, electronic keycards for hotels, etc. For example, almost 350 million new electronic passports have been issued by a hundred countries around the world. The SC 17 standards notably cover:

– the physical dimensions of cards, ensuring they are compatible with the reading terminal (example: the size of the delivery slot in an automatic vending machine; positioning the tracks and reading heads);

32 This date does not take into account its existence as ISO/TC 97/SC 7 in 1984.

33 In reality, from 1984, within ISO/TC 97.

– interoperable technologies, ensuring the compatibility of cards manufactured by different organizations at an international level.

Its current scope is clear and concise: <The current area of work for JTC 1/SC 17 consists of:

– identification and related documents;

– cards;

– security devices and tokens;

– and interface associated with their use in inter-industry applications and international interchange.>

JTC 1/SC 22, Programming languages, their environments and system software interfaces, was also created in 1987[34].

Its current scope: <JTC1/SC 22 is the international standardization subcommittee for programming languages, their environments and system software interfaces. SC 22 is oftentimes called the 'portability subcommittee'.> When it was created in 1984, the question of interoperability between languages was already an essential question. At this time, the main programming languages that SC 22 needed to take into account were low-level languages that needed to be compiled in machine language (binary)[35]. Each language responded to a clearly defined usage typology, and SC 22 took up:

– standardizing the interoperability between these languages and also between different versions of the same language;

– ensuring compatibility between the software environment and the system layers, complementing the work of SC 7.

From the 1990s onwards, a new generation of high-level languages emerged, such as Python (1991), JavaScript, Ruby, Perl and PHP. Unlike low-level languages, these languages were designed such that they could be directly interpreted without any compilation required beforehand. Although they are very easy to use, they are slower to run, which could be a problem

34 In reality, from 1984, within ISO/TC 97.

35 The WGs in SC 22 were in fact groups of experts who specialized in these historical computer languages.

in certain use cases. The increasing number of programming languages[36], however, made it impossible to create a specific WG for each language. Nonetheless, it is essential to maintain expertise over historical low-level languages, especially in critical domains such as:

– industrial and security applications, where compilation optimizes performance;

– coding software directly onto components, which requires compact and efficient code.

JTC 1/SC 23, Digitally recorded media for information interchange and storage, was created in 1987 and is a historical part of JTC 1. Technological progress in terms of digital memory is directly related to the sharing of standardized features, which allow both increased miniaturization and a reduction in costs for the same performance. This standardization applies to internal supports (computation memory) as well as external, fixed supports, which are the specific focus of SC 23. This issue has always required know-how from the IEC. Today, SC 23 has the unique feature of having no WG, which means that it essentially relies on its five liaisons with other standardization groups in the IEC and ISO.

Its current scope is: <Standardization in the field of removable digital storage media utilizing optical, holographic and magnetic recording technologies, and flash memory technologies for digital information interchange, including:

– algorithms for the lossless compression of data;

– volume and file structure;

– methods for determining the life expectancy of digital storage media;

– methods for error monitoring of digital storage media.>

JTC 1/SC 24, Computer graphics, image processing and environmental data representation, was created in 1987 and is also a historical SC within JTC 1.

Its current scope is: <Standardization relating to:

– computer graphics;

36 Over 700 languages listed, as of 2025, on Wikipedia.

– image processing;

– virtual reality, augmented reality and mixed reality;

– environmental data representation;

– visualization of, and interaction with, information.

Excluded: efficient coding of multimedia.>

In its title and scope, the SC 24 experts have identified several axes of standardization, corresponding to two types of activities: one is computer graphics and image processing, and the other is environmental data representation (sometimes called geomatics). The exclusion of standardization of audiovisual information (which is carried out by SC 29) makes it possible to draw this dividing line. While porous, it is nonetheless an important boundary to maintain. SC 24 defines this boundary concisely by mentioning the *efficient coding of multimedia*.

JTC 1/SC 25, interconnection of information technology equipment, was created in 1990. It is often called the subcommittee in charge of standards for *home automation* and *smart industrial buildings*. The standards proposed by SC 25 establish rules for efficient cooperation between all components and services in data networks. These are significant catalysts in the operational technology (OT) and Industry 4.0 (see JTC 1/SC 41 in section 5.6). As with SC 24, there is such a wide diversity of data, flows, producers and clients that it is clear that these applications are only possible with a very large number of pre-defined standards, established through consensus with industrialists, researchers and potential end-users. The WGs in SC 25 clearly reflect the four main areas of standardization within SC 25:

– WG 1: Home electronic systems.

– WG 3: Customer premises cabling.

– WG 4: Interconnection of computer systems and attached equipment.

– WG 5: Taxonomy and terminology for intelligent homes.

Its current scope is: <Standardization of microprocessor systems, interfaces, protocols, architectures and associated interconnecting media for information technology equipment and networks to support embedded and distributed computing environments, storage systems and other input/output components.>

The first years of a new technique and the goals of computer graphics

Computer graphics make it possible to generate new image categories (which may or may not be animated and/or in 3D), which are not necessarily meant to be iconic (Moles 1971, p. 297), but must be as meaningful as possible. This was especially the case with schematic representations, such as technical maps or flowcharts. The earliest computer graphics go back to the 1950s, within the context of the development of war games, with advanced visualization (today we would use the term "enhanced visualization") for radar, as well as aiming tools and trajectory-tracking for rockets. After this initial phase of research and development, which was carried out within the standardized framework of military applications, the industrialists manufacturing these advanced technologies were the first to come together (notably, in organizations such as IEEE) to develop standards.

The real turning point for computer graphics was its convergence with geomatics, in large part thanks to data from NASA and the development of the Global Positioning Systems (GPS). This system, which was implemented by the United States Department of Defense (DoD) for military purposes in 1973, is a system of 24 satellites, which became fully operational in 1995. When it opened up to the mass consumer market, it led to the development of many applications:

– Geographic information systems (GISs), which require many interoperability standards;

– geolocalized advertising;

– devices to help in navigation and steering;

– localization for mobile telephony

Beyond strictly geographical data, the immediate environment is also involved, especially as concerns interactions with the information and its visualization, for example, in medical imaging. Regardless of the purpose for which they are used (civil or military, highly advanced, virtual reality, augmented reality, or more informative and commercial), these software tools and the large volume of associated data cannot be exchanged and effectively used without a set of standards in place. Creating these standards is precisely the objective of SC 24.

Box 5.3. *Computer graphics and geomatics*

Standards for home and building electronic systems in residential and commercial environments to support interworking devices (IoT-related) and applications such as energy management, environmental control, lighting and security.

Cabling system standards for ICT, in all types of residential, commercial and industrial environments for the design, planning and installation, test procedures, automated infrastructure management systems and remote powering.

NOTE.– JTC 1/SC 25 standards reference IEC standards for cables, waveguides and connectors.>

JTC 1/SC 27, Information security, cybersecurity and privacy protection, was created in 1989.

Its scope is: <The development of standards for the protection of information and ICT. This includes generic methods, techniques and guidelines to address both security and privacy aspects, such as:

– security requirements capture methodology;

– management of information and ICT security; in particular, information security management systems, security processes and security controls and services;

– cryptographic and other security mechanisms, including but not limited to mechanisms for protecting the accountability, availability, integrity and confidentiality of information;

– security management support documentation including terminology, guidelines as well as procedures for the registration of security components;

– security aspects of identity management, biometrics and privacy;

– conformance assessment, accreditation and auditing requirements in the area of information security management systems;

– security evaluation criteria and methodology.

SC 27 engages in active liaison and collaboration with appropriate bodies to ensure the proper development and application of SC 27 standards and technical reports in relevant areas.>

This scope clearly explains its methodology, which is reflected in its division into WGs and, even more so, in its partnerships, with 144 liaisons[37].

JTC 1/SC 28 includes office equipment. Its current scope is: <Standardization of basic characteristics, test methods and other related items of products such as 2D and 3D Printers/Scanners, Copiers, Projectors, Fax and Systems composed of their combinations, excluding such interfaces as user system interfaces, communication interfaces and protocols.>

Officially founded in 1990, this subcommittee can trace its roots back to ISO/TC 95 (office equipment), created in the 1960s and merged with ISO/TC 97 in 1981. The years between 1970 and 1990 were marked by spectacular advances in peripheral devices (printers, photocopiers, scanners, etc.) enabled by drastic standardization efforts. These efforts led to a considerable reduction in costs, increased miniaturization and, of course, greater interoperability. However, competition continued, especially through the use of proprietary formats; for inks and toners, for instance. Printers and video projectors must be able to effectively communicate in machine-to-machine mode to allow easy and optimal system settings. Until recently (2015–2020), these configurations were complex. Although these technologies do not depend purely on computing, they are still high-precision systems, with micrometric constraints and sophisticated physicochemical processes. The steady growth of 3D printers justified the creation of ISO/IEC JTC 1/WG 12, 3D printing and scanning, a WG that is directly under JTC 1.

5.3. JTC 1/SC 29: JPEG and MPEG

JTC 1/SC 29 includes coding of audio, picture, multimedia and hypermedia information, the first, fundamental group. This SC is particularly known for its two large families of standards: JPEG and MPEG[38].

Its scope is : <Standardization in the field of:

– efficient coding of digital representations of images, audio and moving pictures, including:

37 This is a large number, in terms of the mobilization of expert-delegates.

38 Joint Photographic Experts Group and Moving Picture Experts Group.

- conventional (natural, computer-generated and immersive) images, moving pictures and audio,

- invisible light and other sensory (such as medical and satellite) images,

- static and dynamic graphic objects;

– efficient coding of other digital information, including:

- multimedia, environment and user-related metadata,

- sensor and actuator information related to audiovisual information,

- other digital data in agreement with the relevant committee, such as genomics;

– digital information support, including:

- synchronization, presentation, storage and transport of single or combinations of media,

- media security and privacy management,

- quality of experience evaluation and system performance metrics.>

The mention of the exclusion of the coding of characters reflects the history of the committee. Indeed, JTC 1/SC 29 was founded in 1991, after JTC 1 decided to dissolve JTC 1/SC 2/WG 8 (coded representation of audio, image, multimedia and hypermedia information) in order to create a dedicated subcommittee for this work. As mentioned earlier, this WG was initially integrated with SC 2, since the initial goal was to develop standardized coding for all information that could be digitized over multiple octets. As with the coding of characters, it was essential to design a common framework of standards to ensure the development of digital audiovisual media and definitely move away from analog technologies (which was the case around 2010).

Analog technologies were clearly hindering evolution in this field. Of course, with the radio, even in analog mode, the Hertzian space was not saturated and signals could be globally broadcast as long as the transmitter was powerful enough and worked on short-wave transmission. On the other hand, analog video signals were much heavier and could only be transmitted in the direct field through a hertzian antenna. This meant that coverage of an entire country required a vast network of relay or infrastructure for analog coaxial cables. The other factor that slowed down the development of digital video was the older standards for cathode tube scanning systems and the number of images per second. These standards have been defined based on the power frequencies in different regions of the world[39], leading to the emergence of three dominant standards: NTSC, PAL and SECAM (the French standard, which went on to be largely replaced by PAL). This diversity in standards complicated the rise of inventions such as high-definition TV, interactive video, video signal processing and storage, as well as digital photography. It was thus imperative to design a global framework for standards, encompassing signal coding, signal processing, storage (compressions) and broadcasting[40].

MPEG, a three-stage rocket

The standardization of the coding of MPEG audiovisual data (ISO/IEC, Moving Pictures and Associated Audio Experts Group) can be compared to the three stages of a rocket[41]. First stage: in 1989, the first version of the CCITT recommendation H.261 was published, relating to video coding and decoding methods for the moving picture component of audiovisual services, and this stirred up a hornet's nest. This document defined the two major tools required for digital television: motion compensation and temporal prediction. This precursor, however (especially the recommendation to Congress in Washington, which led to MARC in 1968) remained rather crude with its fixed framing and uniform background; the specialists were not wrong about the popularity and the interest in the outcome of this work. Taking advantage of this initial push, the researchers who had worked together to produce H.261 already knew what they had to do to correctly code film: take into account breaks in the background related to zoom and traveling effects, multiplex good quality audio and video data. This performance was enabled by a better organization of image flow (I, P, B)

39 Fifty periods in Europe, corresponding to 25 images per second; sixty periods in America and Japan, leading to 30 images per second.

40 The reader can refer to four fundamental texts that serve as a reference for a rational digitization of audiovisual media (Shannon 1948; Huffman 1952; Watkinson 2001; Moffat and Turpin 2002).

41 In an article in the journal Solaris, which the author co-wrote with Jean-Michel Borde, who was then an engineer with AFNOR and in charge of JTC 1/SC 29, we used this metaphor, which was common at the time among MPEG experts (Borde and Hudrisier 1999–2000).

(I = intraframe; P = predicted frames; B = bidirectional frames). Qualifying how the transmitted images were coded, this technique contributed in the desired reduction of flow rate using signal compression and the solution was called MPEG 1. This was the second stage of the rocket, which needed to reach a critical velocity to be released, allowing the world to shift to an effective coding method for radiobroadcasting. This can actually be considered an intermediary stage, as this specification was restricted within a clearly specified stream of bytes at 1.5 Mb/s, which was meant to record the information on the mass distribution media (the digital optical disk). Even before the ink dried on the strategic technical and industrial agreement, radio broadcasting emerged as the new performance to be conquered. This was the third stage of the rocket: MPEG 2. This was the transfer stage and, consequently, this step had a significantly longer industrial life than the preceding stages. This format lasted until its ultimate payload docked: MPEG 4 [...] Compared to the stage that helped launch this rocket, MPEG 4 brought in mobility and brought video into the user's hands, replacing the pen and contributing to the federation of various, highly varied terminals that are still in existence today.

This new writing required a new grammar. Should MPEG 7 be thought of as another new satellite? In keeping with the spirit of its predecessors, it would be better to compare MPEG 7 with a system bus, coordinating the functioning of the various stages of a rocket and its hardware, to ensure that it successfully docks. MPEG 7 multiplied the number of languages to access data based on different specializations, languages and writing, and above all, based on different cultures [...]. Conventional audiovisual media was on its final legs at this time and would probably die out as MPEG 2 reached the end of its obsolescence cycle. However, we can predict that it will have an industrial life of around 30 years, that is, at least the lifespan of the PAL, SECAM and NTSC standards that it is replacing. In this time, new modes of consumption will be established across all products and services that must be invented or reinvented. (Border and Hudrisier 1999–2000)

Box 5.4. *Stages in MPEG standardization*

Although this article predicted that MPEG-2 would remain in use for 30 years before it was replaced, in reality this was an underestimation. Founded in 1991, the MPEG family of standards is still a global reference in 2025. In 2004, a new stage was added with MPEG-21, which was meant for the distribution of audiovisual content within more and more complex environments.

The importance of the JPEG norms, meant for photography, is easier for the general public to comprehend. As with video, the standardization of coding and compression of still images formed the methodological basis for JPEG. The chief difference lay in the introduction of metadata, which facilitated interactivity and archiving. Digital photography represented such a booming global market, that industrialists could soon offer low-cost JPEG components, capable of surpassing the performance of proprietary systems that had earlier been reserved for the military or medical sectors[42].

In this respect, JPEG, MPEG, ISO/IEC-10646 and Unicode are among the JTC 1's biggest successes in ICT standardization. It must be highlighted that a historical entity such as Kodak could not survive this technological transformation.

5.4. The second round of SCs created in JTC 1: 1996–2002

In the first round of SCs (1987–1991), JTC 1 had developed a coherent set of standards. The intervening 5 years allowed various actors within JTC 1 to benefit from these. In 1996[43], the Internet grew tenfold thanks to the development of the Web. Industrialists and users had adopted the Web and its omnipresent interactivity for the past decade. This second round of SC creation was thus focused on the standardization of new modes of entering, storing, processing and exchanging data that were adapted to this new generation of technology, which enforced the use of updated user interfaces.

42 The institutional JPEG standard serves as a textbook example of the economic feasibility of a new generation of industrial imaging technology, notably digital photography. Proprietary digital imaging applications (developed using in-house standards for very high-value uses such as medical, military, and remote sensing applications) were inherently incompatible due to a lack of standardization. Once the design and subsequent marketing of JPEG components became possible, the costs of industrial imaging plummeted, and digital photography became accessible to the general public.

43 Just like a boxing match, the rounds were separated by rest periods that allowed the actors in standardization (industrialists, researchers and users) to benefit from the new technological environment, before regrouping for a new session of defining the guidelines required to regulate the new generation of technology and standards.

The last two SCs in this round were dedicated to specific standard requirements: one was ICT for education and training technologies, while the second was for biometrics, which would mark the end of this second round in 2002.

JTC 1/SC 31, an automatic identification and data capture technique, was created in 1996. Its scope is defined as: <Standardization of data formats, data syntax, data structures, data encoding and technologies for the process of automatic identification and data capture and of associated devices utilized in inter-industry applications and international business interchanges and for mobile applications.>

SC 31 establishes standards for identification processes for a variety of products and objects, thereby facilitating access to information (ticketing, commerce, tracking processes, etc.). Its efficacy essentially arises from its ease of implementation and use. Indeed, there are countless applications and they involve products and processes that are quite cheap as well as high-value devices. SC 31 standardizes, notably, bar codes, radio frequency identification (RFID) and QR codes. In many applications, the standard ISO/IEC 18000-63 allows the RFID of products.

JTC 1/SC 32, Data management and interchange, was founded in 1997. SC 32's objective is to guarantee that network applications using the Internet are not dependent only on the IETF standards, but are also based on standards formally defined by JTC 1. Thus, this subcommittee initiates the definition of standards means for the Internet, especially when there is the risk of data being misused.

Its scope is: <Standards for data management within and among local and distributed information systems environments. SC 32 provides enabling technologies to promote harmonization of data management facilities across sector-specific areas. Specifically, SC 32 standards include:

– reference models and frameworks for the coordination of existing and emerging standards;

– definition of data domains, data types and data structures, and their associated semantics;

– languages, services and protocols for persistent storage, concurrent access, concurrent update and interchange of data;

– methods, languages, services and protocols to structure, organize and register metadata and other information resources associated with sharing and interoperability, including electronic commerce[44].>

SC 32 is especially renowned for the standardization of metamodels to design metadata[45] and also for languages for databases[46].

JTC 1/SC 34, Document description and processing languages, was founded in 1998.

Its scope is: <Standardization in the field of document structures, languages and related facilities for the description and processing of compound and hypermedia documents, including (1) languages for describing document logical structures and their support facilities; (2) languages for describing document-like objects in web environment facilities; (3) document processing architecture and formatting for logical document facilities; (4) languages for describing interactive document facilities; (5) multilingual font information interchange and related service facilities; (6) final-form document architecture and page information interchange facilities; (7) hypermedia document structuring language and application resource facilities; and (8) APIs for document processing.>

SC 34 is in charge of standardizing languages and tools used to describe and process structured documents and hypermedia. It is, therefore, the sub-committee that standardizes markup languages and tools dedicated to interactive documents. While the general public largely knows of markup languages thanks to HTML and XML, these languages originated much earlier in the 1960s (see Box 5.1).

JTC 1/SC 35 includes user interface standards. Established in 1998, SC 35 standardizes user interfaces within ICT environments[47]. The SC's

---

44 ISO family of standards ISO/IEC 15944, base standard ISO/IEC 15944-1:2025 Information technology – Business operational view. Part 1: Operational aspects of open-EDI for implementation.

45 ISO family of standards ISO/IEC 11179, base standard ISO/IEC 11179-1:2023, Information technology – Metadata registries (MDR) Part 1: Framework.

46 ISO family of standards ISO/IEC 13249, base standard ISO/IEC 13249-2:2003, Information technology – Database languages – SQL multimedia and application packages.

47 Especially the family of standards ISO/IEC 11580: Information technology – Framework for describing user interface objects, actions and attributes.

objective is to ensure universal standards for interfaces, notably by including requirements for accessibility[48] and cultural and linguistic adaptability.

Its scope is so clear that it requires no further explanation: <Standardization in the field of user-system interfaces in ICT environments and support for these interfaces to serve all users, including people having accessibility or other specific needs, with a priority of meeting the JTC 1 requirements for cultural and linguistic adaptability.

This includes:

– user interface accessibility (requirements, needs, methods, techniques and enablers);

– cultural and linguistic adaptability and accessibility (such as evaluation of cultural and linguistic adaptability of ICT products, harmonized human language equivalents, localization parameters, voice messaging menus);

– user interface objects, actions and attributes;

– methods and technologies for controlling and navigating within systems, devices and applications in visual, auditory, tactile and other sensorial modalities (such as by voice, vision, movement and gestures);

– symbols, functionality and interactions of user interfaces (such as graphical, tactile and auditory icons, graphical symbols and other user interface elements);

– visual, auditory, tactile and other sensorial input and output devices and methods in ICT environments (for devices such as keyboards, displays, mice);

– user interfaces for mobile devices, hand-held devices and remote interactions.>

5.5. JTC 1/SC 36: information technology for learning, education and training

JTC 1/SC 36 was created in 1999. Its scope, which has evolved greatly, is presently as follows: <Standardization in the field of information

48 Especially the family of standards ISO/IEC 13066: Information technology – Interoperability with assistive technology and ISO/IEC 30150-1:2022: Information technology – Affective computing user interface (AUI), Part 1: model.

technologies for learning, education and training to support individuals, groups or organizations, and to enable interoperability and reusability of resources and tools.

Excluded from this scope are:

– standards or technical reports that define educational standards (competencies), cultural conventions, learning objectives or specific learning content;

– work done by other ISO or IEC TCs, SCs or WGs with respect to their component, specialty or domain. Instead, when appropriate, normative or informative references to other standards shall be included. Examples include documents on special topics such as multimedia, web content, cultural adaptation and security.>

The proposal for a JTC 1 subcommittee dedicated to technologies for teaching and training first came from the pioneering industrialists who had already developed the IEEE's earliest standards for computer-based teaching systems (software tools as well as components) for very specific clients: aircraft manufacturers (Aviation Industry CBT Committee (AICC)); arms manufacturers, buyers and users; and highly innovative universities. Further, it was largely for these applications that computer-based training (CBT) was developed in the 1980s.

And if aviation has today become a safe mode of transport, it is entirely due to the systematic standardization in this field: quality control in aircraft manufacturing, services, equipment and ground infrastructure; training of pilots, crew, air traffic controllers, ground staff, maintenance professionals, etc. Unlike many other sectors of activity in which mechanical failure or human error is admissible, aviation cannot tolerate the smallest failure, nor the slightest error. The market for these activities depends on their absolute safety, and in order to preserve the global aviation market, the standardization of training techniques in all these domains is absolutely essential. Further, the education and training requirements in the defense sector were the same as for aircraft manufacturers, but they were much more interdisciplinary in nature both in terms of training as well as imparting a wider range of knowledge for commanding officers: war games and strategy, for example.

From the beginning, CBT has been closely associated with technical documentation (produced in SGML since the 1960s), which was a major source of pedagogic resources. Three major actors had anticipated the creation of standards in this domain: the AICC, IEEE and Advanced Distributed (or Defense) Learning (ADL), which reports to the Defense Human Resources Activity (DHRA). In 1988, the AICC was first founded by Boeing, Airbus and McDonnell Douglas for the shared development of standardized CBT content and tools. Their first recommendations, published in 1989, related to IT platforms for CBT training media. In 1993, the AICC published guidelines for interoperability in learning management systems (LMS). This initial LMS standard was meant for local interaction with a CD-ROM and in 1998, the standardized specification was improved to add a web interface. The ADl was closely associated with this standardization and development work.

The pioneering promoters of advanced CBT systems were naturally keen on growing their market by proposing to JTC 1 that they develop standards for the entire teaching and training community. There were obvious advantages to this. These standards would allow (1) a worldwide reduction in the cost of education and training, a social need that some countries in the Global South struggled to afford; (2) allowing remote learning (a requirement in countries with very low population densities); (3) maintaining records of the training and education processes, which made it possible to improve evaluation and progress; (4) facilitating self-study, especially at home.

This NWI, which was proposed, was clearly a good project for JTC 1 to undertake. The IEEE was in charge of formalizing the proposal, which was discussed and then adopted, leading to the creation of SC 36 in the JTC 1 plenary session of 1999. The first SC 36 meeting was held in London in March 2000.

Initially, the United States had believed that this was a highly strategic project for the United States. ANSI was in charge of the secretariat and its chair, Frank Farance, was American. In early 2001, the French delegate from Airbus Training, who would go on to be the president of the AICC, predicted the rapid generalization of aeronautic training, which was largely offered on the Web. Unfortunately, he was only too correct. All the kamikaze pilots on September 11, 2001, had trained online, and 9/11 ended America's need to head SC 36. The Americans continued to support the development of these standards, but they prevented standardized interoperability from posing any risks to them.

The BSI and then KATS were successively in charge of the SC 36 secretariat. Another American, Bruce E. Peoples (Raytheon Technologies), was elected as chair in 2003. He was succeeded by Erlend Øverby (Norway) in 2012 and Jon Mason (Australia) in 2020.

As is often the case in other TCs or SCs as well, the first years were spent in bringing all the delegates, from very disparate cultures[49], onto the same page. The fact that the plenary sessions of SC 36 and IEEE[50] were always organized at the same time, every 6 months, made it difficult for industrialists (who could afford to attend both sessions) to work cohesively with the expert-pedagogists, who could often only afford to attend the SC 36 plenary session. This made it hard to put in place the working culture that is essential for consensus-building. Certain experts, who were more educators than technologists, and who had not participated in the IEEE's plenary sessions, felt that they were being forced to accept technical standards that often seemed to them wrong and unsuited to their specific requirements. It is true that the social sciences and literary studies are not necessarily taught in the same manner as engineering sciences, physics or aviation training. However, the fundamentals of education sciences could lead to a consensus being built. There were definite pedagogic styles: behaviorist, constructivist, cognitive, lectures or active and collaborative methods. The basic models and pedagogic resources used by various actors were largely shared by all. Online teaching was clearly most beneficial in blended form (like a blended whisky) – alternating between in-person teaching and remote classes.

49 SC 36 was the other exception, in addition to from JTC 1/SC 2, which required a large number of experts from the social sciences (linguists, paleographists, historians of printing, etc.). SC 36 had experts specializing in CBT alongside specialists or practitioners in the field of pedagogy.

50 The IEEE Learning Technology Standards Committee.

One example of a liaison: the liaison of SC 36 with Agence Universitaire de la Francophonie (AUG)

Although not well known, the role of an SC or TC liaison is essential for preserving inter-coherence, the technical specialization exclusive to the subject of standardization, as well as for contributing to the construction of standards that respond better to the needs of the outside world. There are broadly two or three categories of liaisons:

– *Internal liaisons between committees or subcommittees*, ensuring that interactions and areas of overlap between committees are documented, especially to prevent reinventing the wheel and to prevent the development of standardization processes that diverge from those that already exist or are being developed. These liaisons are formally considered internal liaisons when they are between two committees within the same standardization organization (here, internal to JTC 1). However, it is clear that liaisons with other standardization organizations can be compared to internal liaisons: among others, liaisons between TCs or SCs in the ISO, IEC or ITU.

– *External liaisons with other organizations concerned or already involved in standardization*. These may be scholarly societies or professional societies, centers of research, associations of engineers (IEEE, for example), NGOs or similar bodies, or organizations as diverse as the AICC, Dublin Core Metadata Initiative, etc. In 2025, SC 36 had 16 liaisons with other standardization bodies, *stricto sensu*[51]. SC 36 has four active category A liaisons – 1EdTech Consortium[52]; AUF; the International Information Centre for Terminology (Infoterm)[53]; and IEEE/LTSC – and one category C liaison: the e-Assessment Association (eAA)[54].

---

51 Including a liaison directly established with JTC 1 and eight other liaisons with other SCs in JTC 1: SC 24, SC 27, SC 32, SC 34, SC 35, SC 41, SC 42 and SC 43. Seven other liaisons were activated with TCs in the ISO, including ISO/SC 37 (terminology and linguistic resources) and ISO/SC 46 (documentation).

52 *Liaison A*: organizations making an effective contribution to the TC or SC's work on the questions under consideration. *Liaison B*: unique to governmental organizations wishing to be kept informed of a TC or SC's work. *Liaison C*: organizations making technical contributions and participating fully in the work of a WG.

53 The 1EdTech community brings together leaders from the field of primary, secondary and higher education and suppliers of educational technology. They have committed to creating an open, reliable and innovative digital learning ecosystem.

54 eAA is a professional British organization that promises better evaluation of knowledge, skills and individual capacities through the use of technology.

A liaison does not have the same status as an active member, but that of an observer member within the delegations. When delegates are welcomed at a plenary session of a TC or an SC, all the delegates and the head of the delegations review all national bodies and liaisons (NBLOs). These are the only two categories that are considered during a plenary session. However, the NBs can vote according to the formula "1 vote per NB" while the liaisons are only allowed consultative votes[55]. Often, if there is a lengthy and inconclusive debate, experts stop listening to anyone other than their own camp. Thus, a neutral expert from a liaison can allow the group to arrive at a consensus. As a result, expert opinions from liaisons are highly respected. After a long selection process, the AUF became a category A liaison of the ISO, considering their contributions to SC 36's standard production.

This has, on several occasions, created opportunities for fresh proposals and to bring in active help in consensus-building and protecting minority positions. Of course, in this context, AUF's category A liaison has actively defended the interests of the Francophone world. Thus, as a delegate from the AUF and thanks to his skills, Mokhtar Ben Henda (Bordeaux Montaigne University) became (and continues to be, as of 2025) the *convenor* of SC 36/WG 1, dedicated to terminology. He was able to get the group to accept an onomasiological, and non-semasiological, method that we believe conforms better with the standards of ISO/TC 37 and is especially well-suited for the multilingual terminology used in digital media in education. The AUF liaison also made it possible to defend the idea, which was poorly perceived by certain Francophone activities, that the ISO's official trilingualism (English, French, Russian) need not be systematic. Thus, if a small group of experts (where there are as many different first languages as there are participants) speak to each other, they use new concepts, designated by acronyms for ease of use – and following the earlier logic, these would then have to be expressed in at least three different languages. Thankfully, this is not the case. On the other hand, we have fought for essential standards, such as those produced by SC 36, to be translated into French, and also into other languages that make up or are associated with the French-speaking regions of the world (e.g. Arabic and Vietnamese). But we have always resisted a pointless imposition of Francophonie for the sake of it.

Box 5.5. *A liaison's impact on standardization*

55 Except in more technical instances, such as WGs, where the whole delegation (NB or liaison) participating in the debates will vote with equal votes.

In 2000, three WGs were proposed: (1) SC 36/WG 1 dedicated to vocabulary, (2) WG 2 dedicated to collaborative technology and (3) WG 3 dedicated to learner information[56]. Following this, WG 4 and WG 5 were created in 2002. WG 4 was dedicated to management and delivery of learning, education and training, while WG 5 focused on quality assurance and descriptive frameworks. In 2006, WG 6 was given the responsibility of international standardized profiles and WG 7 focused on culture, language and human functioning. Over the next two decades, other WGs were created. Some of these WGs have evolved in scope and had a change of name, while others have sometimes been dissolved to form Advisory Groups (AGs), which are less autonomous but more agile and able to carry out the common standardizing work of SC 36. We thus have SC 36/AG 2, Emerging technologies (AGET); SC 36/AHG 5, Blockchain in education; and SC 36/AG 6, Artificial intelligence for education (AIEd).

As of 2025, SC 36 had five active WGs: WG 3, Learner information; WG 4 Management and delivery; WG 7, ITLET – culture, language and individual needs; WG 8, Learning analytics interoperability; and WG 9, Online course information model[57]. Two broad families of standards published by SC 36 are particularly of interest: ISO/IEC 19788 and ISO/IEC 20006[58].

JTC 1/SC 37, Biometrics, was founded in 2002 and was the final SC created in the second round of SC creation within JTC 1.

Its scope is: <Standardization of generic biometric technologies pertaining to human beings to support interoperability and data interchange among applications and systems. Generic human biometric standards include: common file frameworks; biometric application programming interfaces; biometric data interchange formats; related biometric profiles; application of evaluation criteria to biometric technologies; methodologies

56 And it was soon suggested that the terminology be jointly developed in French and English, with other languages soon getting added (first Japanese, Korean and Chinese). While these were non-official ISO languages, they were additionally informative publishing languages.

57 A WG that prepares the development of standards for specific requirements (based on country or territory) for culture, languages and individual education needs (disabilities, geographic isolation, nomadic life, etc.).

58 The family of standards ISO/IEC 19788: Information technology for learning, education and training – Part 8: Metadata for learning resources and ISO/IEC 20006: Information technology for learning, education and training – Information model for competency.

for performance testing and reporting and cross jurisdictional and societal aspects. Excluded is the work in ISO/IEC JTC 1/SC 17 to apply biometric technologies to cards and personal identification.

Excluded is the work in ISO/IEC JTC 1/SC 27 for biometric data protections techniques, biometric security testing, evaluations and evaluations methodologies.>

The principal objective of SC 37 is the authentication of personal data, the prevention of identity theft and automatic border control. Its standards collection of human biometric indicators[59] is systematically cross-verified with biometric cards standardized by SC 17.

5.6. The third round of SCs created within JTC 1: 2009–2013

The third round of SC creation began 7 years after the end of the second round. This round also corresponded with a major evolution in the Internet world, marked by the emergence and rise in power of Big Tech.

The goal, therefore, was to establish standards that make it possible to offer alternatives to the dominant models in a context where information and communication escape all regulation. This round of SC creation chiefly aimed to restore downstream control over these new ICTs, so that they could be easily integrated into high-value professional and institutional applications. It also took into account the environmental challenges related to data centers.

JTC 1/SC 38, Cloud computing and distributed platforms, offers an evaluation and standardization system for cloud computing.

This makes it possible to establish a regulated cloud, as opposed to the unregulated paid or free services that are offered by default to general users. SC 38 concentrates on standardizing secure and manageable cloud computing, responding to the needs of demanding clients, such as online

59 For instance: ISO/IEC TR 29195: 2015: Traveler processes for biometric recognition in automated border control systems. Or, more precisely: ISO/IEC 29109-6: 2011: Conformance testing methodology for biometric data interchange formats defined in ISO/IEC 19794 Part 6: Iris image data.

administration, online health, as well as critical applications (such as self-driving cars). The JTC 1 hypothesis is that this standardization will lead to a rapid decrease in costs, which will then promote a large-scale rollout of these solutions to the general public. The goal is to propose standards that facilitate the development of services at attractive prices, encouraging users to no longer depend only on GAFAM[60] (Google, Amazon, Facebook (now Meta) Apple and Microsoft).

Its scope is: <Standardization in the areas of cloud computing and distributed platforms including:

– foundational concepts and technologies;

– operational issues;

– interactions among cloud computing systems and with other distributed systems.

SC 38 serves as the focus, proponent and systems integration entity on cloud computing, distributed platforms and the application of these technologies. SC 38 provides guidance to JTC 1, IEC, ISO and other entities developing standards in these areas.>

JTC 1/SC 39 includes sustainability, IT and data centers. It was founded in 2012. Its principal objective is to maintain a committee of experts within JTC 1 who are in charge of proposing standardization methods for sustainable energy management, especially with respect to data centers[61]. The standardization and control of energy consumption has been a top priority for IEC from the beginning[62]. However, its competencies often clash with those of energy experts in the fossil fuel sector. The brief existence of ISO/IEC JTC 2, dedicated to energy, further illustrates the extreme conflicts in this domain.

The scope of SC 39 is: <Standardization of assessment methods, design practices, operation and management aspects to support resource efficiency,

---

60 For example: ISO/IEC 22123- 3:2023: Cloud computing. Part 3: Reference architecture.

61 For example: ISO/IEC 30134-6:2021: Data centers key performance indicators. Part 6: Energy Reuse Factor (ERF). The ERF score ranges from 0 (no reuse) to 1 (total reuse of energy.

62 The earliest electrical equipment was not as efficient as at present. It would heat up and damage installations.

resilience and environmental sustainability for and by information technology, data centers and other facilities and infrastructure necessary for service provisioning.

To avoid any duplication of work and to support innovation, SC 39 will engage in active liaison and collaboration with:

– other JTC1 entities;

– ISO TC 207, ISO TC 242, ISO TC 257;

– IEC TC 100, IEC TC 111, IEC PC 118, SMB SG 4, IEC/TC 57/WG 2 and IEC/TC 9

– ITU-T SG 5;

– any other appropriate body including external organizations (e.g. consortia).>

JTC 1/SC 40, IT service management and IT governance, was created in 2013.

Its scope is: <Standardization in:

– governance of IT;

– governance of data;

– IT service management;

– IT enabled services – business process outsourcing

Serving as the focal point in these areas, SC 40 communicates, co-operates and collaborates with relevant committees (such as cybersecurity and privacy), external bodies and other stakeholders on topics of mutual interest.>

Its role is specified as follows on the JTC 1 website:

> The current digital age combined with shifting political and economic power has produced a steady stream of innovative technologies and unpredictable ways of conducting business. Business operations are conducted in a data rich environment

> via a complex system of service provision. The governance and management of these arrangements is critical for success, survival and competitive advantage. Our standards provide governance and management guidance to businesses of all sizes on how to benefit from rapid technological advances and live up to the changing expectations of people in the digital world[63].

JTC 1/SC 41, Internet of Things and digital twin, was the last in this third round of SC creation within JTC 1. At the time of its creation in 2013, it inherited the work program of two WGs that were directly attached to JTC 1: JTC 1/WG 7 (sensor networks)[64] and JTC 1/WG 10 (Internet of Things). SC 41 is a perfect illustration of JTC 1's governance strategy, which, for over a decade, has consisted of deferring the establishment of new SCs by first placing them under the direct management of the JTC 1 central bureau. This mode of functioning made it possible to officially integrate them later when a favorable context presented itself[65].

The scope of SC 41 is as follows: <ISO/IEC JTC 1/SC 41 is being supported administratively by IEC. All information related to ISO/IEC JTC 1/SC 41 is available on the IEC website: standardization in the area of Internet of Things and related technologies.

1) Serve as the focus and proponent for JTC 1's standardization program on the Internet of Things and Digital Twin, including their related technologies.

2) Provide guidance to JTC 1, IEC, ISO and other entities developing Internet of Things and Digital Twin–related applications.>

5.7. The fourth round of SCs created within JTC 1: 2017–2025

The founding of the last three SCs in JTC 1 began 4 years after the third round concluded. This break in the creation of new SCs was due to the policy of testing SCs, as was mentioned in the case of SC 41.

---

63 See: https://committee.iso.org/home/jtc1sc40.

64 For example, the standard: ISO/IEC 30101:2014: Sensor networks: Sensor network and its interfaces for smart grid system.

65 See the details at the end of this chapter.

JTC 1/SC 42, artificial intelligence, was created in 2017. Its scope is defined as: <Standardization in the area of artificial intelligence:

– serves as the focus and proponent for JTC 1's standardization program on artificial intelligence;

– provides guidance to JTC 1, IEC and ISO committees developing artificial intelligence applications>[66].

As of March 2025, SC 42 had already published 34 standards[67], while 40 others were underway. Here is an extract from its marketing document ("Prospective Vision of SC 42: 'Why Artificial Intelligence Needs Standards'"):

> Artificial intelligence (AI) is an enabling horizontal technology. Many industry experts and analysts believe that the rapid growth in AI will enable the next digital transformation. While the field of AI is not new, an international standards committee looking at the entire AI ecosystem is a recent development. To better understand why standards are important for AI, it is helpful to identify the diverse stakeholders involved, which include research, academia, industry, practitioners, policy makers, ethics advocates and more. Moreover, there are many different application areas of AI technology, for example, consumer, industrial and commercial amongst others. Regarding the industrial sector, IT is becoming more pervasive in the various industry verticals, including manufacturing, healthcare, robotics, and financial[68].

JTC 1/SC 43, Brain–computer interfaces, was created in 2022. Its scope is as follows: <ISO/IEC JTC 1/SC 43 is being supported administratively by IEC. All information related to ISO/IEC JTC 1/SC 43 is available on the IEC website.

66 In May 2024, the scope stated: <SC 42 has put in place a large number of WGs that will initially study the technical, economic, social, and ethical aspects of various standardization strategies and then structure the future organization of SC 42>.

67 For example: ISO/IEC 23053:2022: Framework for artificial intelligence (AI) systems using machine learning (ML).

68 See: https://jtc1info.org/technology/subcommittees/ai/.

Standardization in the area of brain–computer interfaces for information technology to enable communication and interaction between brains and computers that are applicable across application areas:

– serves as the focus and proponent for JTC 1's standardization program on brain–computer interfaces, including the development of foundational standards;

– provides guidance on brain–computer interfaces to JTC 1, IEC, ISO and other entities developing applications of BCI.

Excluded: standards for human implants and medical applications.>

The first standardization project was to define terminology. This was ISO/IEC CD 8663: Brain–computer interfaces: vocabulary. <This document specifies the terms and definitions commonly used in the field of brain–computer interface (BCI), including basic concepts and classifications of BCI, hardware, experiment setups and protocols used in BCI, related neuroscience concepts of BCI (e.g. coding and decoding, feedback and stimulation) and its applications.>

JTC 1/SC 44 includes consumer protection in the field of privacy by design. Its scope is as follows: <Standardization of consumer protection in the field of privacy by design for products, goods and services, including their data lifecycles.>

The decision to create this new committee was taken during the November 2024 plenary session of JTC 1 and this SC could become a key part of the rebuilding[69] of a standardized digital space that guarantees an ordinary user complete protection of their data, built into the design of platforms and software that comply with this institutional standard[70].

---

69 The term "rebuilding" with regard to a digital space with new standards is deliberately used. Given GAFAM's misuse of our personal data and software, it is important to rebuild a common, shared and secure digital space, negotiated in a collegial manner and representative of techno-cultural diversities. The increasing data breaches, year after year, not only affect individuals but a growing number of organizations and State-run bodies. It is, therefore, valid to believe in this rebuilding and, at the very least, establish an alternative technological offering, whose credibility comes from being officially standardized.

70 Two groups of standards, ISO 31700-1 and 2:2023, are at the public consultation stage: Consumer protection – Privacy by design for consumer goods and services Part 1: High-level requirements. Part 2: Use cases.

Privacy by design is not a new concept. It was first formulated in 2009 by Cavoukian (2009) following a collaboration with the Dutch Data Protection Authority and the Netherlands Organisation for Applied Scientific Research. After 1995, it was integrated into the ISO through ISO/PC 317, a committee that was dedicated to the study of this problem, founded in 2018. This particular standard is a major challenge that will be explored in greater detail in Chapter 6.

5.8. Working groups attached directly to JTC 1

JTC 1 is a one-of-a-kind TC that takes on technical, economic, strategic and complex social challenges. Given these challenges, its governance is far more sophisticated than other TCs in the ISO that deal with more manageable domains. Although it is jointly managed by the ISO and the IEC, it functions almost autonomously and single handedly produces around 20% of ISO's new standards every year. In close to 40 years, what was once a single TC with a constellation of around 10 SCs has become a central organization in the regulation of neo-industrial technologies.

Several groups of experts were directly attached to the JTC's central leadership. They are a special guard that allows the leadership to take clear and rational decisions:

– advisory groups in JTC 1 (JTC 1/AG);

– special WGs in JTC 1 (SGW);

– WGs directly attached to JTC 1's central leadership.

These groups produce documents, formulate recommendations and can evolve into new entities, or even into SCs. This adaptive process reflects JTC 1's ability to guide technological evolution. Thus, although the governance of JTC 1 is similar to that of the ISO or IEC, the fact remains that the ISO (and sometimes the IEC) has a TMB, ultimate editorial control and control over the distribution of standards. Rather than examining the functioning of specific WGs in detail, it would be more helpful to illustrate their impact through a few significant examples.

One of the most interesting is, undoubtedly, JTC 1/AG 2: Emerging technology and innovation (JETI). Its scope is comprehensive and clear: <JETI is mandated to seek opportunities to facilitate JTC 1 standards development for future emerging and innovation technologies with following terms of reference (ToR):

1) assess the opportunities addressing evolving ICT business needs;

2) assess the technology opportunities to identify the relevant standardization issues and priorities that warrant immediate action and those that should be watched for potential consideration later by JTC 1;

3) emphasize reaching out and incorporating input from outside of JTC 1 such as verticals (e.g. financial services and health care);

4) monitor the future considerations from JTC 1 SCs/WGs/AGs (e.g. through their business plans, and/or other alternative information sources) to perform successful execution of standards development and planning with an appropriate coordination in JTC 1;

5) make recommendations on actions to the JTC 1;

6) review and make suggestions to revise SD 4 as appropriate.>

Another key group is JTC 1/AG 14: Systems integration facilitation (SIF), created in 2016. Its role is to leverage JTC 1 expertise and take advantage of the systems integration standardization to meet increasingly complex market needs. The complexity of technologies and their convergence in many new and emerging markets now requires a top-down approach to standardization, starting with a system or system architecture, rather than a product. Increasingly, sectors such as environment, energy, safety and health need system standards rather than standards applicable only to products.

Let us also look at the former JTC 1/AG 16, Brain–computer interfaces, which was dissolved in November 2021 to give way to the present-day SC.

JTC 1/AG 19: along with ISO/TC 20/SC 16, this AG is in charge of coordination in unmanned aircraft systems (UAS). Its goal is to ensure the interoperability of standards for technologies associated with these systems.

And, finally, let us again recall JTC 1/WG 11: Smart cities and WG 12: 3D printing and scanning[71]. There is also JTC 1/WG 15, in charge of JTC 1 vocabulary, created in 2022 to coordinate the development of terminology used in the various SCs under JTC 1.

71 Which is studied in Chapter 6.

6

Consortium Standards and Standardization

At the end of the 20th century, the increase in consortia founded by IT professionals had significantly modified standardization practices. This was not an accidental phenomenon, but the result of the IT world's specific technoculture, which distinguished it from other professions. This included the specific features of electronics and mass media (TV and radio), which were not yet digital at the time. By construction, the tools and main materials available to computer scientists were formal languages, different from natural languages. Natural languages are flexible, rich in polysemy and analogies[1], while computing languages require strict standardization. Consequently, professionals who designed platforms, networks protocols and computing languages had to develop a globalized professional culture with standardization being an intrinsic part of daily life.

Traditional industry was also aware of the importance of standards, which were essential for mass production, modularity, and intercompatibility of products on a global scale. However, their approach to standardization was a long-term process, where the definition of standards took months or even years. This timeframe was completely transformed by the arrival of information technology in the decade from 1970 to 1980. Unlike manufactured products, software and network development relied on intrinsically reactive digital hardware, although designing this hardware required a significant investment in terms of time and human resources.

---

1 This allows mutual understanding between speakers who may not have the same semantic references.

Given this dynamic, computer scientists tended to favor alternative collegial standardization bodies, such as the Internet consortia (W3C) and Unicode, over conventional institutional standardization[2]. This choice, arising from the need to innovate outside the box, was encouraged by large multinationals in this sector. Unlike traditional industry, which tended to converse on unified standards after a phase of innovation, these companies supported digital spaces that were open but largely designed for professionals. It was only the Web that was aimed at the general public.

The consequences of this heterodox approach to consortium standardization of the digital space are evident today: open standards were misused by GAFAM+, whose economic models are based on the massive use (or misuse) of personal data. This data theft by design has allowed these companies to monopolize the benefits of online commerce and exercise unprecedented levels of influence over social and cognitive behaviors.

As we saw in Chapter 5, JTC 1 responded to this by creating several new SCs, especially SC 44, to restore confidence in the institutional and international standardization process. Thanks to these JTC 1 standards, actors who are concerned about data security and labeling of their products and services can benefit from certified and standardized solutions. States have also become aware of this situation, especially in Europe, while public opinion is gradually catching up. While it is true that GAFAM+ dominate the market today, there are alternatives that are emerging.

Internet consortia were initially exceptional drivers of innovation. The emergence of transfer protocols and packet switching completely disrupted the technoculture in the telecommunications sector, which had until then been regulated by the ITU. Because of support from multinationals, academic research centers and military establishments (like ARPA), a transnational community of researchers and engineers could work together to create an open global digital space, built around collaborative standards. Three key factors facilitated this technocultural revolution:

– pre-existing infrastructure at a national and international level;

2 Their impatience with the slow pace of the de jure standardization processes is the main reason for this.

– an electronics industry that could provide affordable (and institutionally standardized!) equipment;

– a digital space that was accessible to all.

It was in this context that the best experts came together in various consortia and created the Internet. These pioneers created the Internet Society, promoting technologies without patents and favoring an open model that could benefit everyone:

– multinationals, which financed these low-cost initiatives;

– industrialists in the electronics field, who anticipated the market growth;

– countries that wished to remain competitive against American domination.

This model of working gradually replaced conventional standardization, establishing de facto standards that competed with de jure standards. Computing science, including the definition of standards, captivated the general public in an unprecedented way, eclipsing other amateur hobbies like the radio or building models. However, for many decades now, too many *consortium standards*, and especially those in the Internet world, have been hugely misused by their sponsors, to the detriment of the users.

This chapter examines the impacts of these changes by studying the consortia that have remained faithful to their founding principles[3], as well as academic consortia within the social sciences, digital humanities and open archives.

Finally, we analyze the reaction of standardization bodies, States and civil society to the inequalities created by GAFAM+, who have exploited these consortia for *global data theft*[4], influencing data as well as minds.

---

3 With the exception of the risks of being misused by their sponsors, especially for AI and machine translation, Unicode seems to remain true to its mission and ethics.

4 From a legal point of view, we cannot use the term *misuse*, strictly speaking. GAFAM+ ensure there is a *return on investment* (however exorbitant) on their initial investments. However, the magnitude of resource appropriation that they carry out is similar to *monopolization*, which is an offence committed by multiple countries.

Consortium: a terminological note

Contrary to popular opinion, a consortium is not, in itself, a legal entity. A consortium is a group formed to carry out activities beyond the resources of any one member. It has no status as a legal entity, but works cooperatively to carry out economic, financial, scientific or cultural operations: purchases, research projects or, of interest to us, standardization. The entities that participate in a consortium can pool together resources but are only liable for the obligations specified in the consortium agreement. Everything depends on agreements between members, who specify, if required, the terms of the activity, its duration and contributions of participants. In practice, a consortium officializes cooperation and strengthens confidence in a structure that may not yet have a clearly established legal basis[5].

Box 6.1. *Judicial definition of a consortium*

6.1. Unicode: standardization of writing systems from around the world

Let us start with a seemingly simple question: What is the difference between the domain of standardization of the subcommittee JTC 1/SC 2 and the Unicode consortium?

As we saw in Chapter 5, the standardization of character codes for all writing systems (ISO/IEC 10646) was jointly carried out by the Unicode consortium and JTC 1/SC 2. Similarly, the Unicode consortium (among others) is the registering authority for the ISO standard 15924 (writing codes) on behalf of ISO/TC 46: Information and documentation[6].

However, beyond participating in the de jure standardization of these references, Unicode also contributed in a way that is unique to them: they

5 It goes without saying that while Unicode, the ISOC and the W3C are consortia founded on formally registered structures, they are legal entities and not-for-profit organizations.

6 ISO/TC 46 had already standardized a two-letter code, then three-letter codes, to designate languages. The standard ISO 15924, managed by Unicode, then introduced a four-letter code, supplementing the earlier codes in order to respond to the more specific requirements of terminology, lexicography, bibliography, linguistics and the vast heritage libraries that are digitizing texts in ancient writing systems (cuneiform, hieroglyphs, etc.).

invented, developed and standardized a whole set of techno-digital characters that was unpatented, allowing rigorous interoperability between all writing systems in the world, current or past. This framework also includes other categories of writing that are not strictly linguistic, such as musical notations (including ancient notations), calculation systems, scientific and technical formulas and emoticons. All these activities were made possible thanks to active collaboration between Unicode members, whether individuals, institutions or companies.

In Chapter 5, we already mentioned the pioneering founders of Unicode, such as Joe Becker and Lee Collins of Xerox and Mark Davis from Apple, working together with the CJK[7] group. The project was first displayed on an Apple computer, modified to function with 16 bits: the Xerox Star (1981). This machine made it possible to simultaneously manage 27 languages, including Japanese, Chinese and English. This was Unicode's birth certificate.

6.2. Partnerships and organization of projects within Unicode

As with other consortia that were founded with the aim of structuring digital space, Unicode was able to organize a partnership made up of large multinationals (chiefly GAFAM+), research centers and NGOs invested in interlinguistic challenges.

They also maintained close relations with global standardization organizations, with whom they actively collaborate. Finally, their partnerships are based on a network of experts. The Unicode consortium is a not-for-profit organization bringing together members from various countries and sectors, including suppliers, national or international organizations, as well as academic and professional institutions[8]. Founded in 1988, it was legally constituted in 1991. Its aim is to produce open source standards, develop data catalogues and design software. The essential point to note: standardization bodies, *stricto sensu*, must never directly supply products or services. Unicode is a perfect illustration of how consortia can act as intermediaries between companies, who have a competitive edge

7 CJK: Chinese, Japanese, Korean. See section 5.1.2 for JTC 1/SC 2.

8 The following pages (governance, work structure and deontology) adapt and include extracts from the Unicode site: https://home.unicode.org/about-unicode/.

thanks to their confidential internal standards or patents, and de jure standardization organizations.

Even before Unicode was founded, the pioneers in this field had seen the need for a balanced discussion, taking into account both the commercial challenges as well as respecting subtle linguistic and cultural nuances within each language. The founders soon included detailed rules regarding voting and functioning in their statutes, along with a concrete charter, which was essential in guaranteeing the durability of their initial project. Unicode thus reflects the importance accorded to large IT multinationals, who were the earliest to develop software with multilingual support and a software environment that was able to process all writing systems and the languages associated with these[9].

6.2.1. *Members and their role*

Unicode has over 30 member organizations, among which are companies, corporate organizations, university organizations and governmental organizations. Several hundred professionals, experts working on a voluntary basis and linguists also contribute as individual members. The consortium is financed through member subscriptions and donations. The collegial structure is complex and there is highly sophisticated voting during debates. All of it is based on a hierarchy of members (companies, organizations, liaisons and individual experts, with or without voting rights: full vote, half vote and then consultative votes (the latter are differentially taken into account depending on the economic influence or competence, evaluated based on the seniority and influence of experts). Its system of governance is based on an explicit hierarchy of member categories:

1) Members with the right to vote, one vote per member:

– *Full members* (eight companies): Airbnb, Amazon, Apple, Google, Meta, Microsoft, Salesforce (specialized in client relations software in the Cloud) and Translated SRL (translation multinational).

– *Supporting members* (half vote): Bloomberg, Stanford Silicon Advancing Digitally Disadvantaged Languages (a Stanford University

9 This distinction is a fundamental one and Latin scripts are a perfect illustration of the multiple languages that use it, most of these languages having different rules of writing.

initiative for the preservation and inclusion of languages), the Tamil Virtual Academy and UC Berkeley.

2) Influential members without voting rights:

– *Associate members* (11 organizations).

– *Industry partners and media* (three organizations).

– *Technological liaisons*: Unicode maintains relations with key entities such as JTC 1/SC 2, ISO/TC 37/SC 2 (Terminology Workflow and Language Coding), OASIS, IETF, W3C and ISO/TC 46 (Information and documentation). There are also specific collaborations for languages such as Vietnamese, Cherokee, Gaelic, Tamil, Breton, Sinhalese, Mongol and various Chinese languages (24 liaison organizations in total).

– *Individual members* (March 2025): 208 experts, whose influence varies based on seniority and experience, following a subtle gradation that prioritizes the most experienced members (81 lifetime members).

6.2.2. *The technical organization of work*

Unicode distributes work over three TCs:

1) *Unicode technical committee (UTC)*: responsible for the development and maintenance of the Unicode standard, as well as the Unicode character database (in coordination with JTC 1/SC 2). This TC manages reports and technical standards. It is divided into five WGs:

– WG on standards and research on emojis;

– WG on coding of scripts[10];

– CJK and Unihan WG;

– WG on properties and algorithms;

– editorial WG: responsible for technical specifications, graphics and open source data for companies and communities around the world.

2) *Common Locale Data Repository technical committee (TC-CLDR)*: a reference for local data and software localization standards. It is estimated

10 Scripts standardize *word processors* (software) conforming to the rules governing the arrangement of characters within a text in each writing system.

that there are around 6,000 languages spoken today around the world, as well as many writing systems. However, there are certain specific characteristics that have not yet been coded. The CLDR is a digital archive that is regularly updated, making available scriptural elements that have already been arranged and codified to interlinguistic processing systems. It is a software suite that is capable of taking charge of all languages of the world.

3) *International Components for Unicode technical committee (TC-ICU)*: thanks to ICU, all users with interscript needs, whether simple or complex, have access to free-to-use software solutions. They can also choose integrated solutions offered by companies. TC-ICU notably takes charge of:

– conversion of pages of codes;

– classification: comparing character strings based on convention and linguistic norms, regional or national[11];

– the formatting of numbers, dates, hours and currencies based on pre-defined regional parameters by integrating multiple types of calendars;

– the processing of bidirectional texts (Bidi, Bidirectional Display): managing texts combining writing systems that write from left to right and from right to left;

– managing text boundaries: the positioning of words, phrases and paragraphs within the text, as well as the detection of sites that are appropriate for line breaks.

6.2.3. *Deontology*

On its website, Unicode lays out two fundamental values underpinning its deontology: confidentiality and consensus.

However, as with other consortia associated with the Internet, Unicode runs the risk of its work being misused, especially with artificial intelligence.

---

11 Focusing on the Latin script alone, the question of how to alphabetically classify accentuated letters (é, à, ô, etc.), letters with a diacritical marks (Ø, Đ, Đ, etc.) and letters with ligatures (Œ, Æ, ß, etc.) is a highly complex one and has seen multiple historical, linguistic and national variations based on the professional habitus of the intended users of this classification: dictionaries, indexes, directories, etc. (see: https://knowledge.exlibrisgroup.com/Alma/Product_Documentation/).

Secure coding for domain names: Punycode

The question of internationalizing domain names had not been foreseen in the first few decades of the Internet. However, Unicode had already made it possible to codify all writing systems in the world, and it would have been logical to apply this coding to domain names. This would have allowed speakers of Chinese, Arabic, Thai and any other language to navigate and create sites using their own writing systems. Nonetheless, it was only in 2010 that country names (first-level domains) could be coded in their national writing systems. This evolution responded to two needs: (1) ensuring compatibility with address tables created by ICANN; (2) avoiding any ambiguity in the shape of characters that could result in serious errors.

Punycode was a coding defined by RFC 3492 of the IETF (ISOC), designed to prevent malicious attacks.

> Malicious attacks exploit visually similar characteristics of different writing systems. For example, a Latin "t" could be replaced by a Greek "τ"[12]. The user finds this symbol almost identical to the one they know. [...] In certain browsers, these misleading characters may be indistinguishable from one another in the address bar. This technique is called a *homograph attack*. The URLs appear to be legitimate and the content of these pages seems identical at first glance. In reality, however it is counterfeit, designed to steal sensitive data or infect the user's device. These attacks are based on classic techniques like phishing, forced downloads, and online fraud. (La Porta 2025)

Box 6.2. *Punycode to secure Internet domain names*

6.3. The Internet: an ideal digital commons at our fingertips

In the 1960s, and until the mid-1970s, computer science was characterized by the size and exorbitant cost of computing centers. However, each computing center had several terminals that were connected through a local network. These centers gradually set up connections between themselves in order to share computing time and exchange data, as long as the machines were installed by the same constructor, had the same software,

12 It is possible to see the difference between the lowercase Greek *tau* and the lowercase Latin *t*, but the capital letters are indistinguishable: T and T.

and, above all, were leased full-time to dedicated digital networks. After two decades of research, groups of researchers, companies and research centers, initially set up on an informal basis, began to emerge. These went on to form the current galaxy of Internet consortia.

Donald Watts Davies, working in the National Physics Laboratory (NPL) in Great Britain, experimented with one of the earliest networks that could go beyond the constraints of dedicated digital networks. He proposed setting up a national network founded on *packet switching* as well as communication nodes (routers) that could ensure the functioning of a telephonic as well as digital national network. Watts Davies was also one of the first to use the concept of *data transfer protocols*, an essential standard for regulating data switching. In parallel, the Cyclades project in France and ARPANET in the United States were working to realize the concept of a national (or even global) digital network based on similar principles. The exchanges between ARPA, the NPL network and Cyclades, as well as Italy, Canada and Germany, increased[13].

Between 1968 and 1992, the institutional framework that had enabled the founding pioneers of the Internet rapidly evolved, testifying to the plurality of their exchanges and alliances. The Defense Advanced Research Projects Agency (DARPA, formerly ARPA[14]) was the first institute to develop and interconnect networks in the United States. In 1966, three ARPA terminals were installed and connected through a common network: one terminal for UC Berkeley's project Genie, another for Massachusetts Institute of Technology's (MIT) Compatible Time-Sharing System and a final one for the System Development Corporation in Santa Monica.

In the early 1970s, inter-network connections multiplied but allowed competition to continue between protocols. File transfer protocols (FTPs) then started being used to exchange computer files and messaging. This proliferation of exchanges inevitably led to sophisticated addressing. In 1972, Jon Postel[15] proposed centralizing the addresses of all ARPANET communications. This thus became the central authority for allocating and

13 Unfortunately, the promising Cyclades project was sacrificed by the French administration in favor of Transpac, but the project remained a France-led one.

14 At certain periods, DARPA temporarily lost its "D" to become "ARPA" (thus, less overtly military in nature). Officially, ARPA was rechristened DARPA in 1971, then again became ARPA in 1993, before going back to being DARPA in 1996.

15 A student at UCLA.

tracking identifiers, while also publishing Requests for Comments (RFC)[16]. It also established an official list of host names and addresses[17].

In 1974, the term "Internet" was used for the first time in RFC 675, which described the Transmission Control Protocol (TCP). This RFC was the reason for the later dominance of TCP/IP (Internet Protocol). Indeed, the first requirement for a network of networks is to develop communication and addressing protocols that are either universal or intercompatible. In concrete terms, the partisans of ARPANET enabled a global discussion of the possibility of making their protocol the universal standard, unifying all global networks. This event marked the birth of the future Internet.

In November 1981, Jon Postel, who was then the director of the Network Working Group (the ARPANET working group), authored a technical note (RCP) initiating a plan to transition from NCP to TCP.

He recommended gradually moving away from the last few addresses that still used NCP and declared:

> The time has come to put these protocols into practice within the ARPANET operational framework and to extend this logical connectivity to other networks participating in the ARPA Internet. [...] The implementation of IP/TCP must urgently be implemented [...] by 1st January 1982 at the latest. In all events, any new host connected to ARPANET must only implement the IP/TCP protocols. (Postel 1981)

In 1984, a final meeting of ARPA and the Internet Configuration Control Board (ICCB) was held at the Royal Signals and Radar Establishment (RSRE[18]) in Malvern, in the United Kingdom. ARPA-ICCB was then dissolved and replaced by the Internet Advisory Board (IAB), made up of the chairpersons of the newly formed research working groups, as well as Jon Postel. In May 1986, the former ARPA-ICCB, which became the Internet Advisory Board (IAB) in 1984, changed its name for the third time and became the Internet Activities Board. In 1992, it took on its fourth and

---

16 The base for future Internet recommendations.

17 Jon Postel had created the forerunner of what would go on to become the Internet Corporation for Assigned Names and Numbers (ICANN).

18 A highly symbolic location: this was the site from which, in 1976, Queen Elizabeth II sent the first transatlantic email.

final name to become the Internet Architecture Board under the aegis of the newly formed Internet Society (ISOC).

6.3.1. *The founding of the IETF, IESG and ISOC*

The IETF, IESG and ISOC were founded consequent to several developments that were important milestones in the history of the Internet, up to the present:

– given the growth and efficacy of the ARPANET network, the Department of Defense (DoD) of the United States no longer wished to finance it indefinitely until it became profitable;

– the Department of Commerce (DoC) saw that this network could become a global network while continuing to promote American industry and, implicitly, preserving the DoD's strategic interests.

Indeed, DoD suppliers were compelled to use TCP/IP protocols. In 1985, the IAB requested Dan Lynch to organize a three-day training. Around 50 DARPA researchers participated in this, and 250 suppliers were registered. This workshop marked the birth of the modern-day Internet Engineering Task Force (IETF) within the ISOC. These arms suppliers had perfectly anticipated the expansion of the global digital market, which could not forever remain a niche military-industrial market. With the extension of the Internet, a zone-wise geographic organization was implemented: the Internet Engineering Steering Group (IESG), a sub-group that brought together regional WGs[19]. The IETF had just been founded but was still dependent on ARPA's and National Science Foundation's (NSF) research contracts. The Internet had demonstrated its potential for commercial profitability, including contexts beyond DoD purchases. The NSF thus decided to stop all subsidies. Vint Cerf then took the initiative of creating a professional organization, which would go on to be called the Internet Society. He announced its imminent creation during the closing session of the INET'91 conference in Copenhagen:

> An Internet Society is being formed to foster the voluntary interconnection of computer networks into a global research and development communications and information infrastructure. The Internet Society will not operate the Internet. Internet operation will continue to be a collaborative activity

19 The present-day chapters of ISOC.

> which the Society will seek to facilitate [...] It will function as a professional society to facilitate, support, and promote the evolution and growth of the Internet as a global research communications infrastructure. (Cerf et al. 1992)

An Internet Society charter was also declared:

> The Society will be a non-profit organization and will be operated for international educational, charitable, and scientific purposes, among which are: to facilitate and support the technical evolution of the Internet as a research and education infrastructure and to stimulate involvement of the academic, scientific, and engineering communities (among others) in the evolution of the Internet; to educate the academic and scientific communities and the public concerning the technology, use, and application of the Internet.

6.3.2. *The W3C and its multiplier effect on the Internet*

The Internet in itself was a revolution within global digital networks. However, it was initially reserved for use among IT professionals and certain academic milieux. In parallel to the development of the Internet, personal computers became easier and easier to use. In 1989, the Web marked a major advance, thanks to its creator, Sir Timothy Berners-Lee, who had invested significantly in the development of a hypermedia layer aimed at simplifying the use of the Internet[20]. This new interface, which would quickly become the Web, was initially meant for use in CERN[21] and for physics researchers around the world.

However, the Web soon outstripped all its initial objectives to become the near-universal interface for Internet networks. In 1991, Berners-Lee launched his WWW software, which included an online browser, Web server software and a library for developers. In March 1991, the software was made accessible to his colleagues using the CERN's specific computers. A few months later, in August 1991, the first "Internet discussion groups" were born and the project grew on a global scale. The first web server in the United States went online in December 1991, in

20 Head of communications between physics researchers at CERN.

21 The European Organization for Nuclear Research. See: https://home.cern

Stanford's particulate physics laboratory, the Stanford Linear Accelerator Center (SLAC) in California. In 1993, CERN made the source code for the World Wide Web freely accessible to everyone. By the end of that very year, there were over 500 servers and the Web represented 1% of Internet traffic. In May 1994, the first international conference on the World Wide Web was held at CERN, bringing together 380 users and developers. By the end of 1994, the Web had 10,000 servers and 10 million users.

The goal was to guarantee that the Web remained an open standard that could not be monopolized by any proprietary system. CERN then considered that the development of the Web was no longer part of its mission. Tim Berners-Lee thus quit the organization and joined MIT, where he founded the international World Wide Web Consortium (W3C). The European Commission worked with INRIA (the French Institute for Research in Computer Science and Automation) and in April 1995 this became the first European host of W3C. In 1996, Japan's Keio University joined the consortium, followed by ERCIM in 2003 (the European Consortium for Research into Computer Science and Mathematics, which had replaced INRIA). In 2013, China's Beihang University also hosted the W3C. As of September 2018, the organization had over 400 members across the world[22].

6.3.3. *Bringing together the W3C, the Internet and data theft by design*

There were almost 20 years between the founding of the World Wide Web Consortium at MIT in 1994 and the founding of a new, not-for-profit organization in 2023, governed by American law and released from MIT's oversight. This intervening period allowed GAFAM+ lobbyists to convince Berners-Lee to join the Internet galaxy, or rather, the Internet nebula. The term nebula seems apt as W3C, ICANN and, above all, ISOC use a communication policy that projects an image that is very different from their reality. They play up the complexity of their partnerships, their industrial interest groups, their chapters and their members and sponsors, whether institutional or private.

In the 2000s, the *chapters of the Internet* could bring together interests that extended beyond the borders of any country, much like the use of

22 This section is based on *A Short History of the Web* (CERN n.d.).

languages such as French, English or Spanish is no longer restricted to a single "home" country. The "Colloques Initiatives, AUF", a series of conferences organized by the AUF, offer a clear picture of this hope for a shared digital world[23]. Today, with the exception of the *Pacific Islands Chapter*, an *Interplanetary Chapter*, and a few urban communities (New York, Washington, San Francisco) and regional communities (especially in Canada and in India), all chapters are now exclusively attached to national bodies. This structure clearly hinders innovative initiatives.

The ISOC presents itself as a benevolent NGO that seeks to finance the spread of the Internet network in developing countries. While this specific action does offer some advantages, it is clear, nonetheless, that the Internet galaxy is making claims that sound politically and ethically correct, while its GAFAM+ partners develop, in parallel, closed, proprietary industrial applications. These applications, however, are derived from the Internet and are based on open-source recommendations. But they make use of software forks, which are variations that are designed to promote proprietary versions of the same source code, often containing a functional aspect whose true purpose is hidden, or sometimes even socially harmful to the user.

Thus, open source code, which is produced by a community of actors who are often benevolent and idealistic, gets reworked into software that allows the proliferation of applications whose use can be described as data theft by design[24].

The collection of personal data (data theft by design) is the true price of our dependence on GAFAM+. This is far from an idealized vision of the Internet economy and we must remember the statement often attributed to Bruce Willis: "If it's free, then you are the product" (Wiseman 2007). From all the evidence, the possibility of being able to communicate from all corners of the world for free via WhatsApp, sending files instantly and accessing high-speed and free search engines are all based on initial costs financed by industrial Internet actors.

---

23 An example followed by many others: Actes du colloque Initiatives 97 : Inforoutes et technologies de l'information, une chance pour le développement dans l'espace francophone (AUPELF-UREF). Paris: Association des universités partiellement ou entièrement de langue française. See: https://www.auf.org.

24 A term that we propose to designate the harmful actions of GAFAM+ (and others), which we hope will be reined in by the concept of privacy by design. It must be noted that this term explicitly references the writings of Cory Doctorow (Doctorow 2025).

Collecting personal data through FOAF

Friend of a Friend (FOAF) is machine-readable ontology that describes individuals, their activities and their relationships with other persons or objects. It thus makes it possible to model social networks without requiring any centralized database. Developed as an open-source project, FOAF was the first Social Semantic Web application, combining the RDF Resource Description Framework technology with social Web concerns. In a 2007 essay, Berners-Lee (2007) redefined the concept of the Semantic Web as a Giant Global Graph (GGG), where relationships transcended networks and documents. He believed that the GGG was on an equal footing with the Internet and World Wide Web, declaring, "I express my network in a FOAF file, and that is a start of the revolution"[25].

Further, although this concept was designed within an open and transparent framework, its open-source nature encouraged some industrial actors, especially GAFAM+, to offer social networks that would capture and then exploit users' personal data.

Box 6.3. *FOAF brought into a network*

The present situation thus results in the growing dependence of users, a loss in their democratic liberty and maybe even cultural and cognitive erosion. Given this situation, several European agencies and institutions have invested in open-source alternatives to GAFAM+ social networks, such as Mastodon and PeerTube. These platforms are decentralized, free and financed through donations, offering a model that is opposed to the GAFAM+ mode of working. Mastodon, for example, does not have any advertisements and does not target users, allowing friends to form connections and networks without any algorithmic influence on who they connect with or exclude.

The European Union launched *EuVoice* in April 2016, a server meant to centralize the communications of various European organizations (European Space Agency, the EU Court of Justice, etc.). In parallel, *EuVideo*, inspired by YouTube, was developed with similar guarantees of respecting user privacy. Thus, ignoring GAFAM+ software forks and promoting European or national alternatives seems a strategic necessity.

---

25 His penchant for triple-letters is evident: WWW, GGG.

6.4. Academic consortium standards

The world of libraries, scientific publishing and scholarly reading soon came together to make use of digital networks and the Internet, all while avoiding the use of consumer software and documentation tools offered by GAFAM+[26]. Academic consortia federated categories of actors with convergent and specific standardization needs:

– bringing together researchers and promoting the production of critical digital editions in domains such as linguistics, literary studies, philology, archival sciences, oral literature, music and musicology. This area of work is notably being carried out through initiatives such as the Text Encoding Initiative (TEI) and the Music Encoding Initiative (MEI);

– setting up open-access or regulated online editions, like those available through the Open Archive Initiative (OAI);

– enhancing the interoperability of cataloguing reference systems and bibliography description tools, as well as document search systems and fund management systems.

Organizing, describing, managing and preserving collections and catalogues, as well as making these available to users, are all domains in which standardization played a key role (ISO/TC 46). The MARC format, created in 1968, was designed for the exchange of digitized bibliographical data. It is complemented by the International Standard Bibliographic Description (ISBD) standard). From the moment it was conceived and all through its life (publishing, bookstore, library), each book is associated with a specialized unique identifier: the International Standard Book Number (ISBN), often coupled with standardized barcodes (JTC 1/SC 31), which makes it possible to uniquely identify each edition of a published book. Beyond this unique and reusable cataloguing structure, there are other document description approaches that are used to create:

– operating standards while guaranteeing interoperability with models that are more flexible than MARC. This was, notably, the objective of Dublin Core, which was designed to structure document databases;

26 On principle, these organizations hide the comprehensiveness of their resources as well as the logic underlying their requests.

– enriched metadata in the form of document headers, as in TEI, in order to have a detailed record of the references and history of the documents. This approach is essential to trace the evolution of a text, its different versions and the multiple contributors to the text.

Dublin Core is a simple and generic description format, created in 1995 at Dublin (Ohio) by the Online Computer Library Center (OCLC) and the National Center for Supercomputing Applications (NCSA). Unlike the strict library standards, this format allows a large variety of resources to be described. It is developed by the Dublin Core Metadata Initiative (DCMI), a non-for-profit NGO based out of Singapore. Dublin Core aims to offer a common base of descriptive elements to improve labeling and enhance the search for resources in an environment with many descriptive formats specific to different disciplines. Its structure is based on 15 fundamental elements, each of which is optional and repeatable, divided into three categories:

– content: title, subject, description, source, language, relation, coverage;

– intellectual property: creator, contributor, publisher, rights;

– instantiation: date, type, format, identifier.

Dublin Core aims to guarantee a minimal interoperability between systems that developed independent of each other based on the combined use of Dublin Core and the encoding schema specific to each project.

The *Open Archives Initiative Protocol for Metadata Harvesting (OAI-PMH)* makes it possible to:

– increase the visibility of digital collections on the Internet;

– virtually reconstitute corpora using resources scattered across different sites;

– provide information to portals with specialized themes.

This protocol is free to use and its specifications can be found on the Open Archives Initiative website. There are two types of actors as follows:

– data providers, who submit their metadata to a web server called a registry;

– service providers, who collect (harvest) these data and integrate them into their digital library indices[27].

The OAI-PMH protocol is based on client-server communications in which the client sends HTTP requests and the server responds with XML flows. There are several academic and research institutes in France, such as the CNRS, INSERM, Institut Pasteur and the Center for Research into the History of Science and Technology, that use this protocol to structure their collections and facilitate the distribution of these collections.

6.5. TEI and MEI: Text Encoding Initiative and Music Encoding Initiative

I will use a long personal citation shared with Laurent Romary to describe the TEI:

> TEI, which can be translated as an initiative for standardized markup of text, is a markup standard for the notation and exchange of electronic documents between corpora, based on SGML. In pragmatic terms, it was developed based on the need for structuring, designing and interconnecting texts. Long years of consensus-based research took place based on the earliest hypotheses postulated during the Vassar College conference (Poughkeepsie, New York, 1987) by scientists interested in the study of texts (specialists in literature, historians, sociologists, linguists, ethnologists, philosophers, etc.) and led to the definition of a set of coding recommendations: the TEI recommendations (TEI guideline). The researchers present at Vassar all agreed on the need to work on defining a new format to code electronic text and postulated the basic principles of this format. The new format had to also be as comprehensive as possible: simple, clear and concrete; easy to use without any particular software; rigorously defined; allow effective processing; open to extension defined by users; compatible with existing standards or those being developed. The major hypotheses postulated by these researchers was that it was possible to use the SGML process to markup texts and note the

27 The same institution may share their metadata and collect metadata from others.

> elements described by this markup in a standardized manner. This markup is organized according to two types of elements: firstly, markups and elements common to all disciplines. For example, the structure of markups and elements specific to each discipline: these allow the user to work on plays, poetry, dictionaries, history, etc.
>
> TEI markup is organized into two complementary but distinct fields: the header, which is a codification not only of the source of the document (a paper book, for example) but also its digital transcription (person and institution responsible for the transcription, transcription format, date, mode of availability, versions and updates, etc.) Codification based on the description modes can be partly automated to transform traditional bibliographical data. The markup, strictly speaking, of the document can be relatively light and strictly formal, which makes it easy to exchange references or corpora. In other cases, the TEI may become a support for much more detailed description, bringing together the form and content of the document (theatrical or poetical literary studies are a good example of this processing) [...] From this first, mandatory cataloguing of the constituents of a primary text in a corpus we go to the second level, which is qualitatively more interesting in scientific terms. Let us reiterate that when analysing a primary document, e.g. a particular digital version of a particular edition of Baudelaire's *Fleurs du mal*, or an integral edition of plays by Tennessee Williams, the author of a critical analysis will generate a new document, referenced in a new header. The key part is not the digitized work, which is digitally available on Gallica, Internet Archive, etc. The central part of a TEI project is the collection of critical editions marked up in TEI. Thanks to their interoperability, these editions can be augmented by the researcher or their colleagues, cumulated, re-annotated, compared, etc. (Romary and Hudrisier 2002, pp. 319–322).

The main challenge is not so much the digitization of works, which are often already available on platforms such as Gallica or Internet Archive, but in the creation of critical editions that use markup language following the TEI guideline. Thanks to the interoperability of the TEI standard, these editions can be enriched, compared and annotated by different researchers, thus promoting collaboration and knowledge building. The TEI Guidelines (TEI 2022) clearly lay out the objectives of the project. The principal categories include Verse, Performance Texts, Transcriptions of Speech, Dictionaries and Manuscript Description.

These categories include markup language designed to structure each type of text. For instance, the Verse section offers a set of tags that make it possible to annotate poetic structures (sonnets, rondos, quatrains, tercets, hemistich, types of meter, etc.) Once this formal base is established, the researcher can add more specific tags to integrate their critical, stylistic or historical comments (e.g. mark a new assonance, flag a recently discovered variant in the manuscript, etc.)[28].

Similarly, Performance Texts offer similar tags for theatrical texts or scripts. The TEI markup standard thus allows researchers to structure entire textual corpora, allowing them to be exchanged, enriched and published. Thanks to this format, critical comments can be directly attached to the relevant textual segments, allowing them to be immediately accessed and making them interoperable. The TEI represents a major advance in the digital humanities. It has radically transformed research methods in literature, by making them more rigorous and, above all, collaborative, while still enabling every researcher to freely analyze the text critically, stylistically, lexically or biographically. It is, therefore, a true standard within the *digital humanities*.

The MEI is similar to the TEI and denotes both an organization, a research community and a markup language. This scientific community, which specializes in studying the history of music, requires a coding system that meets the following requirements:

– representing the semantic and structural complexity of the entire, diversified history of Western notation;

– integrating the expressive characteristics common to traditional facsimile editions, critical editions and sheet music for performances;

28 For example: <text>, <body>, <lg>, </l>, <lg type="quatrain">, <lg type="couplet">, <seg type="hemistich">. Sometimes there are more complex structures: <lg type="chevy-chase-stanza" met="-+-+-+-+/-+-+-+" rhyme="ababcdcd">, etc.

– a public and open standard, managed by the scientific community;

– independent of platforms and founded on open standards;

– taking charge of scientific analysis, as well as a diversity of digital and print rendering of music.

The MEI thus aims to develop a set of tags (MEI 2023) to describe musical notation that meets the following requirements[29]:

– able to code all common Western music, without being limited to this;

– designed by the scientific community for academic and other purposes;

– ensure essential functionalities for traditional publishing, critical editions and sheet music for performances;

– modular in order to fit each researcher's objective;

– founded on open, platform-agnostic standards[30];

– promote the international and sustainable development of annotated musical archives, forming a base for scholarly editions (though not exclusively), analyses, interpretations and other forms of research.

The proximity of both these communities, the TEI and MEI, can be clearly seen and both have ongoing cooperative links. The requirements stated for music are largely transposable to the context of texts for TEI and vice versa. With TEI (and MEI), in certain cases, the references may become a *mille-feuille* of standards[31], with a standardized approach but adapted to each community of researchers.

29 For example: <measure n="2"> <note dur="4" mfunc="ct" oct="4" pname="f" xml:id="analysis.m2e1"/>, indications for harmonies : <chordDef xml:id="harmonychordA"> <chordMember oct="2" pname="a"/>.

30 It is remarkable that from the time it was founded, the TEI (followed by the MEI) has defined its TEI Guidelines to be rigorously independent of any technological software or platform. However, Oxygen XML Editor contains all the style sheets as well as TEI DTD and seems to be the relative exception to this rule.

31 A phrase proposed by Romary (2021).

6.6. Standardizers and GAFAM+

Since the 2000s, it has become clear that certain large ICT multinationals have appropriated Internet standards and W3C standards to profit from these collegial standardization projects. They thus develop products that supposedly conform to Internet and Web recommendations, being effectively interoperable, but with opacity around the origin of the sources and how user data are used. One of the main reasons why this data theft has been able to continue as long as it has is that the majority of users cannot distinguish between the Internet and the derivative applications developed by GAFAM+.

The Internet still retains its reputation for being an open and free digital space, created by an idealistic community that has worked to make it accessible to all. However, the difficulty lies in the fact that apart from W3C, the Internet community never aimed to develop social media tools. Its members designed demonstrators for their recommendations, which were meant for use by IT professionals. This is the stage at which GAFAM+ swooped in. By financing Internet experts, these companies ensured that they would be the first to be able to design free, accessible and high-performing applications.

For almost 20 years now, in exchange for these free applications[32], GAFAM+ companies have accumulated massive quantities of user data. When there is such an imbalance in the exchange on offer, it is valid to speak of "theft" and "monopoly". It must be noted that even the United States, the earliest beneficiary of GAFAM+, is not immune to these consequences. Furthermore, some countries, like China and Russia, are not playing the same game: these states have installed effective digital barriers, while still collecting and misusing data, especially from users abroad, as was seen with TikTok. Today, the issues with GAFAM+ have also caught the attention of the general public. For the past 15 years, professionals concerned about the security of IT systems, as well as many governments around the world, especially in Europe, have stated the need for standards that allow a downstream control of flows through the Internet[33]. JTC 1 has been particularly active on this topic. It is not the only body working on this;

32 Free offers that unsettle the user, as they are difficult to refuse.

33 As things stand, the Internet being dominated by GAFAM+ is an unavoidable reality for clients and citizens and therefore we must contend with this situation.

however, the entire standardization community, *stricto sensu*, has taken this up.

What could the ITU do and what can it do? This body is a diplomatic alliance between States, many of whom used to directly control their telecommunications. The ITU seems almost powerless before the Internet as it is today. Until the late 1980s, the Internet was anecdotal, restricted to small groups. It was only around the 2000s that it became a mass phenomenon. The 2010s accelerated this trend, especially with the generalization of exclusively digital video distribution. By capturing almost all flows on the Internet, GAFAM+ became a blind spot in global telecommunications. The ITU, however, still has some control over global flows, whether in hardware, technical, territorial or satellite terms. It allocates and controls frequencies and ensures the continuity of telecommunications services during natural disasters.

Aware of the new challenges facing it, the ITU organized two World Summits on the Information Society (Sommet Mondial sur la Société de l'Information (SMSI)): in Geneva in 2003 and in Tunis in 2005. Both these summits only highlighted the relative impotence of States vis-à-vis the Internet. The Declaration of Principles, *Building the Information Society: A Global Challenge in the New Millennium*, published in 2004 following the Geneva summit, stopped at an analysis of the situation, with no concrete proposal. Two years later, the *Tunis Agenda for the Information Society* (ITU 2006) showed no significant progress. This second SMSI did, however, lead to the creation of the Internet Governance Forum (IGF). It must be noted that the ITU, like the UNO, to which it is directly attached, as well as most States, have lost control (at least provisionally) given the transformation of the Internet. Periodic meetings of the Internet Governance Forum have not led to any change. As long as the ITU standardized the protocols for known flows, it could guarantee a certain control over the situation. Today, it only controls historical infrastructure.

On the other hand, the founders of the IEC have always had the foresight to base their standards on an international approach that was independent of any country. The IEC was founded 40 years after the ITU, the ISA was founded 60 years after the ITU and the ISO was founded 80 years after the ITU. It seems clear that the IEC and ISO models are more resilient than the ITU model. Strictly speaking, the IEC is only indirectly concerned with derivatives of the Internet. Standardization of IT use is not part of its scope, except in the joint committees that it co-manages with the ISO and ITU, especially JTC 1. In concrete terms, the Internet needs networks, transmission and reception tools, and elements to build standardized and interoperable platforms. The IEC is the only body capable of proposing standards that guarantee increasingly efficient regulation of the Internet while also optimizing costs. Strictly speaking, the IEC only considers volumes, speeds, processing modes, the integrity of information and other standardizing constraints required for actors on the Internet (starting with GAFAM+).

The ISO had already acted to develop certain standards to evaluate, control or offer alternatives to GAFAM+'s deviant practices. The ISO first worked with historical bodies such as COPOLCO, ISO/TC 37 (terminology and linguistic resources) and ISO/TC 46 (information and documentation). From 2016 onwards, several TCs were created within the ISO to respond to the intersectional and societal problems that required the development of standards that could guarantee the security of technologies and services for which transparency in design and functioning was not assured. The most strategic of these were:

– ISO/TC 154: Processes, data elements and documents in commerce, industry and administration;

– ISO/TC 211: Geographic information/geomatics;

– ISO/TC 228: Tourism and related services;

– ISO/TC 268: Sustainable cities and communities;

– ISO/TC 290: Online reputation;

– ISO/TC 307: Blockchain and distributed ledger technologies.

– ISO/PC 317: Consumer protection: privacy by design for consumer goods and services[34];

– ISO/PC 329: Consumer incident investigation;

– ISO/TC 332: Security equipment for financial institutions and commercial organizations;

34 The promising avenue offered by privacy by design, which continues to be the focus of JTC 1/SC 44, has already been mentioned in Chapter 5 and alluded to multiple times.

– ISO/PC 335: Guidelines for organizations to increase consumer understanding of online terms and conditions;

– ISO/WS ESG: Framework for implementing environmental, social and governance (ESG) principles.

Most of the committees we named are able to carry out quality control and help in control, more specifically ISO/PC 317, now transferred into JTC 1/SC 44.

As concerns documentation, the historical primacy of ISO/TC 46, which prevailed till the late 1990s, has been severely tested.

The opacity of search engines offered by GAFAM+ has discouraged users who wish to verify sources. Companies, institutions or individual users who need reliable information requests without their search profiles being used without their knowledge prioritize the documentation standards negotiated and established within ISO/TC 46.

6.7. End of 2025: creation of ISO/IEC JTC 4 dedicated to smart cities

The standardization of smart cities is now the focus of some very promising reorganization. The ISO and IEC decided (end of 2025) to create a new joint technical committee: ISO/IEC JTC 4: Smart and sustainable cities and communities.

As we discussed broadly in Chapter 5, the first ISO/IEC joint technical committee was created in 1987 with JTC 1. After this, it was only in 2024 that the JSyC BDC (IEC/ISO Join Systems Committee on Bio-digital Convergence) and JTC 3 (quantum technologies) were formed. The focus of both these JTCs founded in 2024 is highly strategic and global. However, the experts in both JTCs (in this initial phase of development) are more interdisciplinary than global.

Following these, in 2025, JTC 4: Smart and sustainable cities and communities was founded in order to provide standards and normative guidelines for the basic foundation of the modern human to construct and animate cities and communities using the most innovative digital tools while ensuring that this takes place in perfect harmony with human values as well as a sustainable future for the planet.

JTC 4 could be a fantastic tool to ensure the convergence of all the highly multidimensional standardization challenges faced by our contemporary societies. Information sciences, in the broader sense, from the smartphone to the most specialized industrialized systems within companies and institutions, are at the heart of this convergence to enable dialogue between software, citizens, economic and political decision-makers and service offerings (transport, energy, health, teaching, tourism, etc.), as well as still interacting with the vast amount of statistical data, for example, data flows from smart environmental sensors that can allow a city or region to have a real-time dashboard to track its ecological status.

There are countless functionalities in a smart and sustainable city or community. These may be related to e-government as well as e-democracy (as well as social control within a democracy) the definition and then the tracking of urbanism; monitoring supplies and safety reserves; ensuring that citizens, politicians and regional actors can define a future vision of the city's objectives and then track this development; and choosing similar regions or cities with planning modalities that are well-adapted to typical situations: port city, mountain city, heritage city, tourism-driven city, etc.

Until 2025, and while waiting for JTC 4 to become operation (early 2026), the definition of SSCC standards was divided between the ISO (which is meant to coordinate the whole domain through ISO/TC 268 SSCC, which still existed in late 2025), JTC 1 WG 1 and other standardization committees within the IEC and ITU, which continue to develop standards for smart cities as well as for sustainable regions.

For standardization professionals, JTC 4, which has been founded, now brings together standardization energies that had hitherto been too scattered, especially within ISO/TC 268 and JTC 1/WG 11. JTC 4 now offers a single organizational framework for defining all standards in this domain.

Based on what happened with JTC 1, we can foresee that JTC 4 will define a range of JTC 4/SCs on different topics (transport, energy, etc.) and interdisciplinary topics (especially the UN's SDGs). JTC 4 will facilitate the pooling together of work carried out on standardization, especially work carried out by ISO/TC 268 and JTC 11 WG 11, which will undoubtedly be dissolved. The interdisciplinarity of the experts who are thus brought together will allow standardization to occur more quickly and efficiently.

In the coming decade, it will be essential to reinvent the dynamic between humans, their current, past and future environment, sustainable and ethical economic growth, their social relations and the more reliable use of technical objects, especially with regard to our relations with cybernetics, which can no longer be held hostage by GAFAM+.

6.7.1. *History and objective in an emerging field of standardization: smart and sustainable cities and communities*

For a smart cities approach, a city, or more broadly, a region, must decide to federate, and make interoperable, all its information systems and platforms, all its data and all software (public or with private partners) related to its functioning, both for technical and political management, as well as environmental, sanitary and urban management and for access to energy, transport, education, social services, culture, defense, etc. We must not forget commerce and its relations with other regions and a fortiori, other smart and sustainable cities and communities. This intercompatibility would not exist without standards and brings in many advantages for governance and the management of a city or territory. Urban ontologies and AI allow us to better understand this and make informed choices to create policy with maximal cybernetic support, and also help in automated and smart steering of a city and community, bringing in the various indicators that characterize this community at various levels: human or automated.

This greater visibility of regional needs and challenges does not, however, mean that there is an uncontrolled scattering of strategic information and policies on the city and its citizens, or the commercial and industrial data on its partners. A smart city allows potential, but controlled, access to data that can be useful to various categories of users: either simple citizens (or travelers, shopkeepers, or tourists) or regional professionals or various other actors. These kinds of services have already been developed for over a decade now. Public transport traffic data are now accessible on smartphones and in bus stops and it is possible to reserve vehicles or facilities for differently abled persons or senior citizens via telephone. These are just some of the most visible examples. However, this is not practicable without a drastic standardization of the information systems that were developed earlier without any interoperability. To deploy these services to the full extent of their potential, a smart city must parametrize various levels of access: general public use, professional use, public access versus commercial access, including defining what must be restricted to smart statistical computing systems.

Internal and external access to information from a smart city can only be controlled when applications and social networks are highly secured through standards.

From the founding of ISO/TC 268 in 2012, its secretariat has been managed by AFNOR and, fortuitously, the JTC 4 secretariat is also run by France. ISO/IEC JTC 4 is ready to transform a vast meta-committee to federate the energies of all standardization experts and leaders and to develop standards to respond to current needs. JTC 4, now renamed Smart and sustainable cities and communities, must take up this challenge that will determine our technological, societal, digital and ecological future.

On this topic, we recommend reading Claude Rochet, *Smart Cities: Reality or Fiction?* (Rochet 2018) and *The Smart and Resilient City: Models and Ways of Life*, edited by Gilles N'Goala, Florence Paulhiac Scherrer and Fabien Durif (N'Goala et al. 2025)

The 17 SDGs aim to address this challenge. This development cannot, and absolutely must not, be guided by standards influenced by GAFAM+. sourced and standardized appropriately, notably within the framework of JTC 1SC 42 (AI), digital management of traffic, safety, health, urbanism, etc.; for example, smart sensors to monitor the environment, as well as statistical surveillance thresholds for local reserve stocks, strategic flows (water, energy) or indicators of good governance (health, education, housing, etc.).

Conclusion

Social acceptance of standardization, a growing awareness of the changes caused by GAFAM+ and helplessness in the face of poorly regulated global commerce and the environment have almost immediately become major topics of discussion everywhere.

Of course, standardization is not the alpha and omega of all issues, but it has always been, and remains, an essential means of regulation for our globalized civilization.

It is necessary to study several essential transversal aspects of standardization:

– a geostrategy for standardization, notably including the North–South component as well as the linguistic dimension. This last challenge focuses specifically on the advantages and disadvantages of alphabetic and ideographic languages within ICT and AI;

– the evolution in relations between standards and legislation, a crucial question that concerns, among many other issues, blockchain, which is currently being standardized;

– what is our collective responsibility toward *technological objects*, whether digital or traditional? And what could be the role of expertise in standardization?

	NB	MbP	MbO	Secrt.
Germany	DIN	719	135	135
United States	ANSI	567	8	92
China	SAC	774	3	87
Japan	JISC	663	74	84
France	AFNOR	642	122	81
Great Britain	BSI	703	64	77
Sweden	SIS	474	105	25
Korea (South)	KATS	593	149	24
Italy	UNI	605	115	23
Australia	SA	330	65	22
Switzerland	SNV	449	140	20
Canada	SCC	298	10	18
India	BIS	560	152	11
South Africa	SABS	246	190	11
Netherlands	NEN	452	211	10
Norway	SN	260	90	8
Russia	GOST-R	625	93	7
Spain	UNE	454	236	6
Belgium	NBN	405	153	5
Iran	INSO	365	341	5
Denmark	DS	303	94	5
Austria	ASI	363	217	3
Brazil	ABNT	256	97	3
Malaysia	DSM	176	136	3
Israel	SII	141	147	3
Finland	SFS	331	301	2
Portugal	IPQ	261	225	2
Poland	PKN	219	445	2
Turkey	TSE	151	249	2
Kenya	KEBS	119	155	1
Ukraine	SE UkrNDNC	114	261	1
Argentina	IRAM	103	297	1
Uganda	UNBS	97	34	1
Colombia	ICONTEC	67	100	1
Jamaica	BSJ	16	16	1
Saudi Arabia	SASO	201	161	1 + ANSI
Senegal	ASN	10	25	1 + BSI

Table C.1. *Comparing the performances of national standardization organizations. **NB** = national body; **MbP** = Member Participant; **MbO** = Member Observer; **Secrt** = secretariat. For the full names of the national bodies, please see the National Standards Organizations section of the Abbreviations and Acronyms.*

C.1. The geostrategy of standardization

Standardization is an essential aspect of *technical diplomacy* between States, even though it is a feature the general public is largely unaware of. One example of this is the signing of the free-trade agreement between Mercosur and the European Union. The true challenge lies in the standardization gap between these two large economic zones. The eventual solutions to this differential are not easily understood by the general public, nor by political decision-makers, who often prefer to align themselves on prevailing ideological discourse. Nonetheless, standards allow a region to protect the health and safety of its consumers, workers and residents. On a national or regional scale (Europe, for example), the thoughtful application of national standards generates and preserves an economic, social and environmental ecosystem that must be respected along its borders. However, this is a tricky point, as it often clashes with international free-trade agreements and WTO regulations.

It has already been stated that institutional standards facilitate technology transfers between experts in a given technical committee. However, this process is still an unequal one: large, industrialized nations have a large enough pool of experts, and industrial potential, to participate in many committees, both at the national and international level. Their national standardization bodies (NBs) can thus implement proactive policies by maximizing the number of mirror technical committees and ensuring that these mirror committees have Participant Member (MbP) status rather than simply being Observer Members (MbO). In some cases, when a technical domain is deemed to be highly strategic and when national expertise allows for it, an NB can even apply to manage a TC or SC, an onerous but advantageous responsibility. They can also encourage the nomination of experts from the NB to key posts, such as the chair of a TC or an SC.

Developing countries, on the other hand, who may have economic problems, or even very small developed countries do not have enough monetary or human resources to adopt this strategy. It is impossible for these countries to track all 843 TCs and SCs that are currently active within the ISO. In Europe, the presence of bodies such as the CEN, CENELAC and ETSI makes it possible for Member States within the EU and partner countries (the UK, Norway, etc.) to pool their standardization work.

It is also true that not all TCs and SCs have the same economic and industrial weight. However, the indicators of participation within a technical committee, as well as the number of secretariats managed by an NB, are ways to evaluate standardization work carried out by a country. We use here the same hypotheses and counting methods that we used with Jean-Michel Borde in 2013 for a geography colloquium on standardization (Hudrisier and Borde 2013). In 2013, we had to establish the global statistics for NB participation ourselves[1]. Today, our analysis is limited to the 35 NBs who manage at least one TC or SC secretariat, a relevant criterion for observer actors who are actually involved in standardization. Indeed, managing a secretariat implies total engagement with all processes related to the production of standards. Thus, despite their economic and technological diversity, these countries are all de facto members of an exclusive club of standard producers.

Let us emphasize that within each group, classified based on the number of secretariats it runs, countries are further categorized based on the number of participating TCs[2]. Although this global statistic does not take into account the relative weighting for each country, nor the strategic importance of the standardization carried out, nor the hierarchy between TCs and SCs, it still offers the advantage of revealing certain trends, as well as allowing countries to be broadly grouped based on their standardization policies[3].

An initial group of six countries leads the list, managing between 77 and 135 secretariats. The three historically powerful European countries (France, United Kingdom and Germany) retain their place in this top six; however, Germany is indisputably the world leader in active standardization policy. France and the United Kingdom were in second and third position in 2013 (Hudrisier and Borde 2013) but the United States has now overtaken them to occupy second place. However, if there were a more specific study that also weighted each large domain of standardization based on the volume

1 For the past 4 or 5 years, the ISO has made these data public on its website and it points to them today as an indicator of activity.

2 See: https://www.iso.org/about/members.

3 It is clear that it is difficult to compare ISO/TC 87 (cork) with ISO/TC 85 (nuclear energy), or again with the exceptionally holistic nature of JTC 1.

of international exchanges as well as the hierarchy between TCs and SCs, the top six[4] might look different.

For example, ANSI (United States) has managed the secretariat of JTC 1 since its inception, and thus benefits from a global overview of all sectors of ICT. This means that it can afford to have a reduced presence in certain SCs in JTC 1, no longer being represented in JTC 1/SC 23 (digitally recorded media), JTC 1/SC 35 (user interfaces) or JTC 1/SC 36 (information technology for learning, teaching, and education). This strategic participation, which has been practiced for a long time by the United States, can also be seen in the drastic reduction in ANSI's participation as an observer member (567 committees as a P member, as opposed to only 8 as an O member). This testifies to its desire to develop a global policy of standardization without passive participation: no delegation of experts who "only watch".

Further, we must emphasize how Southeast Asian countries are resetting the balance with greater participation. In our 2013 study, the relative position of these *top six* countries was different from Japan and China. In 12 years, China has seen impressive growth, overtaking neighboring Japan, as well as France and the United Kingdom, and presently ranks third in terms of the number of secretariats. Japan also progressed and now occupies fourth place.

A second group of six countries is distinguished by having held a total of around 20 secretariats each. This group consists of Sweden, South Korea, Italy, Australia, Switzerland and Canada. These countries all have highly active, and highly specific, standardization policies. The number of secretariats they manage is a third, or a fourth, that of the top six. However, taking into account their cumulative partnership as P and O members, they are able to delegate experts to a significant number of TCs and SCs. Canada has made a mark within this group by adopting a policy that is similar to US policy, but adapted to Canada's own scale: 298 instances of participants as P members, with only 10 O member participation.

The final group is much more heterogeneous: the only objective factor is the stark contrast with the previous group. The second group had a lower

4 Health; IT and related technologies; transport; environmental sustainability; management and services; safety, security and risks; energy; buildings and construction; food and agriculture; engineering, materials; inclusion and diversity; and public affairs.

limit of 18 secretariats, while this third group has a maximum of 11 secretariats.

India and South Africa head this group, two BRICS nations that have seen considerable technological progress over the past few years. This evolution is concretized by an increasingly stronger standardization policy. If we were carrying out a deeper analysis, we would wish to group together (or, more precisely, concatenate the participation of) all the actors within the European Standardization Committee (CEN) territories, including Germany, the United Kingdom and France. This would allow us to have a clearer picture, less distorted by the fragmentation of European states, which form a coherent group within CEN associated with the three historical nation-States (Germany, France and the United Kingdom) and, as a group, are able to bring in a geostrategy for standardization. Russia is a special case. Experts from the Soviet-era administration continue to occupy almost all TCs and SCs, with a total of 718 interventions as P or O members, although Russia only runs seven secretariats.

But all differences aside, the fact that unites all the countries who manage a secretariat (whether they run 135, like Germany, or single secretariat, or even a twinned secretariat) is that they belong to the club of members who actively participate in standardization. To attain this, their national body must necessarily structure itself and train its experts in Geneva, which will inevitably transform their industrial vision. Thus, running at least one secretariat is a reliable indicator of a country's industrial and economic development.

Apart from India, South Africa and Israel, this last group also includes Iran, Malaysia, Brazil (for South America) and Kenya and Uganda (from Africa). The last two rows in the table mention twinned secretariats – these are transient bodies that are intended to support the candidate countries as they move toward autonomously managing a secretariat.

North–South relations, oscillating between mutual support and the imposition of standards for neocolonial purposes, are ubiquitous in the practices of standardization experts. It is undeniable that standardization can be used as a devious means for economic, cultural, social and ecological domination. Certain multinationals and certain States unscrupulously exploit standards as means to assert influence over less developed countries.

However, it would be a mistake to generalize these unethical practices, which are unanimously spurned by the vast majority of experts.

Deontologically, standardization experts are chosen for their ability to build consensus. Most of them are benevolent, humanistic, rational and driven by their fascination with the linguistic, cultural, social, technological and scientific diversity in the world. Their work gives them the chance to discover these rich realities, with every journey allowing them to immerse themselves into the local activities around their areas of expertise. From my own modest experience of 20 years in international standardization, being the AFNOR delegate within JTC/1 SC 36 and representing the AUF liaison, I have been able to appreciate the quantum of growth in our knowledge thanks to exchanges with tens of the top global experts in the field. This expertise was able to develop further through many trainings in France and other Francophone countries, as well as through international publications and conferences.

Having had the advantage of being a part of SC 36 right from its inception in London in 2000, I have had the chance to observe the evolution of actors in the field of education. Initially, they had little interest in standardization but they have gradually come to be deeply involved in concretely implementing standards. At my own scale, this allowed me to measure the magnitude of technology transfers, benefitting thousands of experts. Some of these experts exerted greater influence than others, especially those who participated in JTC 1 projects, starting with the successive chairpersons of SC 36.

The development of technical standards was based on a demanding, collective process. During plenary sessions and workshops organized by different working groups (WGs), the chief task is to identify the constants and the universal elements in educational technology and practices. These observations must then lead to guidelines, and after a long process of revisions, comments and amendments, these guidelines will give rise to standards, which are validated through iterative voting before being published. This collaborative work transcends the personalities of the participants: sitting around a table, six or seven experts from five different continents strive to arrive at a consensual formulation that includes the comments put forth by national bodies six months previously. Each contribution adds a fresh perspective and enriches the reflective process, reinforcing the interoperability of the standards being created. Each problem that is raised leads to a better understanding of the diversity around the world. Thanks to these carefully articulated standards, complex technologies become accessible to the communities concerned by the standard, as well as other communities, often represented by an expert.

C.1.1. *The example of learning to write*

Thus, one of the experts of the Standards Australia NB enabled the inclusion of pedagogy that was specific to certain Aboriginal peoples, while experts from the AUF liaison (including the author) have contributed to the inclusion of Francophone partner languages within SC 36 terminology.

Another example to illustrate the rich diversity that must be addressed is that of learning writing, comparing alphabetic and ideographic systems. Learners from regions where ideographic writing systems are used continue discovering new characters *throughout their life*, while also mastering calligraphy and the associated vocabulary[5]. Thus, a Japanese child begins by learning a syllabary of 51 *kana* (*hiragana* or *katakana*) before progressively learning 900 *kanji* (ideograms) over the course of their primary education. As they go through secondary school, they acquire around 2,000 ideograms. Chinese learners, on the other hand, do not have this transition tool and must learn a much larger corpus of characters, although the *pinyin* transcription of characters into the Latin script makes them easier to learn.

Fortuitously, the organization of Chinese characters, like the Japanese *kanji* characters, is based on "keys", constituent elements present in all ideograms. Using around 200 keys, all characters can be organized in an etymographic logic that is similar to an encyclopedic system[6]. This example shows that taking into account cultural diversity, as well as institutional and technical diversity in the world, demands a detailed and rigorously stated description of each specific feature.

---

5 For alphabetic languages, the learner usually learns all the letters by the time they are 7 years old.

6 This specific feature where dictionary entries are organized first according to the Chinese radical, and then by the number of calligraphic strokes added to the radical to form an ideogram (Chinese or *kanji*) demonstrates the complexity of this highly culturally diversified question of classifying and sorting characters. In Japanese, the *hiragana* can even be classified according to the order in which they appear in a mnemonic poem that contains each of them in the initial letter (see section 6.2.2).

C.1.2. A hybrid discussion on standards, recentered on Southeast Asia

Online teaching was one of the first experimental spaces in which the concept of blended learning was theorized (see SC 36, section 5.3.1). It is clear that knowledge transfer is facilitated by online work. However, active, collaborative teaching, as well as the use of flipped classrooms, is more effective when remote learning alternates with in-person classes.

With the Covid-19 pandemic, the companies and organizations that had generalized remote working too quickly swiftly understood the advantages of returning to a blended working model. Work from home days have a negative impact, especially by almost entirely restricting casual chat between workers at all levels in the organization. The effects on creativity, improved work processes and governance are all well-documented today (Beatriz and Erb 2024; Askenazy et al. 2025).

For various reasons related to the geostrategic recentering of the world, leadership in the field of standardization, which was largely Euro-Atlantic, is moving toward Southeast Asia. Standardization organizations, which had to radically reorganize their technical discussions (TC and SC) online, must work with a new dynamic today. This was initiated chiefly by the Standardization Administration of China (SAC), which insisted on prioritizing conducting plenary sessions and WGs in person once again. This recentering, reinforced by the cultural and geographic proximity of the three countries that were in a position to take on global leadership in standardization (China, Japan and Korea), swiftly impacted the future of the founding vision of standardization, which was universal yet Eurocentric.

C.2. From the spirit of the laws to the spirit of standardization

> If I knew something useful to me and harmful to my family, I should put it out of my mind. If I knew something useful to my family and not to my country, I should try to forget it. If I knew something useful to my country and harmful to Europe, or useful to Europe and harmful to the human race, I should consider it a crime. (Montesquieu 1989)

Many political scientists and standardization experts believe that it would be useful to rationally and systematically revisit interactions between standards, regulations and legislation. The fundamental difference between standards and the law is that standards are generally voluntarily adopted and are designed by domain experts either to prevent accidents, risks or defects in quality that have already been observed or to establish a common, pre-competitive base. This basic foundation gives the techno-professional community access to interoperable components, thus facilitating the development of new, more ambitious and convergent technologies, products or services.

Laws, on the contrary, are statutory in nature: in democratic countries, in principle, they are voted in through parliaments and represent the diversity of opinions among a nation. They also, ideally, guarantee peaceful coexistence and solidarity among regions[7]. A government generally works with parliament to propose the reformulation of laws, or to implement new laws that are deemed necessary. However, the crises in the functioning of democracy, affecting many democratic countries around the world, often cause erratic legislative processes or even block them. It becomes difficult to establish consensus and legislation is then based on a corpus of legacy laws, amended or reformulated by successive layers of jurisprudence and legislative adaptations.

As with standards, modernization and the complexification of the world and technologies result in a growing volume of laws and regulations. This often negatively impacts the functioning of democracies. Many political researchers believe that in many cases, the use of voluntary standards would put in place a more flexible legal system, founded on the expertise of the concerned actors rather than periodic ideological battles. In concrete terms, the harmonization and systematic unification of these three domains would simplify the understanding and applications of this ever-growing number of standards (especially in the environment, food and security sectors) by elected representatives, small enterprises and the general public. This difficulty in using standards is even greater when they become mandatory and must be paid for.

Environmental standards are a perfect example of the need for this kind of harmonization. The standardization of smart cities could concretize this legislative-standardization dynamic. Unlike legislation, the corpus of environmental standards can be more easily updated and established through

7 Unfortunately, parliamentary bicameralism is too often underestimated.

consensus between industrialists and insurance professionals[8]. Far from denying democratic reality, the systematic application of consensus-building could profoundly transform our political practices. Each citizen (and, at the minimum, each regional representative) should be able to contribute to the intelligent and sustainable prosperity of their region. However, this legislative-standardization evolution assumes that citizens, entrepreneurs, heads of associations and institutional actors will be personally invested in, or send delegations to, the creation of standards within this new political space, which will be more flexible as it is based on concerted standardization efforts.

There are already initiatives in place to begin this crucial process. This revolution is already taking place in many domains, often without people being fully aware of it. For example, the standards adopted by European bodies (CEN CENELEC) are systematically integrated into corpora of national standards in each of the 27 States, and some of them may be made mandatory through legislation. However, the chief resistance to this transformation is from within the political sphere itself. The jurists who help legislators are more often legal historians than technical experts. Furthermore, in an increasingly technological society, there are many fields related to the law or regulations that will benefit from being examined from a standardization point of view. This need is particularly clear in areas such as the Digital Services Act (DSA), which are highly publicized. This law was the result of standardization and regulation work carried out beforehand by CEN and CENELEC, before being validated by the European Parliament.

Many sectors (urbanism, health, agriculture, food, transport, environment, right to work and education) will benefit from having more diversified expert committees in their ranks. This will facilitate participation from professionals in the field, unionists, elected representatives and representatives from local communities. However, creating this new balance raises questions about the economic model of standardization. While a country's legislators and bureaucrats are paid through revenue from taxes, standardization organizations are largely reliant on subscriptions from companies and from the sale of standards. We can, therefore, imagine how complex it would be to transfer this activity.

8 It is important to emphasize that every year it is becoming increasingly important to have a standardized framework for disasters (fires, floods and pollution).

And yet, it is crucial that we do this, especially given China's increasing geostrategic power in the field of standardization[9]. The rise of smart cities and communities is a perfect illustration of this ongoing transformation. This domain is founded on a constant interaction between laws, regulations and standards. Furthermore, regional governance and associational networks already involve voluntary work, comparable to standardization expertise. Not all countries are equally equipped for this change. Smaller countries, or those containing autonomous regions, will adapt more easily than hypercentralized States like France, where this transition is currently being planned in too bureaucratic a manner.

Parliamentary voting also slows down the process. Unlike standardization committees, parliamentarians often use binary choices (yes or no) without necessarily justifying their choice. They are not bound by a need to go back over texts until they arrive at a consensus, and do not have expertise in all the domains they are voting on. This often leads to their adopting positions based on ideology rather than subject-knowledge. However, a growing number of standards are becoming State mandated.

In France, there are currently around 1,000 standards that are mandatorily applied (as against 400 in 2016). This is a non-negligible number compared to the 22,000 standards in the AFNOR catalogue. Note that 200 of these mandatory standards were transformed into orders or decrees and are available on the official AFNOR and Légifrance websites. (Légifrance is the official French government website with information on laws and regulations.) However, the remaining 800 standards are mandatory but must still be purchased, often at high prices, and some of them are not even translated into French yet. This is quite a paradox with respect to the fundamental legal principle, *Ignorantia juris non excusat* (ignorance of the law is not an excuse). These contradictions, denounced as far back as 2017 in a report prepared by French senator Élisabeth Lamure, have not yet been resolved (Lamure 2017). Slimming down legislative corpora in favor of voluntary standards will not be an easy process. However, the current evolution of the law and standardization makes it possible to identify domains that are a priority in order to accelerate the process.

9 In China, the distinction between laws and standards is not the same as in democratic countries and standards are systematically applied as mandatory.

Another example is that of blockchain (ISO/TC 307), which is a fundamental challenge to sovereign functioning. It is clear that as with many technologies, the recent (2016) work on standardizing blockchain technology allowed politicians to gain a better understanding of the variety of uses it has, beyond its primary objective: bitcoin[10]. The first two lines of this committee's scope emphasize:

<Blockchain technology promises to revolutionize not only the financial world, but also a variety of other sectors, from social inclusion to government efficiency, including health and all enterprise distributed systems as products.>

A quick overview of the various WGs in TC 37 gives us a fascinating glimpse of this highly promising technology – as long as it is regulated by internationally shared standards. These applications include digital money and digital currency, not only bitcoin, but also coins that could be issued by large central banks, as well as local coins, or even demurrage currency[11]. They can also be used for carbon markets and, eventually, other environmental applications (such as land use), smart contracts and their applications, as well as governance. Finally, blockchain may also have an effect on a possible transformation in how electoral delegations are organized and the democratic expression of citizens through blockchain.

C.3. Unification of acronyms for standards: the prerequisite to learning about them

Standardization is a subject that is difficult for the general public to assimilate; however, it is also a discipline, the study of an activity that is

10 See Quiniou (2019).

11 A demurrage currency is a currency that depreciates in value over time. This encourages users to use it up quickly rather than hoarding it, thus stimulating local economies by promoting the circulation of wealth. This is a feature of certain Local Exchange Trading Systems (LETS); however, historically, this was practiced during sieges ("obsidional coins", money issued during a siege, which could not be hoarded since the duration of the siege was uncertain), or for example, in 1932 in Wörgl (Austria), when it was used to revive the economy during a depression. Despite being successful, this experiment was unfortunately stopped by Austria's central bank.

very rarely specified by any university[12]. Nonetheless, the universality of the science of standardization remains an operational concept. This is also the level on which we can envisage studying standardization both as a subject to be taught and also as an area of research. In terms of applied research, this has been happening for a long time. We saw that many of the actors who participated in founding the IEC, for example, were university professors or renowned scholars. On the other hand, although it is slow to be generalized, specific teaching on the theory and practice of normalization is increasingly being seen in engineering schools. Economists, jurists and social scientists in general are also interested in this subject.

Our propositions here are more sectorial and focus on the methodology of standard production, while in universities and in the social sciences, the focus is on the subject matter, its history and the sociology of its actors. In order to rationalize exchanges between researchers, we believe it is essential to have a pre-defined, unique international vocabulary and, especially, to have fixed, universal abbreviations and acronyms independent of the language being spoken. Of course, the experts who work in international standardization use an "ISO dialect" among themselves, which is never ambiguous. Unfortunately, national practices are much more diversified. We have often spoken about the facts that determine these diversities; for instance, the impossibility of dividing the various international bodies (TC, SC and WG) into mirror committees in every country. We have another example: if we wish to maximize the number of experts participating in all national standardization bodies, it is impossible to enforce vocabulary and acronyms that are generally in English right from the outset. Nonetheless, this prerequisite tolerance results in later problems for the experts.

This diversity in vocabulary makes it practically impossible to put in place a rational and exhaustive list of symbols and to include all the objects, processes, productions and standardization bodies. The initial ease of working soon becomes a problem. The assimilation of a large number of abbreviations becomes harder if they depend on a specific language in fundamental documents. For example, the reference for the standard ISO/IEC 10646 (Universal Coded Character Set) may sometimes be translated by institutions themselves, and thus French users will refer to this

12 Knowing that universities, engineering schools and scientific research (fundamental or applied) are organized in highly diverse ways in different countries.

standard as ISO/IEC 10646[13]. Two references for the same standard[14]! Fortunately, using the international abbreviation accompanied by a translated abbreviation is a regular practice almost everywhere, except among Francophones. Thus, this is one pitfall that has been circumvented.

The creation of national mirror bodies distinct from the international reality is a trickier question. However, perhaps this could also be solved by systematically using acronyms or abbreviations from national bodies along with those from the international bodies.

With these few challenges being resolved, we would also then need a systematic clarification of these abbreviations and acronyms. A neophyte is likely to flounder in this sea of letters[15]! Fortunately, the logic behind how these operate is quite simple, with a hierarchic and associative syntax, and with a clear system of prefixes, suffixes, connectors, etc. For example, we have ISO/TC 268, ISO/TC 268/SC 1, and then ISO/TC 268/SC 1/WG 1, and so on. While this must be explained initially, once understood we can see that these abbreviations can be stacked up together like Lego bricks.

Scopes: a question of the stability and traceability of standards. As explained in the preface, scopes are essential definitions that ensure systematic and exclusive information sharing, which alone can allow standards to be interoperable with each other. In this book, we have presented the English versions of the scopes (ISO, IEC and ITU scopes may be available in multiple official languages, with each scope being translated by that body itself, without being a literal translation of any of the other languages). They are presented between brackets. These are not actually fixed statements – scopes may evolve or fluctuate depending on modifications brought in by the standardization body. However, and this is a critical issue, it is difficult and often impossible for even the participating experts to maintain a reliable history of these modifications. This lack of traceability is currently partially remedied within the three large standardization organizations (ISO, IEC and ITU) and in JTC 1, all of which have started archiving their own histories in different ways. However, they almost never include this fundamental history of scopes.

13 Which quickly becomes a necessity.

14 The crucial onomasiological requirement seems to have been forgotten.

15 We do not claim that they are simple to define and resolve by consensus.

It is essential to maintain a history of scopes, as these define the standardization project undertaken by each committee, subcommittee, or working group; they also define the scope of a standard, a set of standards, or preparatory documents developed or proposed by experts. The global community of experts relies on these scopes of action (as well as the titles of the bodies and documents) to ensure rigorous interoperability during standards development. Indeed, as various addenda and updates to a standard are made, and as the scope of standardization activities is addressed by a TC, SC, or WG, their respective scopes will naturally change. However, since by definition the entire community of standards experts cannot know everything, in order to avoid either encroaching on the scope of other TCs or simultaneously developing standards that are dissimilar but have the same objective, it would be highly necessary to have not only the scopes of all committees and all standards, but also the historical data, which alone can ensure true interoperability for all sectors of activity.

If the standardization community could agree on the coordinated interoperability of these few elements (which have been listed and described here very briefly and must be studied in greater detail), it would be much easier to communicate how standard production functions and how it can be used.

C.4. Digital refounding through transparent and certified standards

Only 1 or 2 years ago, from a straightforward, humanistic point of view, it looked as though our society was being held hostage by GAFAM+[16]. However, for over 10 years now, standardization organizations, *stricto sensu*, have been developing new families of standards, which are redefining what truly reliable and sincere ICT standards should be, as prescribed by Lord Balfour[17] in his 1908 speech in London: "So to describe the qualities of different machines that, whilst the man who buys and the man who sells will know exactly what each, respectively, is doing, there will yet be the freest initiative left to both" (Balfour 1908). Our neo-industrial civilization in this third decade of the 21st century is greatly dependent on electrical, electronic

16 As with the founding of standardization organizations in the 19th and early 20th centuries, this assertion has its limits, those of European democratic universality.

17 Concretely, it concerns the creation of TCs or SCs.

and information technologies, and it is therefore imperative for these machines to be transparent, with no "black box"[18]. However, GAFAM+ have completely violated Balfour's founding pact.

The majority of the families of standards proposed over the last two rounds by JTC 1 reiterate these rules. The corpus of recommendations proposed to construct the Internet is not in question. These recommendations exist and may serve as the basis for rebuilding ICT in the second quarter of the 21st century. It is heartening to see that certain industrial actors, who have been profiting from data theft and addicted minds for the past 15 years, are now beginning to feel threatened. By openly siding with purveyors of falsehoods and science denialism, Elon Musk is indisputably accelerating people's loss of confidence in all GAFAM+ companies. It is probable that almost all users will abruptly stop placing their confidence in GAFAM+. What will democratic nations do? What anti-trust laws can be used by future governments of the United States? How will GAFAM+ carry out their transformation? Some applications will continue with the *status quo*, undoubtedly, retaining their faithful clientele of conspiracy theorists and addicts to the original network.

However, a transparent digital refoundation, certified by standards and guaranteeing privacy, may occur sooner than we hope. It is true that today this is just a niche market for professional and institutional users largely; however, it could soon grow. These standards have become indispensable for many Cloud applications, IoT, AI, health, and e-governance, which are the pioneering clientèle of these standards. Products and applications for the general public, and whose transparency will be certified, could soon follow. This could prevent profits from e-commerce and e-tourism from being unduly snatched away from their sites of production. A considerable share of GAFAM+ capital and expertise will necessarily be redistributed into this new offering. At present, GAFAM+ sponsor Unicode and Internet consortia, while also being shareholders in a large number of undersea cables and satellites. How will these consortia work if they are no longer sponsored? Will they be welcomed within standardization organizations? Integrated into JTC 1? Taken into ITU for a true renewal of this body?

18 Buyers who use ICT for industrial, commercial or service purposes, as well as end consumers.

With certain aspects changed, this digital refoundation that is already underway could be compared to the early years of the Electrical Congresses and then the IEC. Thanks to standards, the trust reposed in the digital sector by industrialists as well as users has made this the central industry of the 20th and now the 21st century. Like mechanical machines, which had to move beyond their "Wild West" developmental period, the digital world is also likely to enter an era of transparency and privacy, guaranteed by standards.

It is urgent to push back against GAFAM+ using targeted technological standards; however, this is not the only challenge posed by globalization, which grows ever more complex every year. We have seen that the interactions between laws and standards have become very strategic. Modern nations can no longer burden parliamentarians alone with the task of developing regulation for a technoculture and technological environment that is often beyond their competencies. The use of standards that have been discussed within a voluntary framework can relieve parliamentarians of overly specialized tasks. Further, the need to cooperate with standardization experts will help evolve decision-making models that are too centered on archaic rules favoring a majority, without requiring consensus or justifications. This question is one that is expected to respond to today's democratic crisis.

Smart and sustainable cities and communities are another promising standardization challenge, complementing what we just saw. Ancient cities were able to invent democracy because their forum was the focal point of debates and exchanges of all kinds. And indeed, it is because of the meta-convergent nature of smart cities that the different branches of standardization TCs or SCs, who have thus far developed their standards in a vertical manner, will be forced to rapidly change their strategy. For example, it will become impossible for highly polluting factories to monitor their waste percentage all by themselves. In order to remain competitive and prosperous, cities must integrate all manner of indicators (environmental, as well as cultural, health, education, economic balance, etc.).

All the data generated or used by AI, IoT, home automation and smart sensors in a city or region can thus be oriented to serve the interests of a city or region and help them achieve their social, economic or environmental goals. Democratic expression itself is concerned as software can be used to modulate votes, synthesizing questions that are often contradictory in nature, to ultimately "make society". But to stay on the topic of standard production, we are convinced that smart cities are the optimal focal point for a meta-convergence of activities that must be standardized and which are essential for this neo-industrial civilization.

In his profound work *On the Mode of Existence of Technical Objects*, Simondon laid out the philosophical and ethical framework for our technoculture:

> Recognition of the modes of existence of technical objects must be the result of philosophic consideration; what philosophy has to achieve in this respect is analogous to what the abolition of slavery achieved in affirming the worth of the individual human being [...] Culture behaves towards the technical object much in the same way as a man caught up in primitive xenophobia behaves towards a stranger [...] Still, the machine is a stranger to us, it is a stranger in which what is human is locked in, unrecognized, materialized and enslaved, but human nonetheless. The most powerful cause of alienation in the world of today is based on misunderstanding of the machine. The alienation in question is not caused by the machine but by a failure to come to an understanding of the nature and essence of the machine. (Simondon 1980, pp. 9–10)

References

André, J. (2002). Caractères, codage et normalisation : de Chappe à Unicode. In *Unicode, écriture du monde*, André, J. and Hudrisier, H. (eds). Hermès Science Publications, Paris.

Andries, P. (2008). *Unicode 5.0 en pratique. Codage des caractères et internationalisation des logiciels et documents*. Dunod, Paris.

Archives parlementaires (1795). Loi du 1er vendémiaire an IV.

Ariffin, Y. (2015). Les expositions universelles comme communautés émotionnelles imaginées : du bon usage des émotions dans l'art d'instruire et de divertir. *Relations internationales*, 164(4), 9–26.

Aristotle (1895). *The Nicomachean Ethics of Aristotle*. G. Bell, London.

Askenazy, P., Di Nallo, U., Ramajo, I., Thiounn, C. (2025). Télétravail et présentiel : le travail hybride, une pratique désormais ancrée dans les entreprises. *INSEE Analyses*, 105, 1–4.

Azémard, G. (2013). *100 Notions for Crossmedia and Transmedia*. Éditions de l'Immatériel, Paris.

Azémard, G., Hudrisier, H., Ben Henda, M. et al. (2015). Mutations et continuités du document numérique : similarités historiques et approche déconstructiviste de la grammatologie post-numérique. In *Actes du dix-huitième colloque international sur le document électronique (CIDE 18)*, Montpellier.

Balfour, A. (1956). Speech for IEC delegation [1908]. In *History of the International Electrotechnical Commission*, Ruppert, L. (ed.). International Electrotechnical Commission, Geneva [Online]. Available at: https://www.iec.ch.

Barchietto, R. (1997). Le travail du Secrétariat central. In *L'Histoire d'une amitié partagée : souvenirs à propos des 50 premières années de l'ISO*. ISO, Geneva.

Barny, A. (1863). *Traité historique des poids et mesures et de la vérification*. Hachette, Paris.

Beatriz, M. and Erb, L. (2024). Comment évolue la pratique du télétravail depuis la crise sanitaire ? *Dares Analyses*, 64, 1–8.

Ben Henda, M. (2013). Can ICT be standardized? An overview from an educational perspective. In *French-Chinese Bioethics Symposiums – 2nd Wuhan Seminar: Ethical, Legal and Social Issues Raised by Emerging Technologies*, Wuhan, 7–8 November.

Ben Henda, M. (2015). Adaptation normative des big data et du learning analytics. In *Big data – Open data. Quelles valeurs ? Quels enjeux ?*, Broudoux, E. and Chartron, G. (eds). De Boeck Supérieur, Louvain-la-Neuve and ADBS, Paris.

Ben Henda, M. (2017). La normalisation du "bien numérique commun" dans la coopération internationale. In *Coopération à l'ère du numérique*, Laulan, A.-M. (ed.). L'Harmattan, Paris.

Berners-Lee, T. (2007). Giant global graph. Decentralized Information Group [Online]. Available at: https://web.archive.org.

Berners-Lee, T. and Cailliau, R. (1990). Proposal for a HyperText project [Online]. Available at: http://cds.cern.ch/record.

Blandin, B., Mason, J., Neville, L. (2012). Standards et gouvernance : l'expérience du SC 36 de l'ISO/IEC. *Distance et médiation des savoirs*.

BnF (n.d.a). Naissance du mot et de la phrase dans les manuscrits occidentaux. *BnF Essentiels* [Online]. Available at: http://essentiels.bnf.fr/fr/litterature.

BnF (n.d.b). Une histoire de la typographie des origines à l'ère industrielle. *BnF Essentiels* [Online]. Available at: http://essentiels.bnf.fr/fr/litterature.

Borde, J.-M. (2005). Interopérabilité et normalisation dans les systèmes d'information pour l'éducation. In *Colloque EIAH'2005. Environnements informatiques pour l'apprentissage humain : Actes de la conférence EIAH 2005*, Tchounikine, P. (ed.). ATIEF, Lyon.

Borde, J.-M. and Hudrisier, H. (1999/2000). Au cœur de la technologie du document. *SOLARIS*, 6.

Borde, J.-M., Vaucelle, A., Hudrisier, H. (2014). La normalisation : dynamique opaque ou bonne gouvernance mondiale ? *Pensée plurielle*, 2(36), 9–35.

Bourda, Y., Mason, J., Neville, L. (2013). SC36 and the future of e-learning standards. *International Journal of IT Standards and Standardization Research.*

Bourda, Y., Cho, Y.-S., Guay, J.-J. et al. (2017). Metadata for learning resources (MLR, ISO/IEC 19788). In *Initiatives 2015: Standards for Digital Learning Resources: Publishing, Referencing, Delivery, Tracking*, Ben Henda, M. (ed.). Les Éditions de l'Immatériel, Paris.

Boyé, M. (n.d.). Introduction du système métrique. Académie Montesquieu [Online]. Available at: https://www.academie-montesquieu.fr/introduction-du-systeme-metrique-par-michel-boye/ [Accessed 17 February 2025].

Bracha, O. (2005). Owning ideas: A history of Anglo-American intellectual property. SJD Dissertation, Harvard Law School, Cambridge [Online]. Available at: http://www.obracha.net/oi/oi.htm.

Brasseul, J. (1998). Une revue des interprétations de la révolution industrielle. *Région et développement*, 7, 45–47.

Brossard, L.E. (1924). *Le correcteur typographe.* Arrault et Cie, Tours.

Broudoux, E. and Scopsi, C. (2011). L'enjeu des métadonnées dans un contexte de "re-documentarisation". *Études de communication*, 9–22.

Burnard, L. (2014). *What Is the Text Encoding Initiative? How to Add Intelligent Markup to Digital Resources*. Open Edition Press, Marseille.

Cavoukian, A. (2008). Privacy in the clouds. *Identity in the Information Society*, 1(1), 89–108 [Online]. Available at: https://scispace.com/papers/privacy-in-the-clouds-xydtgkqnrl.

CCNR (n.d.). Historique du CCNR [Online]. Available at: https://www.ccr-zkr.org/11010100-en.html.

Cerf, V., Kahn, B., Chapin, L. (1992). An oral history of the Internet Society's founding [Online]. Available at: https://www.internetsociety.org/history/oral-history-of-the-internet-societys-founding/ [Accessed 17 February 2025].

CERN (n.d.). A short history of the Web [Online]. Available at: https://home.cern/science/computing/birth-web/short-history-web.

Champion, B. (2007). La mesure du monde : Ératosthène et Ptolémée. *Travaux & documents, Journées de l'Antiquité 2005-2006*, 29, 135–160 [Online]. Available at: https://hal.archives-ouvertes.fr/hal-01170184.

Chapelle, J.-B., Jaucourt, L., Rousseau, J.-J., Venel, G.-F. (1751). Mesure. In *L'Encyclopédie*, volume 10, Diderot, D., d'Alembert, J.L.R. (eds). Édition Numérique Collaborative et Critique de l'Encyclopédie (1751–1772) (ENCCRE), Académie des Sciences, Paris [Online]. Available at: https://enccre.academie-sciences.fr/encyclopedie.

Condorcet (1791). Lettre de M. Condorcet au nom de l'académie des sciences concernant le choix d'une unité de mesure, lors de la séance du 26 mars 1791. In *Archives parlementaires de la Révolution Française, Première série (1787-1799), Tome XXIV – Du 10 mars 1791 au 12 avril 1791, Assemblée nationale, 26 mars 1791, Séance du matin, Rapport par M. Talleyrand-Périgord et décret relatif à l'établissement d'une unité de mesure*. Parliamentary Archives, Paris.

CRHST/CNRS (2013). Histoire des unités électriques : le premier congrès internatio-nal des électriciens à Paris en 1881. Site Ampère [Online]. Available at: http://histoires-de-sciences.over-blog.fr/2013/11/histoire-des-unités-électriques.html [Accessed 17 February 2025].

Davis, M. (n.d.). 10 years of unicode [Online]. Available at: https://www.unicode.org.

Davis, M. and Wideburg, L. (1998). Mark Davis: Interview by Laura Wideburg [Online]. Available at: https://www.unicode.org.

Dcode (n.d.). Code Chappe : télégraphe optique/aérien – Décoder et encoder en ligne [Online]. Available at: https://www.dcode.fr [Accessed 17 February 2025].

De Naucratis, A. (1789–1791). *Banquet des savants, Livre XII*. Lamy, Paris [Online]. Available at: https://www.digitale-sammlungen.de/en/view/bsb10215752.

Decramer, L.R., Elhaj, R., Hilton, R., Plas, A. (2002). Approche géométrique des centuriations romaines : les nouvelles bornes du Bled Segui. *Histoire et mesure*, 17(1/2), 137–150.

Delambre, J.B.J. (1814). *Astronomie théorique et pratique*. Veuve Courcier, Paris.

Delemontey, Y. (2020). Industrialiser le bâtiment sous l'Occupation : un repli prolifique entre restrictions et substitutions. In *Architecture et urbanisme*, Cohen, J.-L. (ed.). Éditions du Collège de France, Paris.

Destrez, J. (1923). La pecia dans les manuscrits du Moyen Âge. *Revue des sciences philosophiques et théologiques*, 13(2), 182–197.

Diderot, D. and d'Alembert, J.L.R. (1751–1772). *Encyclopédie ou dictionnaire raisonné des sciences, des arts et des métiers*. Chez Briasson, Paris [Online]. Available at: https://fr.wikisource.org/wiki/Encyclop%C3%A9die,_ou_Dictionnaire_raisonné_des_sciences,_des_arts_et_des_métiers [Accessed 17 February 2025].

Doctorow, C. (2025). *Le rapt d'Internet*. C&F, Caen.

Dumas, J.-B. (1869). Rapport sur les prototypes du système métrique : le mètre et le kilogramme des Archives. *Comptes Rendus des Séances de l'Académie des Sciences, Paris*, 69, 514–518 [Online]. Available at: http://sites.mathdoc.fr/cgi-bin/rbsm?au=DUMAS.

Eisenstein, E.L. (1989). *The Printing Revolution in Early Modern Europe*. Cambridge University Press, Cambridge.

English, B. and Wideburg, L. (1998). Bill English : premier directeur financier du consortium Unicode [Online]. Available at: https://www.unicode.org.

Février, D. (n.d.). Histoire du mètre : des débuts de l'ère chrétienne à nos jours – Histoire d'une unité de mesure. Métrologie légale et industrielle [Online]. Available at: https://metrologie-francaise.lne.fr/fr/metrologie/histoire-des-unites.

Fielden, J. (1836). Speech in the House of Commons (9 May 1836). *Spartacus Educational* [Online]. Available at: https://spartacus-educational.com/IRpiecers.htm.

Figuier, L. (1867–1891). *Les merveilles de la science ou description populaire des inventions modernes*. Furne, Jouvet et Cie, Paris [Online]. Available at: https://fr.wikisource.org/wiki/Les_Merveilles_de_la_science.

Figuier, L. (1868). *Les merveilles de la science ou description populaire des inventions modernes : le télégraphe électrique*. Furne, Jouvet et Cie, Paris.

Fraboulet, D. (2007). *Quand les patrons s'organisent : stratégies et pratiques de l'Union des industries métallurgiques et minières 1901–1950*. Presses universitaires du Septentrion, Villeneuve-d'Ascq.

Frey, E. (1909). Les quatre Bureaux internationaux de Berne. In *Conférence donnée à Berne aux étudiants de l'École supérieure de commerce de Berlin* [Online]. Available at: https://www.itu.int/net/.

Frontard, R. (1994). Histoire de la norme. *Culture technique, La normalisation technique*, 29, 19–27.

Frontard, R. (1997). Standards-related activities: "The global view". In *Friendship Among Equals: Recollections from ISO's First Fifty Years*. ISO, Geneva.

Gall, E. and Chacon, M.-J. (2015). ScoLOMFR and ScoLIE: Two complementary projects from the French Ministry for Education, Higher Education and Research (MENESR). In *Initiatives 2015: Standards for Digital Learning Resources: Publishing, Referencing, Delivery, Tracking*, Ben Henda, M. (ed.). Les Éditions de l'Immatériel, Paris.

Gerspach, É. (1860). Histoire administrative de la télégraphie aérienne en France. *Annales télégraphiques* [Online]. Available at: https://www.itu.int/net/.

Gille, B. (1986). *The History of Techniques. Vol 1: Techniques and Civilizations; Vol 2: Techniques and Sciences*. Gordon and Breach Science Publishers, New York.

Goodrich, J. (2023). How the computer graphics industry got started at the University of Utah. *IEEE Spectrum* [Online]. Available at: https://spectrum.ieee.org [Accessed 17 February 2025].

Goody, J. (1977). *The Domestication of the Savage Mind.* Cambridge University Press, Cambridge.

Grey, V. (1997). Setting standards: "A phenomenal success story". In *Friendship Among Equals: Recollections from ISO's First Fifty Years*. ISO, Geneva.

Grison, E. (2000). Gaspard Monge. *Bulletin de la Sabix*, 23 [Online]. Available at: http://journals.openedition.org/sabix/216 [Accessed 27 April 2024].

Guillaume, J. (1909). Les sextiles de l'ère républicaine. In *Études révolutionnaires, 20e partie* [Online] Available at: https://www.antimythes.fr/individus/guillaume_james/gj_etudes_revolutionnaires_20.pdf.

Hacquard, G. (1952). *Guide romain antique*. Hachette, Paris.

Havelock, E.A. (1981). *The Literate Revolution in Greece and its Cultural Consequences*. Princeton University Press, Princeton.

Herrenschmidt, C. (1999). Écriture, monnaie, réseaux. Inventions des Anciens, inventions des Modernes. *Le Débat*, 4(106), 17–36.

Hoel, T. (2017). An exploration of standardisation options for the new field of learning analytics. In *Initiatives 2015: Standards for Digital Learning Resources: Publishing, Referencing, Delivery, Tracking*, Ben Henda, M. (ed.). Les Éditions de l'Immatériel, Paris.

Hudrisier, H. (1997). La norme de codage des caractères sur plusieurs octets (ISO/IEC 10646), un enjeu pour le Sommet francophone de Hanoi. In *MED'IACOM inforoutes 97*, Beirut [Online]. Available at: https://www.auf.org/.

Hudrisier, H. (1999). Distinguer technique et technologie, un préalable à la réflexion NTIC. *Passerelles Paris*, 8(24), 54–56.

Hudrisier, H. and Borde, J.-M. (2013). L'indicateur normalisation technique industrielle dans la géopolitique du développement économique global. In *CANAL 2013 : circulations et appropriations des normes et des modèles de l'action locale*. Agropolis, Montpellier.

Hudrisier, H. and Lucas, N. (1991). Des idéogrammes dopés par l'ordinateur. *Le Monde diplomatique*, 12, 44–46.

Huffman, D.A. (1952). A method for the construction of minimum-redundancy codes. *Proceedings of the IRE*, 40, 1098–1101.

Humbley, J. (2007). Vers une réception plurielle de la théorie terminologique de Wüster : une lecture commentée des avant-propos successifs du manuel Einführung in die allgemeine Terminologielehre. *Langages*, 168(4), 82–91.

IAB (n.d.). History of the IAB [Online]. Available at: https://www.iab.org/about/history/ [Accessed 17 February 2025].

IEC (n.d.). History of IEC [Online]. Available at: https://www.iec.ch/history [Accessed 17 February 2025].

IEC (1938). International electrotechnical vocabulary [Online]. Available at: https://www.iec.ch.

IEC (1981). Bulletin spécial IEC [Online]. Available at: https://www.iec.ch [Accessed 17 February 2025].

ISO (1997). *Friendship Among Equals: Recollections from ISO's First Fifty Years*. ISO, Geneva [Online]. Available at: https://web.iso.org/files/live/sites/isoorg/files/about%20ISO/docs/en/

ITU-WSIS (2003). Declaration of principles: Building the information society: A global challenge in the new millennium. World Summit on the Information Society, Phase 1.

ITU-WSIS (2005). Top global experts on information technology expected to take part in Tunis conference on bridging "digital divide". World Summit on the Information Society, Phase 2.

Kant, E. (1796). *Projet de paix perpétuelle*. Jansen et Perronneau, Paris [Online]. Available at: https://gallica.bnf.fr/ark:/12148/bpt6k55798317.

Kuert, W. (1997). The founding of ISO: "Things are going the right way!" In *Friendship Among Equals: Recollections from ISO's First Fifty Years*. ISO, Geneva.

Kuhn, T.S. (1957). *The Copernican Revolution: Planetary Astronomy in the Development of Western Thought*. Harvard University Press, Cambridge.

Kuhn, T.S. (1962). *The Structure of Scientific Revolutions*. University of Chicago Press, Chicago.

La Condamine, C.-M. (1751). *Mesure des trois premiers degrés du méridien dans l'hémisphère austral*. Imprimerie royale, Paris [Online]. Available at: https://gallica.bnf.fr/.

La Nature (1881–1895). Le Congrès international des électriciens [Online]. Available at: https://www.cnam.fr/portail/conservatoire-national-des-arts-et-metiers.

La Porta, L. (2025). What is Punycode? Fake domains that deceive the human eye. *JAMF*.

Lamure, É. (2017). Impact de la normalisation. Report 627, Senate, Paris [Online]. Available at: https://www.senat.fr/rap/r16-627/r16-6271.pdf.

Lapointe, S. (2000). L'histoire des brevets [Online]. Available at: https://www.robic.ca/wp-content/uploads/2017/05/174-LHistoire-des-brevets.pdf.

Lefebure, A. (1992). *Havas, les arcanes du pouvoir*. Grasset, Paris.

Légifrance (n.d.). Site officiel du droit français [Online]. Available at: https://www.legifrance.gouv.fr.

Lemoine, B. (1986). *L'architecture de fer : France XIXe siècle*. Champ Vallon, Seyssel.

Lespinet-Najib, V. and Pinède, N. (eds) (2021). *Fractures corporelles, fractures numériques, de l'accessibilité aux usages*. Maison des sciences de l'homme d'Aquitaine, Pessac.

Lucas, N. (2002). Le retour des idéogrammes : Unicode CJC vu du Japon. *Document numérique*, 6(3–4).

Luce, J.H. (1953). Géométrie de la perspective à l'époque de Vitruve. *Revue d'histoire des sciences et de leurs applications*, 6(4), 308–321 [Online]. Available at: https://www.jstor.org/stable/23905531.

Maréchal, R. (1997). The early years: "We had some good times". In *Friendship Among Equals: Recollections from ISO's First Fifty Years*. ISO, Geneva.

Marquet, L. (1975). Il y a cent ans : Jean-Baptiste Dumas et la Convention du mètre. *Revue d'histoire de la pharmacie*, 227, 559–567..

Martin de Guise, S. (2013). La MEI (Music Encoding Initiative) : un standard au service de la musique kabyle. In *Iles Dimesli*, Tigziri, N. (ed.). Université Mouloud Mammeri, Tizi-Ouzou.

Mason, J. (2007). Standards, services, models, and frameworks: Trends in ICT infrastructure for education and research. In *Next Generation Photonics and Media Technologies*, Yoshida, J. and Sasabe, H. (eds). PWC Publishing, Chitose.

Mason, J., Peoples, B.-E., Lee, J. (2020). Questioning the scope of AI standardization in learning, education and training. *Journal of Web Engineering*, 8(2), 107–122 [Online]. Available at: https://journals.riverpublishers.com/index.php/JICTS/article/view/2643/1737.

MEI (2023). MEI guidelines version 5 [Online]. Available at: https://music-encoding.org/guidelines/v5/content/introduction.html.

Moffat, A. and Turpin, A. (2002). Minimum-redundancy coding. *Compression and Coding Algorithms*, 669, 51–90.

Moles, A. (1971). Image, schématisation iconale. In *La communication. Les dictionnaires du savoir moderne*. Centre d'études et de promotion de la lecture, Paris.

Monge, G. (1820). *Géométrie descriptive*. Veuve Courcier, Paris [Online]. Available at: https://gallica.bnf.fr/ark:/12148/bpt6k96811234.

Montesquieu, C.L. (1989). *The Spirit of the Laws*. Cambridge University Press, Cambridge.

Mouren, R. and Hudrisier, H. (2018). Éthique et Storytelling : une co-construction démocratique des normes techno-numériques de la Smart City. In *International Digital Storytelling Conference: Current Trends in Digital Storytelling*, Zakynthos Island.

Mouren, R. and Marneffe, T. (2022). Normalisation internationale de la gouvernance numérique des systèmes de mobilité durable : enjeux et perspectives. *TIC et société*, 16(1), 11–45 [Online]. Available at: https://journals.openedition.org/ticetsociete/7219.

Navier, C.L.M.H. (1826). *Leçons sur l'application de la mécanique à l'établissement de la construction des machines*. L'École des ponts et chaussées, Paris [Online]. Available at: https://archive.org/details/rsumdesleconsdo00saingoog.

Nguilla-Kooh, F. and Doyen, S. (2021). *Transport ferroviaire intelligent et sécurité numérique : enjeux et challenges dans l'espace européen*. EGE, Paris.

Nora, S. and Minc, A. (1980). *The Computerization of Society: A Report to the President of France*. MIT Press, Cambridge.

Normand, J.-M. (2019). L'éclatante Jamais Contente. *Le Monde* [Online]. Available at: https://fr.wikipedia.org/wiki/Histoire_du_véhicule_électrique.

Noyer, M. (2002). *Normes et standards : de la stratégie à la pratique*. Hermès, Paris.

Noyer, M. (2004). Les normes dans la société de l'information. In *La société de l'information : nouveaux enjeux politiques et sociaux*, Proulx, S. (ed.). Hermès, Paris.

Oillo, D. (2018). L'innovation en éducation, un enjeu majeur pour les pays francophones. *Communication, technologies et développement*, 5, 11 [Online]. Available at: https://journals.openedition.org/ctd/366.

OIML (n.d.). Scope [Online]. Available at: https://www.oiml.org/fr/front-page.

Panckoucke, C.-J. (1782–1832). *Encyclopédie méthodique : recueil des planches du Dictionnaire de chimie et de métallurgie*. Hassenfratz, Paris.

Parisot, J.P. and Suagher, F. (1997). *Calendriers et chronologie*. Masson, Paris.

Paucton, A.-J.-P. (1780). *Métrologie ou traité des mesures, poids et monnoies des anciens peuples & des modernes*. Veuve Desaint, Paris.

Peoples, B.-E. (2015). Center of gravity analysis for international standards published by ISO/IEC JTC 1/SC 36. In *Initiatives 2015: Standards for Digital Learning Resources: Publishing, Referencing, Delivery, Tracking*, Ben Henda, M. (ed.). Les Éditions de l'Immatériel, Paris.

Perriault, J. (1989). *La logique de l'usage. Essai sur les machines à communiquer*. Flammarion, Paris.

Perriault, J. (1996). *La communication du savoir à distance*. L'Harmattan, Paris.

Perriault, J. and Cécile Vaguer, C. (eds) (2011). *La norme numérique. Savoir en ligne et Internet*. CNRS Éditions, Paris [Online]. Available at: https://www.cnrseditions.fr/.

Pinault-Sørensen, M. (2003). Le dessin technique. In *L'Europe des sciences et des techniques*, Hilaire-Pérez, L., Simon, F., Thébaud-Sorger, M. (eds). Presses Universitaires de Rennes, Rennes.

Porat, M.U. (1977). *The Information Economy: Definition and Measurement*. US Department of Commerce Office of Telecommunications, Washington, D.C.

Porte, D. (1993). *Rome : l'esprit des lettres*. La Découverte, Paris.

Postel, J.B. (1981). RCP 801. ISI.

Preteux, F., Vaucelle, A., Ben Henda, M. et al. (2008). MPEG-21 : base normative pour les TICE du XXIe siècle. In *CIDE 2011 : 11e Colloque international sur le document électronique "Interactions & usages autour du document numérique"*, Rouen.

Procès-verbaux du Comité d'instruction publique de la Convention nationale (1793). *Les merveilles de la science ou description populaire des inventions modernes : le télégraphe aérien*. Furne, Jouvet et Cie, Paris.

Quiniou, M. (2019). *Blockchain: The Advent of Disintermediation*. ISTE Ltd, London and Wiley, Hoboken, NJ.

Raeburn, A. (1949). *The First 50 Years: IEC Technical Committee Creation: The First Half-century (1906–1949)*. IEC, Geneva [Online]. https://www.iec.ch/history/first-50-yearshttps://www.iec.ch/history/first-50-years.

Rafidinarivo, E. and Randrianarison, A. (2017). Towards the integration of norms and standards for digital educational resources in an adequate digital policy. In *Initiatives 2015: Standards for Digital Learning Resources: Publishing Referencing, Delivery, Tracking*, Ben Henda, M. (ed.). Les Éditions de l'Immatériel, Paris.

Romary, L. (2021). Normes et patrimoine numérique [Online]. Available at: https://hal.science/hal-03598115v1.

Romary, L. and Hudrisier, H. (2002). Définition rapide de la TEI. *Études et documents berbères*, 19/20(1), 319–322.

Rousseau, J.-J. (1997). *Julie or the New Heloise*. Dartmouth College Press, Hanover.

Ruppert, L. (1956). *History of the International Electrotechnical Commission*. IEC, Geneva [Online]. Available at: https://www.iec.ch.

Salles, C. (1992). *Lire à Rome*. Les Belles Lettres, Paris.

Salomon-Bayet, C. (1970). Un préambule théorique à une Académie des arts. *Revue d'histoire des sciences et leurs applications*, 23(3), 229–250.

Say, L. and Chailley, J. (1900). *Nouveau dictionnaire d'économie politique*. Guillaumin et Cie, Paris.

Shannon, C.E. (1948). A mathematical theory of communication. *Bell System Technical Journal*, 27, 379–423.

Shon, J.-J. (2010). SC 36 ISO/IEC activities and the future of educational technology standards. In *Asia-Pacific Educational Technology Conference*.

Shon, J.-J., Mason, J., Blandin, B. (2011). Standardization of learning technology and international collaboration in SC36. ED-MEDIA.

Simkin, J. (1997). Interview by Michael Sadler and his House of Commons committee on 10th July, 1832. *Spartacus Educational*.

Simondon, G. (1980). *On the Mode of Existence of Technical Objects*. University of Western Ontario, London, ON.

Sinisgalli, R. (2011). *On Painting. A New Translation and Critical Edition*. Cambridge University Press, Cambridge.

Snyder, J., Komaitis, K., Robachevsky, A. (2016). The history of IANA [Online]. Available at: https://www.internetsociety.org/ianatimeline.

Soudanne, J. and Maupetit, L. (2016). Normalisation DIN : de la lettre au mobilier. [Online]. Available at: http://indexgrafik.fr/normalisation-din-de-la-lettre-au-mobilier/.

Sturen, O. (1997). The expansion of ISO: "Decade by decade". In *Friendship Among Equals: Recollections from ISO's First Fifty Years*. ISO, Geneva.

Talleyrand-Périgord, C.-M. (1884). Proposition sur les poids et mesures. In *Archives parlementaires de 1787 à 1860 : recueil complet des débats législatifs et politiques des Chambres françaises. Première série, 1787 à 1799.* Imprimerie du Sénat, Paris [Online]. Available at: https://archives-parlementaires.persee.fr/prt/5cdd98d2-c976-442e-a3af-817c443b3699.

TEI (2022). TEI P5: Guidelines for electronic text encoding and interchange [Online]. Available at: https://guidelines.teipublisher.com/.

Turgot, A.-R.-J. (1775). Lettre à Messier de l'Académie des sciences sur la recherche d'un étalon commun pour les poids et mesures. In *Œuvres de Turgot et documents le concernant*, volume 5. Guillaumin, Paris [Online]. Available at: https://www.institutcoppet.org/oeuvres-de-turgot-et-documents-le-concernant-volume-5/.

Turgot, A.-R.-J. (1844). Lettre à l'abbé Terray sur la marque des fers (à Limoges, le 24 décembre 1773). In *Œuvres de Turgot*. Guillaumin, Paris [Online]. Available at: https://fr.wikisource.org/wiki/Page%3AOeuvres_de_Turgot.

Venel, G.-F. (1775). *Instructions sur l'usage de la houille, plus connue sous le nom impropre de charbon de terre, pour faire du feu ; sur la manière de l'adapter à toutes sortes de feux ; et sur les avantages tant publics que privés, qui résulteront de cet usage.* G. Regnault, Avignon [Online]. Available at: https://gallica.bnf.fr/ark:/12148/bpt6k96737936.

Vian, B. (2022). *Vercoquin and the Plankton*, Bradford, T. (trans., ed.). Wakefield Press, Cambridge.

Vine, A. (2008). Unic-Ode: Lyrics [Online]. Available at: https://www.unicode.org/uni2book/unicode-ode.html.

Vitruvius (1914). *The Ten Books on Architecture*, Morgan, M.H. (trans.). Harvard University Press, Cambridge.

Watkinson, J. (2001). *The MPEG Handbook: MPEG-1, MPEG-2, MPEG-4.* Focal Press, Oxford and Boston.

Wiener, N. (1948). *Cybernetics: Or Control and Communication in the Animal and the Machine.* MIT Press, Cambridge.

Wikipedia (n.d.a). Entrées : code Chappe; dessin; union latine; union postale universelle [Online]. Available at: https://fr.wikipedia.org.

Wikipedia (n.d.b). Ancient Roman units of measurement [Online]. Available at: https://en.wikipedia.org/wiki/Ancient_Roman_units_of_measurement.

Wild, A. (1995). La typographie de la Bible de Gutenberg. In *Cahiers Gutenberg*. INRIA, Rennes.

Wiseman, L. (2007). Die Hard 4: Live Free or Die Hard. Movie.

Wüster, E. (1923). *Enciklopedia vortaro esperanta-germana*. Hirt, Leipzig.

Wüster, E. (1931). *Internationale Sprachnormung. in der technik besonders in der Elektrotechnik*. VDI Verlag, Berlin.

Young, T. (1807). Lectures on natural philosophy. In *L'architecture de fer : France XIXe siècle*, Lemoine, B (ed.). Champ Vallon, Seyssel.

Zauner, A. (1902). *Die Romanischen Namen der Körperteile: Eine Onomasiologische Studie ; La désignation des parties du corps dans les langues romanes : une étude onomasiologique*. Forgotten Books, Vienna.

Zenkouar, L. (2004). L'écriture amazighe tifinaghe et Unicode. *Étude et documents berbères*, 22, 185–202.

Zreik, K. (2012). Enjeux de l'aménagement de la ville hybridée : une 4e dimension. In *HyperUrbain 3 : villes hybrides et enjeux de l'aménagement des urbanités numériques*. Europia, Paris.

Index

J, K, L

M, N

O, P

Other titles from

iSTE

in

Information Systems, Web and Pervasive Computing

2026

BRÉZILLON Patrick
Context-based Modeling of Activity in Real-World Projects

CARRÉ Dominique, VIDAL Geneviève
Connected Digital Devices in Health
(Computing and Connected Society Set – Volume 4)

2025

ABEL Marie-Hélène, MATTA Nada, KARRAY Hedi, SAAD Inès
Ethics and Digital Transition

BATTA Priya, KUMAR Abhishek, MANOJ S. Oswalt, CHINNATHAMBI Dhaya, RAVI Srivel
Sustainable Supply Chains and Carbon Footprint Reduction: The Blockchain Advantage

DJOUAD Anaïs
The Hypermodernity Factory: Working with Relational Technologies
(Intellectual Technologies Set – Volume 10)

KUMAR Abhishek, BATTA Priya, MANOJ S. Oswalt, CHINNATHAMBI Dhaya, RAVI Srivel
Blockchain and the Water Supply Chain: Opportunities, Challenges and Innovations

STOCKINGER Peter
The Art of Communication: Semiotic Foundations and Strategic using Applications

2024

ALBAN Daniel, EYNAUD Philippe, RICHET Jean-Loup, VITARI Claudio
Information Systems Management: Governance, Urbanization and Alignment – 2nd edition

PINET François, BATTON-HUBERT Mireille, DESJARDIN Eric
Geographical Data Imperfection 2: Use Cases

SEDKAOUI Soraya
Automated Data Analytics: Combining Human Creativity and AI Power using ChatGPT

2023

POMEROL Jean-Charles
Action in Uncertainty: Expertise, Decision and Crisis Management

REVEST Valérie, LIOTARD Isabelle
Digital Transformation and Public Policies: Current Issues

2022

ACCART Jean-Philippe
Library Transformation Strategies

BEN REBAH Hassen, BOUKTHIR Hafedh, CHÉDEBOIS Antoine
Website Design and Development with HTML5 and CSS3

BOADA Martí, LAZARO Antonio, GIRBAU David, VILLARINO Ramón
Battery-less NFC Sensors for the Internet of Things

BRÉZILLON Patrick, TURNER Roy M.
Modeling and Use of Context in Action

CHAMOUX Jean-Pierre
The Digital Era 3: Customs and Practices

KARAM Elie
General Contractor Business Model for Smart Cities: Fundamentals and Techniques

LAURENT Sébastien-Yves
Conflicts, Crimes and Regulations in Cyberspace
(Cybersecurity Set – Volume 2)

2021

EL ASSAD Safwan, BARBA Dominique
Digital Communications 1: Fundamentals and Techniques
Digital Communications 2: Directed and Practical Work

GAUDIN Thierry, MAUREL Marie-Christine, POMEROL Jean-Charles
Chance, Calculation and Life

LE DEUFF Olivier
Hyperdocumentation
(Intellectual Technologies Set – Volume 9)

PÉLISSIER Maud
Cultural Commons in the Digital Ecosystem
(Intellectual Technologies Set – Volume 8)

2020

CLIQUET Gérard, with the collaboration of BARAY Jérôme
Location-Based Marketing: Geomarketing and Geolocation

DE FRÉMINVILLE Marie
Cybersecurity and Decision Makers: Data Security and Digital Trust

GEORGE Éric
Digitalization of Society and Socio-political Issues 2: Digital, Information and Research

HELALI Saida
Systems and Network Infrastructure Integration

LOISEAU Hugo, VENTRE Daniel, ADEN Hartmut
Cybersecurity in Humanities and Social Sciences: A Research Methods Approach (Cybersecurity Set – Volume 1)

SEDKAOUI Soraya, KHELFAOUI Mounia
Sharing Economy and Big Data Analytics

SCHMITT Églantine
Big Data: An Art of Decision Making (Intellectual Technologies Set – Volume 7)

2019

ALBAN Daniel, EYNAUD Philippe, MALAURENT Julien, RICHET Jean-Loup, VITARI Claudio
Information Systems Management: Governance, Urbanization and Alignment

AUGEY Dominique, with the collaboration of ALCARAZ Marina
Digital Information Ecosystems: Smart Press

BATTON-HUBERT Mireille, DESJARDIN Eric, PINET François
Geographic Data Imperfection 1: From Theory to Applications

BRIQUET-DUHAZÉ Sophie, TURCOTTE Catherine
From Reading-Writing Research to Practice

BROCHARD Luigi, KAMATH Vinod, CORBALAN Julita, HOLLAND Scott, MITTELBACH Walter, OTT Michael
Energy-Efficient Computing and Data Centers

CHAMOUX Jean-Pierre
The Digital Era 2: Political Economy Revisited

COCHARD Gérard-Michel
Introduction to Stochastic Processes and Simulation

DUONG Véronique
SEO Management: Methods and Techniques to Achieve Success

GAUCHEREL Cédric, GOUYON Pierre-Henri, DESSALLES Jean-Louis
Information, The Hidden Side of Life

GEORGE Éric
Digitalization of Society and Socio-political Issues 1: Digital, Communication and Culture

GHLALA Riadh
Analytic SQL in SQL Server 2014/2016

JANIER Mathilde, SAINT-DIZIER Patrick
Argument Mining: Linguistic Foundations

SOURIS Marc
Epidemiology and Geography: Principles, Methods and Tools of Spatial Analysis

TOUNSI Wiem
Cyber-Vigilance and Digital Trust: Cyber Security in the Era of Cloud Computing and IoT

2018

ARDUIN Pierre-Emmanuel
Insider Threats
(Advances in Information Systems Set – Volume 10)

CARMÈS Maryse
Digital Organizations Manufacturing: Scripts, Performativity and Semiopolitics
(Intellectual Technologies Set – Volume 5)

CARRÉ Dominique, VIDAL Geneviève
Hyperconnectivity: Economical, Social and Environmental Challenges
(Computing and Connected Society Set – Volume 3)

CHAMOUX Jean-Pierre
The Digital Era 1: Big Data Stakes

DOUAY Nicolas
Urban Planning in the Digital Age
(Intellectual Technologies Set – Volume 6)

FABRE Renaud, BENSOUSSAN Alain
The Digital Factory for Knowledge: Production and Validation of Scientific Results

GAUDIN Thierry, LACROIX Dominique, MAUREL Marie-Christine, POMEROL Jean-Charles
Life Sciences, Information Sciences

GAYARD Laurent
Darknet: Geopolitics and Uses
(Computing and Connected Society Set – Volume 2)

IAFRATE Fernando
Artificial Intelligence and Big Data: The Birth of a New Intelligence
(Advances in Information Systems Set – Volume 8)

LE DEUFF Olivier
Digital Humanities: History and Development
(Intellectual Technologies Set – Volume 4)

MANDRAN Nadine
Traceable Human Experiment Design Research: Theoretical Model and Practical Guide
(Advances in Information Systems Set – Volume 9)

PIVERT Olivier
NoSQL Data Models: Trends and Challenges

ROCHET Claude
Smart Cities: Reality or Fiction

SALEH Imad, AMMI, Mehdi, SZONIECKY Samuel
Challenges of the Internet of Things: Technology, Use, Ethics
(Digital Tools and Uses Set – Volume 7)

SAUVAGNARGUES Sophie
Decision-making in Crisis Situations: Research and Innovation for Optimal Training

SEDKAOUI Soraya
Data Analytics and Big Data

SZONIECKY Samuel
Ecosystems Knowledge: Modeling and Analysis Method for Information and Communication
(Digital Tools and Uses Set – Volume 6)

2017

BOUHAÏ Nasreddine, SALEH Imad
Internet of Things: Evolutions and Innovations
(Digital Tools and Uses Set – Volume 4)

DUONG Véronique
Baidu SEO: Challenges and Intricacies of Marketing in China

LESAS Anne-Marie, MIRANDA Serge
The Art and Science of NFC Programming
(Intellectual Technologies Set – Volume 3)

LIEM André
Prospective Ergonomics
(Human-Machine Interaction Set – Volume 4)

MARSAULT Xavier
Eco-generative Design for Early Stages of Architecture
(Architecture and Computer Science Set – Volume 1)

REYES-GARCIA Everardo
The Image-Interface: Graphical Supports for Visual Information
(Digital Tools and Uses Set – Volume 3)

REYES-GARCIA Everardo, BOUHAÏ Nasreddine
Designing Interactive Hypermedia Systems
(Digital Tools and Uses Set – Volume 2)

SAÏD Karim, BAHRI KORBI Fadia
Asymmetric Alliances and Information Systems:Issues and Prospects
(Advances in Information Systems Set – Volume 7)

SZONIECKY Samuel, BOUHAÏ Nasreddine
Collective Intelligence and Digital Archives: Towards Knowledge Ecosystems
(Digital Tools and Uses Set – Volume 1)

2016

BEN CHOUIKHA Mona
Organizational Design for Knowledge Management

BERTOLO David
Interactions on Digital Tablets in the Context of 3D Geometry Learning
(Human-Machine Interaction Set – Volume 2)

BOUVARD Patricia, SUZANNE Hervé
Collective Intelligence Development in Business

EL FALLAH SEGHROUCHNI Amal, ISHIKAWA Fuyuki, HÉRAULT Laurent, TOKUDA Hideyuki
Enablers for Smart Cities

FABRE Renaud, in collaboration with MESSERSCHMIDT-MARIET Quentin, HOLVOET Margot
New Challenges for Knowledge

GAUDIELLO Ilaria, ZIBETTI Elisabetta
Learning Robotics, with Robotics, by Robotics
(Human-Machine Interaction Set – Volume 3)

HENROTIN Joseph
The Art of War in the Network Age
(Intellectual Technologies Set – Volume 1)

KITAJIMA Munéo
Memory and Action Selection in Human–Machine Interaction
(Human–Machine Interaction Set – Volume 1)

LAGRAÑA Fernando
E-mail and Behavioral Changes: Uses and Misuses of Electronic Communications

LEIGNEL Jean-Louis, UNGARO Thierry, STAAR Adrien
Digital Transformation
(Advances in Information Systems Set – Volume 6)

MONINO Jean-Louis, SEDKAOUI Soraya
Big Data, Open Data and Data Development
(Smart Innovation Set – Volume 3)

NOYER Jean-Max
Transformation of Collective Intelligences
(Intellectual Technologies Set – Volume 2)

VENTRE Daniel
Information Warfare – 2nd edition

VITALIS André
The Uncertain Digital Revolution
(Computing and Connected Society Set – Volume 1)

2015

ARDUIN Pierre-Emmanuel, GRUNDSTEIN Michel, ROSENTHAL-SABROUX Camille
Information and Knowledge System
(Advances in Information Systems Set – Volume 2)

BÉRANGER Jérôme
Medical Information Systems Ethics

BRONNER Gérald
Belief and Misbelief Asymmetry on the Internet

IAFRATE Fernando
From Big Data to Smart Data
(Advances in Information Systems Set – Volume 1)

KRICHEN Saoussen, BEN JOUIDA Sihem
Supply Chain Management and its Applications in Computer Science

NEGRE Elsa
Information and Recommender Systems
(Advances in Information Systems Set – Volume 4)

POMEROL Jean-Charles, EPELBOIN Yves, THOURY Claire
MOOCs

SAAD Inès, ROSENTHAL-SABROUX Camille, GARGOURI Faïez
Information Systems for Knowledge Management

SALLES Maryse
Decision-Making and the Information System
(Advances in Information Systems Set – Volume 3)

SAMARA Tarek
ERP and Information Systems: Integration or Disintegration
(Advances in Information Systems Set – Volume 5)

2014

DINET Jérôme
Information Retrieval in Digital Environments

DUBÉ Jean, LEGROS Diègo
Spatial Econometrics Using Microdata

HÉNO Raphaële, CHANDELIER Laure
3D Modeling of Buildings: Outstanding Sites

KEMBELLEC Gérald, CHARTRON Ghislaine, SALEH Imad
Recommender Systems

MATHIAN Hélène, SANDERS Lena
Spatio-temporal Approaches: Geographic Objects and Change Process

PLANTIN Jean-Christophe
Participatory Mapping

RIGO Michel
Formal Languages, Automata and Numeration Systems 1: Introduction to Combinatorics on Words
Formal Languages, Automata and Numeration Systems 2: Applications to Recognizability and Decidability

TORRES-MORENO Juan-Manuel
Automatic Text Summarization

VENTRE Daniel
Chinese Cybersecurity and Defense

2013

BERNIK Igor
Cybercrime and Cyberwarfare

CAPET Philippe, DELAVALLADE Thomas
Information Evaluation

LEBRATY Jean-Fabrice, LOBRE-LEBRATY Katia
Crowdsourcing: One Step Beyond

SALLABERRY Christian
Geographical Information Retrieval in Textual Corpora

TURENNE Nicolas
Knowledge Needs and Information Extraction: Towards an Artificial Consciousness

2012

BUCHER Bénédicte, LE BER Florence
Innovative Software Development in GIS

GAUSSIER Eric, YVON François
Textual Information Access

STOCKINGER Peter
Audiovisual Archives: Digital Text and Discourse Analysis

VENTRE Daniel
Cyber Conflict

2011

BANOS Arnaud, THÉVENIN Thomas
Geographical Information and Urban Transport Systems

DAUPHINÉ André
Fractal Geography

LEMBERGER Pirmin, MOREL Mederic
Managing Complexity of Information Systems

STOCKINGER Peter
Introduction to Audiovisual Archives

STOCKINGER Peter
Digital Audiovisual Archives

VENTRE Daniel
Cyberwar and Information Warfare

2010

BONNET Pierre
Enterprise Data Governance

BRUNET Roger
Sustainable Geography

BUFFET Olivier, SIGAUD Olivier
Markov Decision Processes in Artificial Intelligence

CARREGA Pierre
Geographical Information and Climatology

CAUVIN Colette, ESCOBAR Francisco, SERRADJ Aziz
Thematic Cartography – 3-volume series
Thematic Cartography and Transformations – Volume 1
Cartography and the Impact of the Quantitative Revolution – Volume 2
New Approaches in Thematic Cartography – Volume 3

LANGLOIS Patrice
Simulation of Complex Systems in GIS

MATHIS Philippe
Graphs and Networks – 2nd edition

THERIAULT Marius, DES ROSIERS François
Modeling Urban Dynamics

2009

BONNET Pierre, DETAVERNIER Jean-Michel, VAUQUIER Dominique
Sustainable IT Architecture: the Progressive Way of Overhauling Information Systems with SOA

PAPY Fabrice
Information Science

RIVARD François, ABOU HARB Georges, MERET Philippe
The Transverse Information System

ROCHE Stéphane, CARON Claude
Organizational Facets of GIS

VENTRE Daniel
Information Warfare

2008

BRUGNOT Gérard
Spatial Management of Risks

FINKE Gerd
Operations Research and Networks

GUERMOND Yves
Modeling Process in Geography

KANEVSKI Michael
Advanced Mapping of Environmental Data

MANOUVRIER Bernard, LAURENT Ménard
Application Integration: EAI, B2B, BPM and SOA

PAPY Fabrice
Digital Libraries

2007

DOBESCH Hartwig, DUMOLARD Pierre, DYRAS Izabela
Spatial Interpolation for Climate Data

SANDERS Lena
Models in Spatial Analysis

2006

CLIQUET Gérard
Geomarketing

CORNIOU Jean-Pierre
Looking Back and Going Forward in IT

DEVILLERS Rodolphe, JEANSOULIN Robert
Fundamentals of Spatial Data Quality

Printed and bound by CPI Group (UK) Ltd, Croydon, CR0 4YY
13/09/2026
14961048-0006